# MOTOR CYCLE RESTORER'S WORKSHOP COMPANION

Patrick Stephens Limited, a member of the Haynes Publishing Group, has published authoritative, quality books for enthusiasts for a quarter of a century. During that time the company has established a reputation as one of the world's leading publishers of books on aviation, military, model-making, motor cycling, motoring, motor racing, railway and railway modelling subjects. Readers or authors with suggestions for books they would like to see published are invited to write to:
The Editorial Director, Patrick Stephens Limited, Sparkford, Nr Yeovil, Somerset, BA22 7JJ.

# MOTOR CYCLE RESTORER'S WORKSHOP COMPANION

## The complete guide to techniques and tools for bike restoration and repair

## GEOFF PURNELL

**PSL**

Patrick Stephens Limited

This book is based on the author's highly
successful *Car Restorer's Workshop Companion*,
published by Patrick Stephens Limited in 1989.

© Geoff Purnell 1992

First published in 1992

**British Library Cataloguing in Publication Data**
A catalogue record for this book is available
from the British Library.

ISBN 1-85260-393-3

Library of Congress Cataloging in Publication
No. 92-81444

Patrick Stephens Limited is a member of the
Haynes Publishing group, Sparkford, Nr Yeovil,
Somerset, BA22 7JJ.

Printed in Great Britain by J. H. Haynes & Co. Ltd.

# Contents

# Introduction

So many books on motor cycle restoration assume that those undertaking the work are familiar with all the practical skills and processes that are necessary in the sometimes complex work involved. Unfortunately this is rarely the position, and while most people have had the opportunity at school to learn some of the basic skills needed, this may have been some time ago and the memory now needs a jog or two.

I hope that the following pages will help you to undertake the processes involved in restoration with confidence and success. Don't be deterred if you lack some of the equipment mentioned in this book. Many colleges and night schools are beginning to be aware that there are an increasing number of people undertaking restoration work and that these people are willing to join classes and pay for the use of the machines. If there is no suitable class in your area, approach the local college and see if they are willing to provide a course or workshop facilities. Lastly, don't be afraid to attempt jobs that you have put off in the past; with careful thought, planning and ingenuity, it is surprising what can be achieved. The sense of satisfaction that can come from a job well done, especially if it is something attempted for the first time, is one of life's real pleasures. If this book helps you to achieve that satisfaction, it will have been well worth the writing.

# CHAPTER 1

# A place to work and tools to work with

In theory, the ideal place to restore your machine would be light, airy, spacious and full of all the equipment that might ever be needed. Unfortunately not many people are blessed with this ideal and have to make the best of what they have, be it a garage, garden shed or spare bedroom.

However, a great deal can be accomplished in a small space with a little care and thought. The most important item is a strong, rigid bench of a height best suited to you; as a guide if you are making one from scratch, 33 inches (840 mm) is the height of the average bench. The top should be at least $1\frac{1}{2}$ inches (38 mm) thick and firmly attached to the legs, which in turn should be bolted or screwed to the floor or wall. The top should extend beyond the underframe by at least $1\frac{1}{2}$ inches (38 mm) so that work can be clamped to the top by a G-clamp or similar. It is also beneficial to let into the edge of the top a piece of angle iron fixed with countersunk screws; this will be found useful for bending sheet metal as described in the relevant chapter. Another useful tip is to cover the top with hardboard, well varnished to prevent it soaking up liquids, to protect the main top from damage. When this becomes too tatty, it can be removed and a fresh piece put in its place.

Figure 1 shows the basic plan of a suitable bench. As its construction does not have any woodworking joints, it can be made quickly and easily. If a long bench is made, the number of legs should be increased, 4 feet (1200 mm) being the furthest they should be apart for rigidity.

The essential engineer's vice should be bolted to the bench, not screwed, as it invariably comes loose, and as near to a leg as possible to give extra

Basic frame – side rails glued and screwed. Cross rails can be added to the bottom rails.

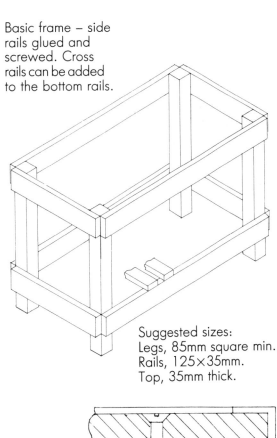

Suggested sizes:
Legs, 85mm square min.
Rails, 125×35mm.
Top, 35mm thick.

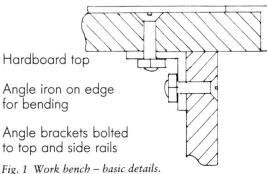

Hardboard top

Angle iron on edge for bending

Angle brackets bolted to top and side rails

*Fig. 1 Work bench – basic details.*

support. The top of the jaws should be level with your elbow. The height of the vice subtracted from the height of your elbow from the floor will give you the ideal height for the top of the bench. When fixing the vice, make sure that the fixed jaw is beyond the edge of the bench top; this will enable you to hold long pieces of work vertically in it.

While on the subject of vices, buy the best you can afford; cheap vices are often made from an inferior grade of iron and will not stand up to any heavy usage. If you intend to do a great deal of heavy hammering on the vice, it is important to buy one that has been designed for that purpose — these usually incorporate an anvil in their design — otherwise you could find the casting cracked after use.

The jaws of the vice will be serrated, and though this is very useful for gripping work very securely, it will leave marks on it. To prevent this happening a pair of fibre soft jaws can be bought to clip over the vice jaws. Another method is to remove the jaws and place thin sheet steel or aluminium behind them; the jaws are then bolted back in place and the thin sheet folded over the front of them, covering the serrations.

As far as tools go, there is no end to achieving a full set. Perhaps the most important thing is to ensure that those you buy are the best you can afford. Resist the temptation to buy a full set of, for example, taps and dies or reamers, unless you have plenty of spare money. Some of these you will probably never use and the money would be better spent on your bike. The one exception I would make to this rule is where the tools themselves may become unobtainable. It is, for example, still possible to buy taps and dies for obsolete threads, but how long this situation will last is impossible to tell.

While on the subject of these tools, I would not advise anyone to buy second-hand taps, dies or reamers unless you are certain they have not had much use. Tools such as these are useless when they are blunt and cannot be sharpened without special equipment. When buying cutting tools, it is preferable to buy those made from high-speed steel (H.S.S.); they are more expensive than those made from carbon steel (C.S.), but they will keep their edge much longer. The only exception I would make would be taps and dies if they are not likely to be used very often.

A set of drills $\frac{1}{16}$ inch to $\frac{1}{2}$ inch, or 1 mm to 13 mm, is ideal and if kept sharp and stored carefully will last for years. The old letter and number drills have now been superseded by metric sizes and are more expensive to buy. The tables at the end of the chapter on drills show that many of these have a metric equivalent.

Files come in a bewildering array of shapes and sizes but, for a start, the following will be most useful:

10 inch hand file (second cut), one edge safe
10 inch half round (second cut)
8 inch round
8 inch three square
6 inch half round
6 inch flat
$\frac{1}{4}$ inch round
10 inch Millenicut or Dreadnought
A set of needle files

Make sure that you use good-quality file handles such as the 'Python'; these are much stronger and there is less chance of the handle splitting.

A senior and junior hacksaw complete with adaptor clips for 'Abra' saw blades will satisfy most of your sawing needs. For marking out and measuring, the following are the minimum necessary: scriber, centre punch, 4 inch (100 mm) engineer's square, 6 inch (150 mm) or 12 inch (300 mm) steel rule, and 4 inch (100 mm) or 6 inch (150 mm) dividers. For accurate measuring, a micrometer or a pair of vernier callipers are needed. Micrometers are either metric or imperial, whereas vernier callipers are usually dual measurement.

As for the rest of the tools, apart from the basic ones needed to dismantle the bike, they are best bought as and when you need them. Power tools are an invaluable help to the restorer and anyone who tackles any major work without the minimum of an electric drill is going to find the working that much harder. An electric drill with a $\frac{1}{2}$ inch (13 mm) chuck is ideal, preferably one with a variable speed control; even two-speed drills revolve too quickly for large-diameter drills on their slowest

*An angle grinder, a useful tool to have in the workshop.*

*Good quality open-ended, ring and combination spanners will last a lifetime. (Britool Ltd.)*

speed. For accurate drilling, a drill stand is very useful, together with a good-quality drill press vice. When buying such a vice, check that the moving jaw is a good fit where it slides on the base and does not lift up as it tightens onto the work, so presenting it to the drill out of true. Obviously a pedestal drill is the ideal solution and these can be found at auctions and second-hand machine dealers. A small bench grinder is very useful, not only for grinding pieces of work but also for

sharpening drills, cold chisels, etc. If you are contemplating a lot of welding, an angle grinder is invaluable for dressing up welds; with a wire brush attachment it will also clean rust from metal with ease.

The ultimate machine tool is of course the lathe, a most versatile machine that can be a boon to the restorer. If you are in a position to be able to afford a lathe, careful consideration must be given as to the work you hope to achieve with it. A model

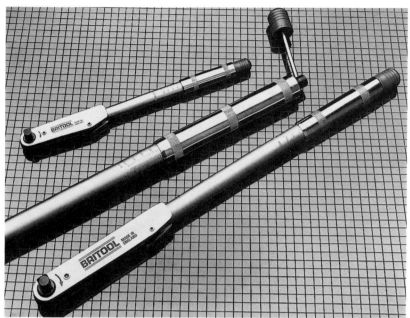

**Left** *Torque wrenches give peace of mind and security for those important fixings.* (Britool Ltd.)

**Below left** *A variety of pliers for holding, cutting and turning.* (Britool Ltd.)

**Below** *A selection of screwdrivers suitable for most needs.* (Britool Ltd.)

**Right** *A hydraulic work bench.* (R & R Ltd.)

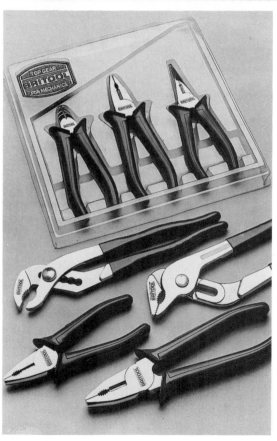

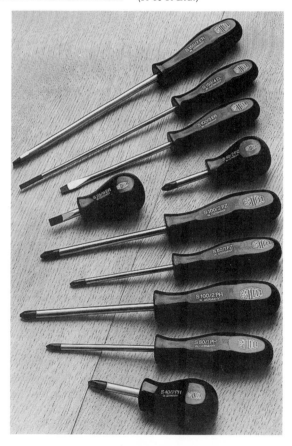

maker's lathe is excellent for small work, but does not have the capacity to handle anything of any size, whereas a $7\frac{1}{2}$ inch lathe capable of turning a 15 inch diameter piece of work will take up a great deal of space and will most likely require three-phase electricity to run it. Perhaps the best size of lathe is 5 inch or 6 inch, and the chapter on lathes includes a check-list of points to look for when buying second-hand.

Should you just be starting out on the road of motor cycling and restoration, you will need the basic tools for dismantling your machine. In my opinion it is best not to be taken in by some of the cheap universal tool kits that are advertised as containing everything the motor cyclist needs for life. In many cases the tools are cheap imports dressed up in fancy boxes and will not stand the test of time. They are often a poor fit on the nut or bolt head and will slip at the wrong moment, rendering a tight nut or bolt even more difficult to loosen because the hexagon has had its corners rounded.

A socket set and a set of combination spanners suited to the fixings on your machine, i.e. metric, B.S.F/B.S.W., etc., plus the appropriate screw-drivers, etc., will be sufficient for almost all the work you are likely to undertake. Particular special tools for dismantling parts of the engine are best bought as and when they are needed; some one-make clubs have a loan scheme where such tools can be borrowed against a small deposit. Make sure that you buy good quality tools from a well-known manufacturer—they will last a life-time and repay your investment many times over.

A luxury for many but a necessity for some, particularly those with back problems, is a work-bench that will lift the bike to a suitable working height. The illustration shows a factory-produced example, but after having read this book and gained the necessary skills and techniques, you may feel perhaps you could design and make your own.

Should you be restoring a sidecar that has a wooden frame, the necessary tools and materials to tackle this particular aspect of restoration are included in Chapter 15.

# CHAPTER 2

# Metals for motor cycles

## Composition and usage

All metals, whatever their composition, have physical properties which make them suitable or unsuitable for particular applications on a motor cycle.

**Brittleness** is the property of breaking without much permanent distortion. Cast iron is a brittle metal because its structure is split up by flakes of graphite, which is a brittle material. Shortness is another expression used instead of brittleness. Hot or red shortness in a metal is when it is brittle in the red hot state. Cold shortness means that a metal is brittle when cold.

**Toughness** is the resistance to fracture or deformation. Toughness decreases as metals become hot.

**Elasticity** The elasticity of a metal is its ability to return to its original shape after being deformed by a force, e.g. as in a road spring. The elastic limit of a metal is expressed in tons per square inch or newtons per square millimetre. If the elastic limit of a bar of metal was 20 tons per square inch and this force was exceeded, the bar could take on permanent stretch, often called permanent set.

**Hardness** This is the resistance of a metal to being scratched, worn or indented by harder materials. There are a number of standard tests (e.g. Brinell) by which hardness of metals can be compared.

**Malleability** The property which allows a metal to be rolled or hammered without breaking. Lead, for instance, is a very malleable metal.

**Plasticity** This is a similar property to malleability and involves permanent deformation without rupture. Plasticity is necessary for forging, and most metals become plastic when hot.

**Ductility** The ability to be drawn into fine wire. Ductility often increases with heat. It bears little relation to malleability, e.g. lead is very malleable but not ductile as it does not have the strength to be drawn out without breaking.

**Strength** The strength of a metal is its ability to resist the application of a force without rupture. In use, a metal may have to withstand forces in compression, torsion, tension or shear, or a combination of these. The ultimate tensile strength (U.T.S.) of a metal is the load necessary to fracture a sample one square inch in cross-section, and is expressed in pounds or tons per square inch or newtons per square millimetre.

## Forms of supply

### Cast iron
This is an alloy of iron and carbon where the carbon content is in the range of 2% to 4%. Other elements present in much smaller percentages are silicon, manganese and phosphorus.

Cast iron is a brittle metal that has relatively little strength except in compression, and care should be taken when working with it. Its great

*Cast iron barrel and aluminium alloy crankcase, on mid-vintage AJS 350.*

advantage is its good fluidity when molten, making it ideal for complex castings such as cylinder barrels. It is easily machined, once the hard outer layer is cut through, and it is also a good bearing surface, e.g. for cylinder bores where the free graphite in its structure seems to act as a lubricant.

Cast iron engines are often quieter than those of aluminium alloy because the density of the metal reduces noise transmission.

Special cast iron alloys have been developed in recent years; these contain small percentages of nickel, copper, chromium or molybdenum. This produces a tough metal which casts well, resists shock loadings and is ideally suited for crankshafts.

Cast iron is not used a great deal in motor cycles, its main uses being cylinder barrels and crankshafts; it is also not usually available from normal retail outlets.

## Steel

This is also an alloy of iron and carbon but in this case the carbon content ranges between 0·05% and 1·4%. Above this figure carbon cannot be contained in the combined state with the iron and will exist as free graphite, and the metal merges into the group of cast irons.

Carbon steels fall into five main groups: dead mild, 0·05%–0·15% carbon; mild steel, 0·1%–0·3% carbon; medium carbon, 0·3%–0·6% carbon; high carbon, 0·6%–0·9% carbon; and tool steel, 0·9%–1·4% carbon. Typical uses of these steels may be seen in Figure 2.

**Alloy steel** To improve the properties of these plain carbon steels, they are frequently alloyed with small quantities of other elements. Nickel, for example, improves tensile strength and toughness, while chromium in small quantities will increase the hardness of the steel and in large quantities will produce stainless steel which is corrosion resistant. 18/8 stainless steel refers to 18% chromium and 8% nickel in the composition of the metal.

Molybdenum reduces the brittleness of the steel and improves machinability. Among the alloy steels, the nickel-chrome-molybdenum steels possess perhaps the best all-round combination of properties useful for motor cycle work.

Vanadium in small quantities improves the forging and stamping properties of the alloy, and chrome-vanadium steels are widely used for drop forgings, e.g. drop-forged spanners and sockets. The table in Figure 3 gives some alloy steels and their uses. The British Standard designation, which has replaced the old E.N. numbers, is included.

| TYPE OF STEEL | % CARBON | USES |
|---|---|---|
| DEAD MILD | 0.05–0.10 | RIVETS NAILS CHAIN. HOT AND COLD ROLLED STRIP, SEAM WELDED PIPE. |
| MILD | 0.10–0.20 | RSJ, SCREWS, MACHINE PARTS, STAMPINGS, SHEET, DROP FORGINGS. |
| | 0.20–0.30 | FREE CUTTING STEELS, SHAFTING, GEARS, FORGINGS, STRUCTURAL WORK. |
| MEDIUM CARBON | 0.30–0.40 | HIGH TENSILE TUBES, AXLES, CON-RODS, FORGINGS, CRANE HOOKS, WIRE. |
| | 0.40–0.50 | CRANKSHAFTS, GEARS, AXLES, SHAFTS, DIE-BLOCKS, HEAT TREATED MACHINE PARTS. |
| | 0.50–0.60 | LAMINATED SPRINGS, WIRE ROPES, RAILS. |
| HIGH CARBON | 0.60–0.70 | SCREWDRIVERS, SAWS, SET SCREWS. |
| | 0.70–0.80 | HAMMERS, LAMINATED SPRINGS, CAR BUMPERS. |
| | 0.80–0.90 | COLD CHISELS, PUNCHES, SOME HAND TOOLS. |
| TOOL STEELS | 0.90–1.00 | SPRINGS, KNIVES, DIES, SILVER STEEL. |
| | 1.00–1.10 | DRILLS, TAPS, SCREWING DIES. |
| | 1.10–1.20 | BALL BEARINGS, LATHE AND WOOD TOOLS. |
| | 1.20–1.30 | FILES, REAMERS, BROACHES. |
| | 1.30–1.40 | SAWS, RAZORS, MACHINE PARTS WHERE RESISTANCE TO WEAR IS ESSENTIAL. |

**Above** *Fig. 2 Typical uses of carbon steels.*

**Left** *A very exotic crank assembly made for a BSA racing Gold Star, employing an aluminium alloy con-rod and alloy steel flywheels with a large diameter high tensile steel parallel crankpin.* (M. Adams.)

| TYPE OF STEEL | B.S. 970 DESIGNATION | USES |
|---|---|---|
| LOW CHROME 1% | 530 M 40 | AXLES, CON-RODS, STEERING ARMS. |
| LOW NICKEL LOW CHROME | 653 M 1 | HIGHLY-STRESSED PARTS IN AUTO-ENGINEERING, E.G. CON-RODS, DIFFERENTIAL SHAFTS. |
| LOW CHROME LOW NICKEL | 640 M 40 | CRANKSHAFTS, CON-RODS, DIFFERENTIAL GEARS, AXLES. |
| 1% CHROME MOLYBDENUM | 709 M 40 | CRANKSHAFTS, CON-RODS, STUB AXLES, ETC. |
| 1½ NICKEL CHROME MOLYBDENUM | 817 M 40 | DIFFERENTIAL SHAFTS, ETC, WHERE FATIGUE AND SHOCK RESISTANCE ARE IMPORTANT. |
| 4½% NICKEL CHROME MOLYBDENUM | 835 M 30 | AIR-HARDENING STEEL FOR HIGHLY-STRESSED PARTS CAN BE SURFACE-HARDENED BY CYANIDE. |

**Above** *Fig. 3 Typical uses of some alloy steels.*

| S.W.G. | IMP. | METRIC | S.W.G. | IMP. | METRIC |
|---|---|---|---|---|---|
| 6 | 0.192 | 4.90 | 16 | 0.064 | 1.60 |
| 7 | 0.176 | 4.50 | 17 | 0.056 | 1.45 |
| 8 | 0.160 | 4.10 | 18 | 0.048 | 1.23 |
| 9 | 0.144 | 3.70 | 19 | 0.040 | 1.05 |
| 10 | 0.128 | 3.30 | 20 | 0.036 | 0.92 |
| 11 | 0.116 | 2.95 | 21 | 0.032 | 0.82 |
| 12 | 0.104 | 2.65 | 22 | 0.028 | 0.72 |
| 13 | 0.092 | 2.35 | 23 | 0.024 | 0.61 |
| 14 | 0.080 | 2.05 | 24 | 0.022 | 0.56 |
| 15 | 0.072 | 1.85 | 25 | 0.020 | 0.51 |

**Right** *Fig. 4 Imperial and metric equivalent to S.W.G.*

Steels are readily available in a great variety of sections: round, square, hexagonal, rectangular (known as flats), angles, sheet and tube of different sections.

**Black mild steel** in flat or square form has rounded corners and comes coated with scale which looks like a brown skin. It is softer than **bright drawn mild steel** (B.D.M.S.) which is pickled in a 3% to 10% solution of sulphuric acid to remove the oxide, and then drawn through a series of dies. This produces a more accurately sized metal and the flats and squares have 90° corners. The metal is harder because of the drawing process. **Freecutting mild steel** (F.C.M.S.) is produced by the addition of small quantities of lead to the metal which improves machinability.

The standard lengths of these sections is 10 feet (3 metres) and most steel stock holders are loath to cut bars into smaller lengths. If you only want small quantities, local engineering works are probably the best place to try.

**Steel tube** is available in a variety of sections and properties but falls into two main groups: seamed, which is made by forming a flat sheet into the shape required and then electrically welding the seam, thus being known as electric resistance welded (E.R.W.); and cold drawn seamless (C.D.S.) tube, which is drawn from a solid block of

metal through dies to the required shape. This type of tube is much stronger than E.R.W. size for size, and should be used where strength is of paramount importance.

**Sheet steel** comes in two basic sizes, 8 ft × 4 ft (2,400 mm × 1,200 mm) and 6 ft × 3 ft (1,800 mm × 900 mm). The thickness of sheet steel or any other sheet metal is measured in standard wire gauge (S.W.G.). Figure 4 shows the metric and imperial equivalents of S.W.G. Sheet steel can also be coated in various materials to provide a

corrosion-resistant or decorative surface. Steel coated with tin is known as tinplate and is widely used for petrol tanks. Lead-coated steel can also be used for this purpose and is known as terne plate. Galvanised steel has a zinc coating. It is also possible to buy steel sheet coated with plastic.

**Aluminium**

In its pure state aluminium is a relatively soft and weak metal. For use in industry it is usually alloyed with other elements, mainly copper, to increase its hardness and strength. Aluminium has two main

| TRADE NAME | CHARACTERISTICS AND USES |
|---|---|
| LM 4 | GENERAL PURPOSES. WITHSTANDS MODERATE STRESSES. |
| LM 9 | SUITABLE FOR INTRICATE CASTINGS. GOOD CORROSION RESISTANCE. |
| LM 13 | LOW THERMAL EXPANSION. USED FOR PISTONS FOR HIGH-PERFORMANCE ENGINES. |
| LM 14/Y-ALLOY | PISTONS AND CYLINDER HEADS FOR LIQUID AND AIR COOLED ENGINES. GENERAL PURPOSES. |
| LM16 | USEFUL FOR INTRICATE SHAPES AND PRESSURE TIGHTNESS. CYLINDER HEADS; VALVE BODIES; WATER JACKETS. |

*Fig. 5 Some typical uses of common aluminium casting alloys.*

*A nice early example of a sand-cast crankcase, on a 1911 Henderson 4.* (F. Farrington)

uses in motor cycles: sheet material for sidecar body panels, mudguards and petrol tanks, and castings of various types. Extrusions are also available in a wide variety of shapes for many different purposes.

**Sheet aluminium** is available in the same sizes and thicknesses as sheet steel but a basic difference is that it can be ordered in various stages of hardness: soft, half-hard and hard. In the soft condition it can be easily shaped but is perhaps too prone to denting to be useful for body panels of sidecars or mudguards. Half-hard will still work fairly easily and is much more resistant to dents, while hard sheets are best used for panels that require little or no shaping.

Aluminium is also available with a variety of raised patterns to produce a non-slip surface; this is often referred to as tread plate.

**Aluminium casting alloys** fall into two main groups: sand casting and die casting. To increase their strength, some of these alloys can be heat treated. The table in Figure 5 gives some of the most widely used alloys.

**Magnesium alloys**
Often called Elektron, these are found in the form of castings on some high performance and racing machines where the extra cost can be offset by the advantage of saving weight.

**Zinc-based alloys**
These are often known by the trade name 'Mazak', and are mainly used for gravity or pressure die-casting of components which have to take relatively little stress, e.g. carburettors, light fittings, etc. The alloy can be easily chrome-plated but suffers from a major drawback in the swelling and cracking of the casting during use. This is most noticeable in the earlier forms of zinc casting before metallurgists discovered that the presence of impurities in the zinc were causing the problem. The situation has improved in recent years by the use of 'four nines' zinc, i.e. 99·99% pure metal.

**Other metals**
Other metals used in motorcycles include copper, mainly used for gaskets and electrical wiring, and brass, often used for decorative mouldings and small castings on earlier machines. Both these metals can be obtained in sheets or tube. Brass can also be bought in the usual range of sections, while copper is not usually available in these forms because of its soft nature and cost.

Bearing metals will be dealt with separately in a later chapter.

# CHAPTER 3

# Heat treatment

Although heat treatment of metal is often considered beyond the scope of the amateur restorer, there is a certain amount that can easily be accomplished in the home workshop.

## Annealing

All metals, when they are worked in the cold state by bending or hammering, harden as the work progresses, so need to be re-softened, or annealed as it is called, so that work can continue without the metal cracking. Annealing involves heating the metal to a certain temperature, then allowing it to cool slowly.

**Steel** should be heated to red heat, held at that temperature until the heat has soaked right through the metal, then left to cool slowly, preferably in a container of vermiculite granules or, failing this, dry sand.

**Aluminium** must first be coated with a thin film of soap. The reason for doing this is that aluminium does not change appearance when it is heated until it begins to melt, making it very difficult to judge its temperature. The layer of soap will turn a dark brown colour when the annealing temperature has been reached; the metal should then be left to cool.

**Copper** should be heated until a rainbow effect of colours appears on the surface; this indicates that the correct temperature has been reached. The metal can be either left to cool or can be quenched in water without affecting its softness.

**Brass** should be heated to red heat and allowed to cool slowly.

## Hardening

The only metal that can be hardened in the home workshop is steel, and the two methods used depend on its carbon content. Steel with more than 0·3% carbon can be hardened by heating to red heat and quenching vertically, with a swirling figure-of-eight movement, in water or brine. This will produce an extremely hard and brittle metal that is of little use in this state; some of this brittleness must therefore be removed by the process known as tempering.

**Tempering** a metal means re-heating it to a specified temperature then quenching it. Fortunately it is possible to assess the temperature of the metal by observing the changing colour of the oxide film on its surface as it is heated. Obviously the surface must be cleaned up with emery cloth after it has been hardened so that this change in colour can be seen. When the correct colour is reached, the metal is again quenched in water or brine. Care must be taken not to heat the metal too quickly as the oxide film changes colour rapidly and it is very easy to overheat the work. The table in Figure 6 shows the correct colour and temperature for different applications.

**Case hardening**   It is not possible to harden steel with less than 0·3% carbon in its structure, i.e. mild steel, by heating and quenching. In this

*Fig. 6 Tempering temperatures.*

| TEMPER COLOUR | TEMP. CENT. | ARTICLES |
|---|---|---|
| PALE STRAW | 230 | TURNING TOOLS, SCRAPERS. |
| DARK STRAW | 240 | DRILLING, MILLING TOOLS. |
| BROWN | 250 | TAPS, SHEAR BLADES. |
| BROWNISH-PURPLE | 260 | PUNCHES, REAMERS. |
| PURPLE | 270 | AXES, PRESS TOOLS. |
| DARK PURPLE | 280 | COLD CHISELS. |
| BLUE | 300 | SPRINGS, SCREWDRIVERS. |

instance it is necessary to introduce extra carbon into the outer layer of the metal.

This is achieved by heating the steel to red heat and rolling it in carbon-rich powder (available commercially under the trade name 'Kasenite'). The metal then has to be re-heated and rolled again. After this process has been repeated two or three times, the surplus powder should be brushed off with a wire brush, the metal heated to bright red and then quenched. This will leave a case of high carbon steel around a tough mild steel core.

In commercial operations the parts to be case hardened are packed in special refactory boxes full of carbon powder and heated in a furnace for several hours before being quenched.

**Normalising** This process returns work-hardened metal to its normal condition after forging or bending. The metal has to be heated to red heat and allowed to cool naturally in still air.

## Commercial heat treatments

While it is not possible to undertake the following processes in the home workshop, it is important to have some knowledge of commercial methods of heat treatment so that parts that are produced can be given the appropriate treatment. It must be stressed that it is important for you to know and to be able to tell the heat treatment firm the precise material from which the component is made.

**Nitriding** This process will produce a surface on the metal that has a high resistance to wear. Components are placed in airtight containers and heated for a period of 24 hours after the introduction of dry ammonia. This process is ideal for crankshafts, gears, etc., as very little distortion is produced.

**Induction hardening** The component being hardened is placed inside an electric coil. When a high frequency current is passed through the coil the component is heated by induction. Having reached the correct temperature, the component is quenched in oil or by water spray.

**Cyanide hardening** Components to be hardened are heated in a bath of molten sodium cyanide, a hazardous process that no amateur should attempt. This hardening process produces very little surface scale on the component.

**Flame hardening** The surface of the component is heated by a very intense flame before being quenched. Because of the localised position of the flame, it is possible to harden particular parts of a component while leaving the rest untreated. Sprockets, for example, can have the teeth hardened to resist wear while the rest of the sprocket is left in its normal state. Only certain steels can be treated by this method.

# CHAPTER 4

# Bearings and bearing materials

Wherever moving parts come into contact with each other or with a stationary surface, friction will try to prevent the movement between them. Heat is generated and efficiency will be impaired unless an attempt is made to reduce the friction. The purpose of a bearing is to reduce this friction to an acceptable amount, usually in conjunction with some kind of lubrication.

Bearings can be separated into two main groups: plain bearings and rolling element bearings.

## Plain bearings

Plain bearings are the simplest type of bearings, ranging from a bronze bush that carries a slow-moving shaft to a high-performance white metal shell that can support a connecting rod revolving thousands of times a minute.

**Bronze** is used for bushes that carry a moderate load at medium speeds. The bush can be machined from cast bronze bar and, to save a large amount of waste, bar above 1 inch (25 mm) diameter can be bought hollow in a range of sizes.

Self-lubricating or porous bronze bushes are used in situations where regular lubrication would be difficult and an excess of oil undesirable. These bushes are made from bronze powder which is formed to the required shape in a die on a hydraulic press and cold welded together under the pressure of the press. The bush is then sintered in an oven to give it its final strength. These bushes should be soaked in oil for 24 hours before fitting; the lubrication should then last the lifetime of the bush.

**White metal** Plain bearings for high speed and high loadings are made from white metal, a blanket description which covers a range of different alloys of tin and lead. The original alloy was called 'Babbit' metal, the name of the original patentee, and it contained a large proportion of lead. As crankshaft speeds became higher, the lead was replaced by tin to form an alloy of 88% tin plus 8% antimony and 4% copper.

**Lead-indium** In the mid-1960s lead-indium bearings were developed for high-speed engines. This bearing material consists of a bronze layer on a steel shell; a layer of pure lead is then plated on the bronze. Finally a layer of indium is electrolytically and thermally fused over the bearing surface to give it good anti-frictional qualities.

**Aluminium** In recent years the rising price of tin has forced bearing manufacturers to experiment with other metals, particularly aluminium. Reticular tin aluminium bearings have been developed

which do not require the overlay of indium or other materials. The crystals of aluminium are coated with tin and the material is bonded onto the steel strip. This is followed by a heat treatment process during which the tin aluminium structure is modified and the tin forms a continuous network through the aluminium.

**Plastics**, particularly nylon, have been used as plain bearings for some years. Their use is limited to medium-speed, low-load applications where heat is not a problem. Plastics technology is, however, progressing rapidly and it may not be long before new plastics will be able to take over the role of more traditional materials.

### Fitting moulded bearings

Up until the late 1930s big-end bearings were cast direct onto the con-rod and then machined to size. This type of bearing must be carefully fitted by hand-scraping to match the corresponding crankshaft journal.

The process of scraping is not difficult but requires patience and care to achieve a good result. The crankshaft journal must be clean and then a thin coating of engineer's blue should be applied to the whole of it. The con-rod should then be bolted to the journal and the crankshaft rotated by hand for one or two revolutions. The con-rod is then removed and the white metal inspected; the high spots of the bearing will show blue where they have rubbed the crankshaft journal, and these must be carefully removed using a half-round scraper; only a very small amount of metal should be removed at a time as it is very easy to go too far.

The bearing should then be bolted up again after it has been cleaned, the journal re-coated with the engineer's blue and the crankshaft rotated again. The scraping of the bearing should continue until an even coating of blue is transferred to the whole surface of the big-end bearing. The con-rod should also rotate freely round the crankshaft. Do not forget that there needs to be clearance between the sides of the bearing and the cheeks of the crankshaft to allow for expansion when the engine gets warm. It is foolish to cheat at this stage and add a little extra engineer's blue to the crankshaft to make the bearing appear a better fit; you are only storing up trouble for yourself later on. If the crankshaft has been re-ground at the same time as the bearings have been re-metalled there should not be much scraping to do to provide a perfect fit.

More modern engines fitted with shell bearings are a much easier proposition; replacement is a matter of fitting new shells. Naturally the crankshaft should be checked both visually and with a micrometer for signs of scoring and wear.

Manufacturers' workshop manuals usually give the maximum allowance for ovality and there should be no taper from one end of the journal to the other. If the crankshaft is oval or scored it will need to be reground and the next undersize big-end bearings fitted.

Some manufacturers of more recent machines do not provide undersize bearing shells, so allowing the crankshaft to be re-ground, their belief being that the crankshaft should last for the usable lifetime of the machine. To those of us interested in

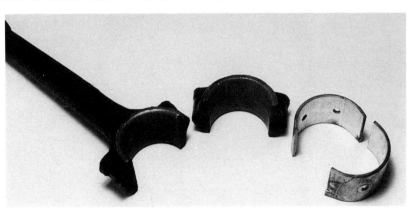

**Left** *Hollow bronze bar for making plain bushes.*

**Right** *A moulded white metal big-end, and big-end sheels.*

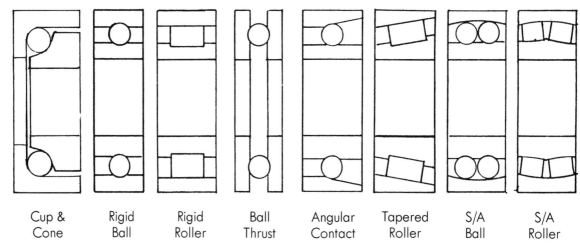

| Cup & Cone | Rigid Ball | Rigid Roller | Ball Thrust | Angular Contact | Tapered Roller | S/A Ball | S/A Roller |

**Top** *Fig. 7 Some typical rolling element bearings.*

**Above left** *A rigid ball bearing.*

**Above** *A rigid roller bearing.*

**Left** *A needle roller bearing.*

**Top right** *A ball thrust bearing.*

**Middle right** *Angular contact bearings, showing thrust and non-thrust faces.*

**Bottom right** *A tapered roller bearing.*

preserving older machines this seems a short-sighted attitude to say the least. Fortunately there are some engine re-conditioners who offer a crankshaft service complete with undersize bearings, but this does mean shopping around for a firm that offers the service for your particular machine. This is an area where one-make clubs can be a very useful source of information.

Failing this, it is possible to have the worn journal built up by either metal spraying or plating and then ground back to the standard size. Again this service is carried out by some engine re-conditioners.

## Rolling element bearings

Although plain bearings have many uses in motor cycles, they are quite inefficient compared to rolling element bearings. These convert the sliding friction of plain bearings to rolling friction, which requires less power to overcome.

There are many types of rolling element bearings available and Figure 7 shows the main types of anti-friction bearings found on motor cycles.

The **rigid ball** bearing shown opposite is probably in greater use than any other type. It will carry radial and axial loads with combinations of both, and has many uses in gearboxes, crankshafts, big-ends and wheel bearings.

**Rigid roller** bearings are capable of carrying very high radial loads but they cannot be used to locate a shaft as the design of the bearing allows free lateral movement of the shaft. Where the rollers are of a small diameter the bearing is referred to as a needle roller bearing.

**Ball thrust** bearings are designed to take axial loads only and are most suited for use at low speeds. They can be found in some types of steering head to take the thrust at the bottom of the shaft.

**Angular contact** bearings are dual-purpose bearings, capable of taking thrust in one direction only or combined thrust and radial loads. Ideally two

such bearings should be fitted to the shaft, set in opposite directions. Because it is the axial load that keeps the balls in their tracks, the bearings must be carefully adjusted to eliminate end play. Their use is not very common on motor cycles but a knowledge of them could prove useful on the rare occasions you may come across them.

**Tapered roller** bearings are designed to take high axial loadings in one direction only, and are often used in the steering head of more modern machines. Older-type bearings are adjusted so that there is a small amount of play in the system. Some newer types of these bearings are designed to be set up with some pre-load on the system.

The **cup and cone** bearing is one of the oldest types of ball bearing, and is used frequently for wheel bearings in older machines and also in the steering head. Some types have a cage for locating the balls while the majority rely on the balls spacing themselves around the bearing surfaces. It is important when fitting these bearings to ensure that the balls used are the right diameter for the tracks and that only the correct number are fitted. There should be a space equivalent to approximately half the diameter of a ball left when the correct number are in place.

All the bearings described so far rely on the accurate alignment of the shaft and bearing housing to work correctly. Where this cannot be achieved, or where the shaft is likely to deflect, a **self-aligning ball bearing** should be chosen. It should not be used where axial loading is present though it will take moderate radial loads. Where higher radial loads are anticipated, the **self-aligning roller bearing** should be used.

## Ball and roller bearing maintenance

Whenever a component that has a ball or roller bearing in it is stripped down, the bearing should be inspected carefully for signs of wear or damage.

Wash the bearing carefully in white spirit, making sure it is completely clean. Examine the tracks and rolling elements for pitting or scoring, and also look for any signs of overheating. Hold the outer ring firmly and turn the inner ring with pressure first on one side, then the other. If there is any gritty or rough feeling as it is turned, it should be scrapped; similarly, if any signs of wear are present it should also be scrapped. If you are in any doubt, scrap the bearing anyway — it has probably been in place for years and the cost of a new one is worth the peace of mind it brings.

Take care when removing bearings from their shafts or housings. A sustained attack with a large

*A self-aligning ball bearing.*

*A self-aligning roller bearing.*

hammer will only serve to ruin what could have been a perfectly serviceable bearing. A press or a set of claw extractors are the correct tools for the job, but if you cannot borrow or hire them, then, with care, a hammer can be used.

It is usual for the rotating part of the bearing to be an interference fit and the stationary part of the bearing to be a firm push fit. In the majority of cases, where a shaft rotates the inner ring must be an interference fit on the shaft, and the outer ring a firm push fit into the housing. In this instance the inner ring of the bearing must be used to drive the bearing off the shaft. Use a brass drift and a heavy hammer, working round the ring to even out the pressure. It is essential that the bearing is kept square to the shaft to prevent damage to either. Obviously the outer ring of the bearing will be driven out of the housing in the same way.

Re-fitting the bearing must also be done with care. A press is the best method, but if one is not available a hammer can be used. When fitting a bearing onto a shaft, a short length of thick-walled tube, slightly larger than the diameter of the shaft, will help to drive the bearing on square.

Where a bearing is fitted into a housing, it is often a good idea to warm the housing first. If it is small it can be warmed in a domestic oven, or a small blowlamp can be used. However, take care with the heating, particularly if the housing is made of aluminium or other low-melting-point alloy. If the housing is small enough it may be possible to use the bench vice as a small press to fit the bearing. Obviously it is essential to keep everything very clean during this operation, to prevent dirt or grit finding their way into the bearing.

If the outer or inner ring of the bearing has been rotating in the housing or on the shaft, the fault will have to be rectified before reassembly. Should the wear be small, it is possible to use an adhesive such as 'Perma Bond A11B' retainer; correctly applied, this will give up to four times the shear strength of an interference fit. Where the wear is great, the shaft or housing will have to be built up either by metal spraying or by electro-plating. Under no circumstances try to rectify the problem by using a centre punch to raise the surface of the shaft or housing. It may appear to work but the bearing will soon fret loose again.

Most bearings located in an external casing of a component are fitted with an oil seal of some description. These should always be renewed before reassembly; their low cost does not warrant trying to make do with a worn seal. Ensure that the seal is fitted the correct way round and that it is seated squarely in its housing. The older type of felt seal which was used to retain grease should be renewed if it shows any sign of hardening or leakage. New felt seals should be soaked in oil before fitting.

When buying a new bearing it is important to be able to quote the reference numbers that are stamped or engraved on the ring of the bearing. This will allow the stockist to cross reference the numbers and find the correct type and size. Bearings are also graded by manufacturing and fitting tolerances on the scale 0 to 0000. For most purposes 00 grade will be suitable for almost all motor cycling purposes. You may never be asked about these grades but if you are, and you have at least heard of them, you will not feel totally ignorant!

If you have a friend in the engineering trade, now is the time to buy him a pint and ask a favour. Considerable discounts are given by bearing stockists and manufacturers to the engineering trade and a friend in the right place could save you a fair bit of money.

# CHAPTER 5
# Hand tools for metalworking

This chapter describes some of the more common hand tools that could be useful to the motor cycle restorer; it is not intended as a comprehensive guide to all hand tools — to achieve that would require a book in itself.

## Marking out and measuring tools

**Steel rule**   Available in a range of sizes and choice of graduations. Much preferred to a wooden rule for measuring.

**Scriber**   Made of high-carbon steel and available in several sizes and types. The point should be ground to a 30° angle and kept sharp for accuracy.

**Centre punch**   Made of high-carbon steel, the point should be ground to 90°. Used for marking the position of a hole before drilling. A dot punch is similar in shape and size but the point is ground to 60°.

**Engineer's square**   Used for checking squareness and marking lines at right-angles to an edge.

**Combination set** is four tools in one — a grooved steel rule along which three other tools can slide. The square head has one face to 90° to the rule, another at 45°. It also incorporates a spirit level. This can be used as a mitre square, square, or depth gauge, etc. The protractor head enables the rule to be set at any angle for marking out or

*A scriber and dot punch.*

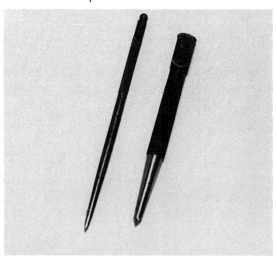

*A transfer centre punch. This is very useful for marking centres through one component into another.*

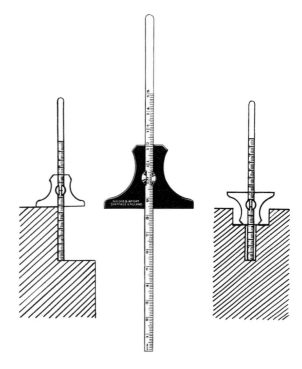

Above *A selection of marking out tools. The combination set and engineer's square are in the centre.* (James Neill Ltd.)

Above right *Fig. 8 A depth gauge and its uses.* (James Neill Ltd.)

Right *Spring dividers.* (L.S. Starrett Ltd.)

measuring angles. The centre square is used to locate the centre of a round bar.

All the heads can be locked onto the rule with knurled nuts; the spirit levels can be used for setting up work before machining.

**Depth gauge**  This tool consists of a steel body with a narrow rule running through the centre of it. The rule can be locked in any position by means of a knurled nut. It is used to measure the depth of holes, recesses, etc. (see Figure 8).

**Dividers**  Used for scribing arcs and circles, also for stepping off measurements.

**Trammels**  For drawing large-diameter circles

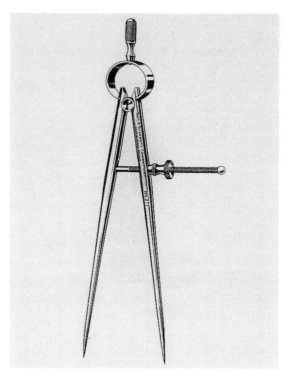

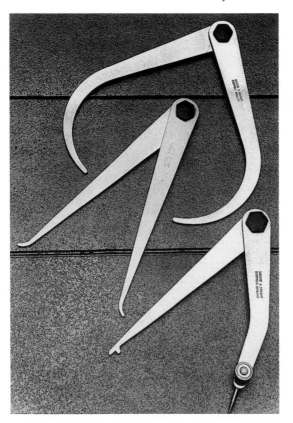

and stepping off measurements beyond the scope of dividers. Two heads are used on a beam of suitable length; some types have a fine adjustment mechanism on one head for accurate setting.

**Inside callipers**   Used for measuring inside diameters or slots. One leg is held in contact with the metal while the other is rocked through an arc to get the right 'feel'.

**Outside callipers**   Used for measuring outside diameters. They must be held square to the work or a false reading will be obtained.

**Odd-leg callipers**   These are used for scribing a line parallel to an edge. Care must be taken to ensure that they are held square to the edge otherwise the line will be inaccurate. They can also be used to find the centre of a bar by estimation from four positions. Also known by the name Jenny or hermaphrodite callipers.

### Micrometers

The appearance and construction principles of the micrometer are the same whether it is for imperial or metric measurement. The micrometer consists

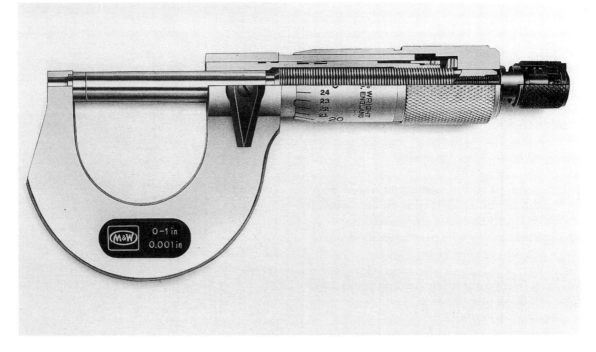

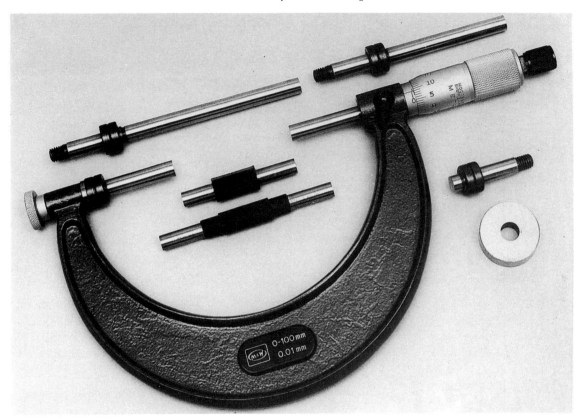

**Above left** *From top to bottom, outside, inside and odd-leg callipers.* (James Neill Ltd.)

**Left** *A cutaway view of a micrometer.* (James Neill Ltd.)

**Above** *A 0-100 mm micrometer with extension bars.* (James Neill Ltd.)

**Right** *Digital micrometer. This gives a visual display of the reading, which reduces the risk of error.* (James Neill Ltd.)

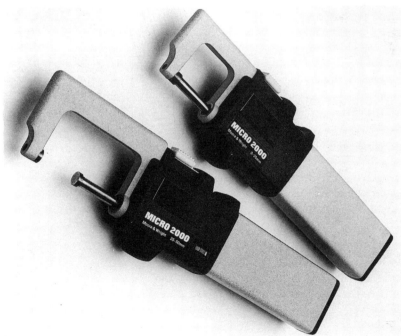

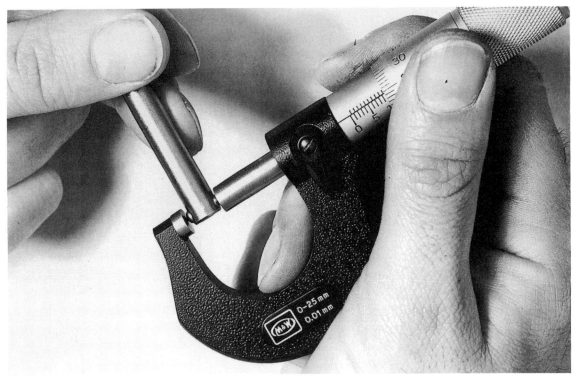

**Above** *The correct way to hold a micrometer when taking readings.* (James Neill Ltd.)

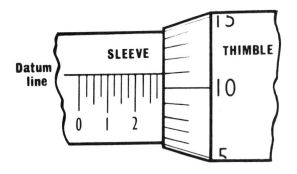

*Fig. 9 Reading the imperial micrometer.* (James Neill Ltd.)

| | |
|---|---:|
| 1 *Read the largest number on the sleeve* | ·200 *inch* |
| 2 *Add the number of fortieths visible on the sleeve* (3 × 0·025) | ·075 *inch* |
| 3 *Add the number on the thimble level with the datum line* | ·011 *inch* |
| *Total* | ·286 *inch* |

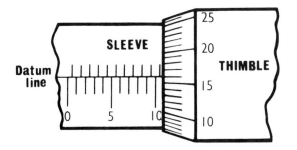

*Fig. 10 Reading the metric micrometer.* (James Neill Ltd.)

| | |
|---|---:|
| 1 *Read the largest number on the sleeve* | 10·00 *mm* |
| 2 *Add half millimetres if necessary* | ·50 *mm* |
| 3 *Add the number on the thimble level with the datum line* | ·16 *mm* |
| *Total* | 10·66 *mm* |

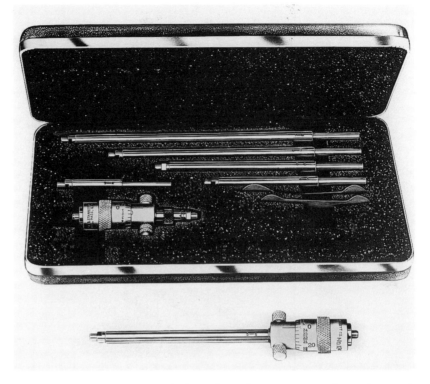

*A full set of internal micrometers for measuring cylinder bores etc.* (L. S. Starrett Ltd.)

of a frame which is roughly semi-circular in shape and carries at its left-hand end the anvil and at its right the barrel, or sleeve, which is graduated in either tenths of an inch or millimetres for a length of 1 inch or 25 mm. The thimble rotates around the barrel and is divided on its circumference into 25 divisions (imperial) or 50 divisions (metric). Micrometers only measure a total of 1 inch (25 mm) so the next size will measure 1 inch to 2 inches (25-50 mm). For larger sizes the frame and the barrels are in two parts and the measuring unit can be clamped into different frame sizes each 1 inch (25 mm) bigger than the last.

**The Imperial micrometer** The screw of the imperial micrometer is threaded 40 teeth per inch (40 TPI). Thus, in one revolution of the thimble the spindle moves $\frac{1}{40}$ inch, or 0·025 inch.

The thimble is divided on its circumference into 25 parts; if the thimble moves along one of these divisions the spindle will move $\frac{1}{25}$ of 0·025 inch, or 0·001 inch. Therefore each division on the thimble represents 0·001 inch.

The barrel, or sleeve, carries a datum line with each tenth of an inch divided into four parts, i.e. 0·025 inch. When the micrometer is closed, the 0 of the barrel should coincide with the 0 on the thimble. If it does not, the micrometer should be adjusted so that it does. Alternatively the discrepancy should be allowed for when calculating the measurement. See Figure 9.

**The metric micrometer** The screw has a pitch of 0·5 mm, therefore the spindle moves 0·5 mm for each revolution of the thimble. The thimble is divided into 50 parts, each division representing a 0·01 mm movement of the spindle. The barrel or sleeve is graduated in millimetres and half millimetres. See Figure 10.

**Internal micrometers** These are used for measuring internal diameters. The head is similar to the external micrometer but its range of adjustment is only $\frac{1}{2}$ inch (13 mm). Its total length is 1 inch (25 mm) which means that 1 inch (25 mm) is the smallest bore it will enter.

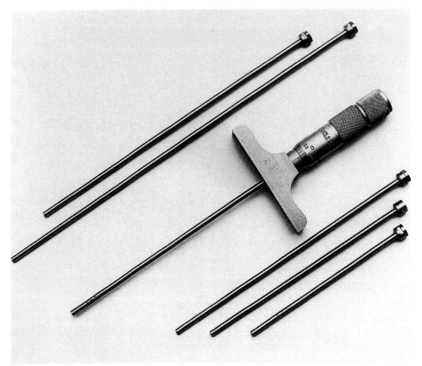

**Left** *A micrometer depth gauge with extension bars.* (James Neill Ltd.)

**Below** *A vernier calliper.* (L.S. Starrett Ltd.)

**Right** *A digital vernier showing the read-out. The 'ears' on the back of the vernier are for measuring internal sizes.* (James Neill Ltd.)

**Below right** *Feeler gauges. These can be used for measuring small gaps, not just valve adjustments,* (James Neill Ltd.)

Extension rods of different lengths are available to increase the range of bore sizes, and a spacing collar $\frac{1}{2}$ inch (13 mm) long can be fitted between the head and the extension rods to give intermediate measurements.

**Micrometer depth gauge**   This is used for the accurate measuring of holes, shoulders, etc. The range of measurement is usually 0–1 inch (0–25 mm) which can be increased by extension rods.

All micrometers should be used with care, and the faces of the anvil and spindle should be cleaned prior to use. Never force the barrel into the work as this will give a false reading. If the micrometer is

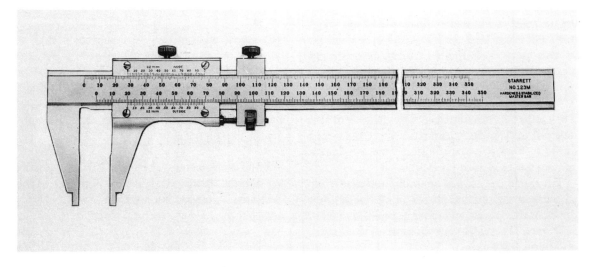

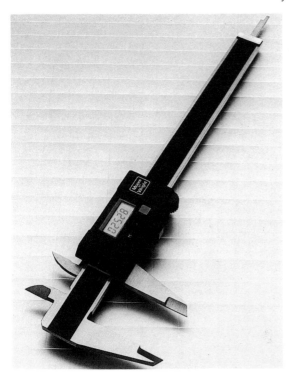

fitted with a rachet, use it and so apply the same correct amount of pressure every time.

When not in use, the micrometer should be stored somewhere safe away from any possible damage.

### Vernier callipers

This tool is capable of reading accurate measurements over a wider range than the micrometer. Vernier callipers are made in sizes from 6 inches (150 mm) upwards and are used for measuring internal and external diameters.

Care should be taken when using the callipers to make sure that the jaws are not strained in any way, which would make them inaccurate. The fine adjustment screw should always be used to produce an accurate reading.

**Reading the vernier** Vernier scales make use of two scales that are slightly different and set alongside each other. They can be used on any scale to enable fine measurements to be made, e.g. micrometer, protractor, etc.

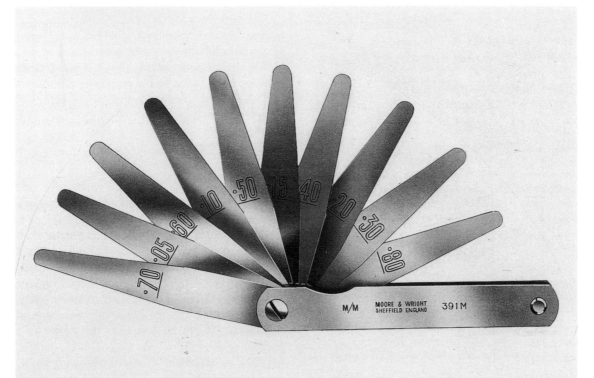

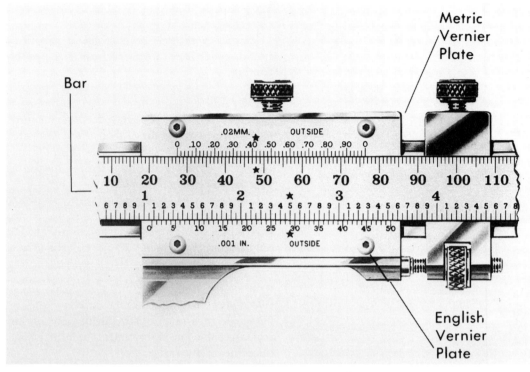

*Fig. 11 Reading a vernier calliper scale.* (L.S. Starrett Ltd.)

*Imperial*

**1** *Read the biggest whole number on the main scale*  1·000 inch

**2** *Read the number of tenths on the main scale before the 0 on the vernier scale (0)*  0·000 inch

**3** *Read the number of twentieths on the main scale before the 0 on the vernier scale (1)*  0·050 inch

**4** *Look for a line on the vernier scale that corresponds with any division on the main scale. The number where this occurs is in thousandths. It is indicated by the star on the diagram (29)*  0·029 inch

Total  1·079 inch

*Metric*

**1** *Read the number of mm on the main scale before the 0 on the vernier scale.*  27·00 mm

**2** *Look for a line on the vernier scale that corresponds with any division on the main scale. This is the number of 0·2 mm, and is indicated by the star (41)*  0·82 mm

Total  27·82 mm

The vernier scale is read in the same way irrespective of the number of divisions on it. Figure 11 explains how it should be read.

When measuring internal sizes, the width of the jaws must be added to the measurements shown on the callipers. It is usual to find the dimensions of the jaws marked on them.

## Cutting tools

### Files

The file is probably the most commonly used cutting tool in any metalworker's workshop and comes in a great variety of shapes and sizes.

Files are made from high-carbon steel; the blade is hardened and tempered while the tang is left soft for strength. The handle, usually of wood, should be a tight fit on the tang; split or loose handles should be replaced to prevent accidents.

The teeth on the file blade can be single or double cut. Single cut files have the teeth cut in parallel rows at 70° to one edge. Double cut files have one set of teeth at 70° to one edge and another set running across them at 45° to the other edge.

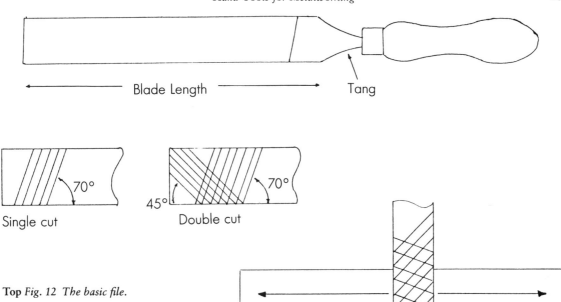

Blade Length — Tang

Single cut

45° Double cut

70° 70°

**Top** *Fig. 12 The basic file.*

**Above** *Fig. 13 Single and double cut files.*

**Right** *Fig. 14 Draw filing.*

The grade of the file indicates the coarseness of the teeth, the grades being: rough, bastard, second cut, smooth, and dead smooth. The number of teeth per 25 mm (1 inch) of the blade varies not only with the grade but also in proportion to the length of the file. A 150 mm (6 inch) second cut file will have more teeth per 25 mm than a 250 mm (10 inch) second cut file.

Files are specified by length, cut and cross-section. Figure 15 shows the main types of file and their uses. Riffler files are small double-ended files; often the blade is curved for filing in awkward places where little material needs to be removed.

Hold metal firmly in a vice with the surface to be filed being horizontal, if possible, and as close to the vice jaws as practicable. Your weight should be balanced evenly on both feet; the left foot should be forward of the right if you are holding the handle of the file in the right hand, or vice versa if you are left-handed. The wrist of the hand holding the handle of the file should be kept rigid and the forearm horizontal and level with the work. The other hand should grasp the tip of the file, with the palm resting on top of the blade.

Apply pressure on the forward stroke, relieving it on the backward stroke, as files only cut on the forward stroke. To produce a flat surface, the file should be used diagonally across the work, changing direction frequently; always use the full length of the file if possible. Once the surface has been filed to the line by cross-filing, a smooth, fine-grained surface can be produced by draw-filing (Figure 14). A smooth file should be used, held at right-angles to the work; the blade should be held with the hands as close together as possible to reduce wobble. The file is then pushed to and fro along the length of the metal until all the cross-filing marks have disappeared.

Files should be looked after carefully; if the teeth become 'pinned' or clogged with pieces of metal they should be cleaned out, as the file will not cut efficiently and the work will become scored. File teeth are brittle and easily chipped, so files should be stored carefully and not thrown together in a box.

If you often work on brass, keep a new file to one side for that purpose as worn files will not cut very well.

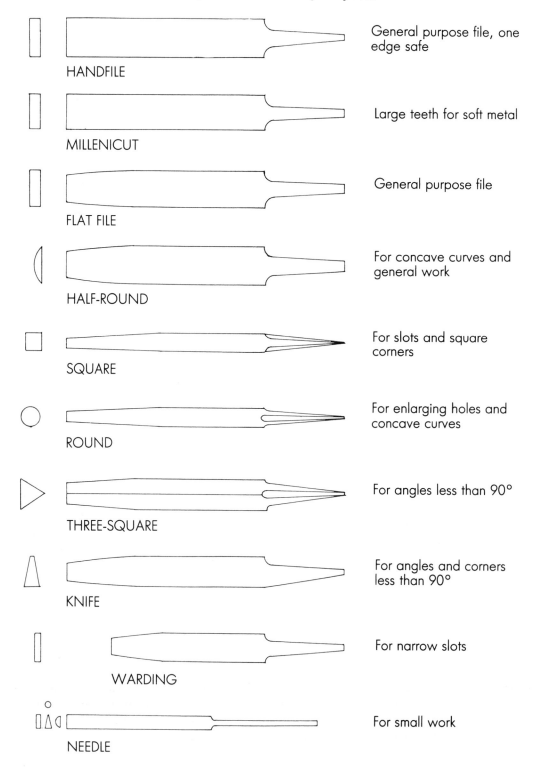

HANDFILE — General purpose file, one edge safe

MILLENICUT — Large teeth for soft metal

FLAT FILE — General purpose file

HALF-ROUND — For concave curves and general work

SQUARE — For slots and square corners

ROUND — For enlarging holes and concave curves

THREE-SQUARE — For angles less than 90°

KNIFE — For angles and corners less than 90°

WARDING — For narrow slots

NEEDLE — For small work

Left *Fig. 15 Files and their uses.*

| TEETH PER 25 mm | USES |
|---|---|
| 14 | LARGE SECTIONS OF SOFT MATERIALS. |
| 18 | SMALL SECTIONS OF SOFT MATERIALS, LARGE SECTIONS OF HARD MATERIALS – GENERAL PURPOSE SIZE. |
| 24 | SMALL SECTIONS OF HARD MATERIALS, eg 3–6 mm TUBE, SHEET AND SECTIONS. |
| 32 | VERY SMALL SECTIONS, eg LESS THAN 3 mm TUBE, SHEET AND SECTIONS. |

Right *Tooth sizes of hand hack-saw blades.*

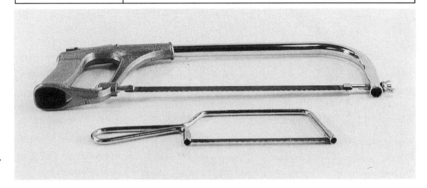

Right *A hacksaw and junior hacksaw.*

## Metal-cutting saws

**Hacksaws** normally have adjustable frames to accommodate blades of different lengths. The blade holders can also be rotated in the frame so that the blade can be held at 90° to it, to enable a long cut to be taken or for sawing in a confined space.

Hand hacksaw blades are 10 inches (250 mm) or 12 inches (300 mm) long and $\frac{1}{2}$ inch (13 mm) wide. The length is measured by the distance between the centres of the fixing holes. The teeth on the blade are 'set' so that the teeth cut a wider slot than the thickness of the blade, to prevent jamming.

Hacksaw blades come in a variety of types and are designated by the material from which they are made and the number of teeth per 1 inch (25 mm). This ranges from 18 to 32 teeth per 1 inch (25 mm), and as a basic guide there should always be at least three teeth in contact with the metal. A thin material will therefore need a greater number of teeth per inch than a thicker one (see the table above).

Junior hacksaws use blades 6 inches (150 mm) long, with pinned ends. The tension on the blade is applied by either the spring of the frame or by tightening the handle. They are used for general-purpose work where the standard hacksaw is too large.

**Tension files** are made from steel wire with spiral teeth which will cut in any direction. They can be used in a special frame or in a standard hacksaw frame, using special links to hold the blades. There are three grades of blade: fine, medium and coarse, each 200 mm (8 inches) long. They should be fitted in the frame with the coloured end of the blade at the handle end of the frame.

**Piercing saws** use a very fine-toothed blade available in different numbers of teeth per 1 inch (25 mm), ranging from 32 to 80. They are used for cutting thin sheet material, where intricate shapes are needed.

### Scrapers
These tools are made from high-carbon steel and are used where only a very small amount of metal needs to be removed. Normally scrapers are not used until a surface has been worked as accurately as possible by other methods.

**Above** *Hand scrapers. From left to right: half-round, flat and triangular.*

**Below** *Ball and cross pein hammers.*

**Bottom** *A selection of hammers for beaten metal work. Left to right: combined blocking and planishing hammer, raising hammer, blocking hammer, and planishing hammer.*

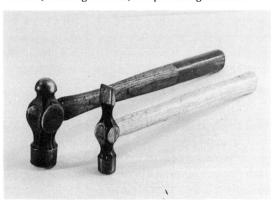

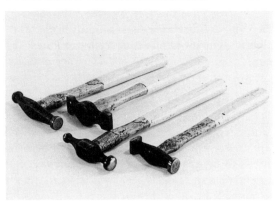

There are three types of scraper: flat, half-round and triangular. The flat scraper is used to make a surface flatter than can be achieved by a file; the half-round scraper is for concave surfaces and is ideal for fitting bearings to a shaft; and the triangular scraper is used for working into awkward corners where the use of the other shapes would be impossible. Old worn-out files can be converted into useful scrapers. They should be first annealed and ground to the shape required and the blade hardened and tempered to a straw colour. The final edge is then achieved by grinding on an oilstone.

# Hammers and mallets

Hammer heads are made from high-carbon steel with the pein and face hardened and tempered; that is why it is dangerous to hit hammer heads together as the hardened faces can chip and fly anywhere.

Hammers are classified by weight from $\frac{1}{4}$ lb (0·1 kg) to 3 lbs (1·35 kg). For general benchwork a hammer of about 1 lb (0·4 kg) is probably best; a heavy hammer can be unwieldy and tiring to use for any length of time.

Hammers used for beaten metalwork come in a variety of shapes and sizes depending on their purpose. The faces of these hammers should be smooth and polished, otherwise any imperfection will be transferred to the metal being beaten. For this reason they should never be used for anything other than beaten metalwork.

**Wooden mallets** are used for sheet metalwork. Their heads are made of boxwood or lignum vitae and the shafts from cane. The tinman's mallet is used for bending sheet metal, while the bossing mallet is used for the initial shaping of concave curves.

**A rawhide mallet** consists of a tightly rolled length of rawhide fixed to a shaft. This mallet gives a softer blow than a boxwood mallet.

**Soft-faced hammers** are available in a variety of materials: copper, brass, lead, rawhide or plastic.

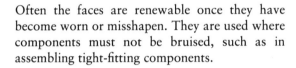

*A selection of mallets. From left to right: tinman's, rawhide and bossing.*

*Cross-cut and flat cold chisels.*

Often the faces are renewable once they have become worn or misshapen. They are used where components must not be bruised, such as in assembling tight-fitting components.

A useful soft hammer can be made by melting some lead in a suitable container. A steel tube for the handle can be stood in the centre of the container and the lead will set round it. It is important that the tube has holes drilled across the diameter so that the lead can flow into the handle and make a mechanical bond between the two. This will prevent the two parting company, usually at a most inappropriate time!

# Cold chisels

Cold chisels are made from high-carbon steel; the cutting edge is hardened and tempered, but the head is left soft otherwise it would crack or splinter when hit with a hammer.

There are four types of cold chisel and the size is denoted by the width of the cutting edge. When the head of the chisel begins to form a mushroom shape after a lot of use, this should be ground off. If it is left there is the danger that pieces of it will fly off when being hit and cause injury.

Cold chisels should be kept sharp, but care must be taken when grinding not to overheat the cutting edge and draw the temper; this will soften the edge and leave it useless for cutting. Flat chisels are most commonly used for general cutting work, while cross-cut chisels are used for cutting slots or grooves. The half-round chisel is used for cutting circular grooves and the diamond chisel for cleaning out corners.

# CHAPTER 6
# Drills and reamers

## Drills

Drills are normally made of high-speed steel (H.S.S.) and have either a parallel or taper shank. They can also be bought in different lengths: the standard length, known as 'jobbers drills', for general-purpose work; long series drills, for deeper hole drilling; and stub drills, which are much shorter than jobbers drills, making them more robust.

Two of the most important aspects of drilling are to ensure that the drill is sharpened correctly and that it is revolving at the right speed. A small bench grinder is essential for sharpening drills properly. The drill must be presented to the grinding wheel at the correct angle of 59° and then rotated so that the tip clearance is produced at the right angle. Figure 17 shows the effects of incorrect grinding.

A grinding attachment can be bought to fit on the grinding machine; this will give quick and accurate results. Attempting to drill holes with a blunt drill will normally result in an inaccurate hole, with the possibility of the drill overheating and becoming useless for further work.

Before drilling a hole, the position should be carefully marked with a centre punch; this will locate the point of the drill and prevent it skidding over the surface of the metal. The work piece should be securely fixed to prevent vibration producing an irregularly shaped hole. When drilling large-diameter holes it is best to use a small drill first to act as a pilot, otherwise the chisel point of the large drill will have difficulty in penetrating the surface of the metal. The pilot drill should be just bigger than the chisel point of the large drill.

Drilling small pieces of sheet metal calls for some care. It is essential to hold the work firmly with a hand vice or mole grips onto a piece of wood; if practicable a G-cramp could be used instead. This is because there is always the possibility that the drill will 'catch' as it breaks through the underside of the sheet; this would be sufficient to pull the sheet from the grasp of bare hands and

*Taper shrank and straight shank drills (left), and (right) large drills with reduced shanks for use in ½ in (13 mm) chucks.*

*Fig. 16 Twist drill nomenclature.* (S.K.F. Dormer Ltd.)

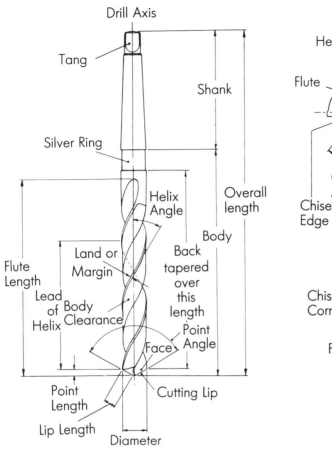

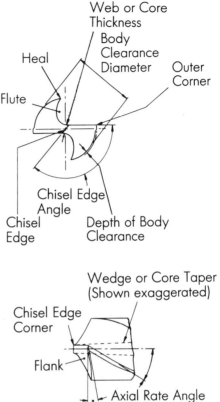

**Right** *A machine vice for use with a drill stand or machine.*

**Below right** *A hand vice for holding sheet metal while drilling.*

**Below** *Fig. 17 The effects of incorrect grinding.*

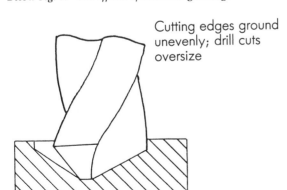

Cutting edges ground unevenly; drill cuts oversize

spin it round on the point of the drill to the obvious detriment of your hands!! The drill catches because the point breaks through the metal before the full diameter of the drill has entered the sheet, a possibility that increases with the size of the drill.

If a lot of drilling in sheet metal is contemplated, the point angle of the drill should be modified to 140° as shown in Figure 18. To protect painted or polished surfaces it is a good idea to use a wide strip or strips of clear sticky tape to prevent the swarf from the drill scratching the surface of the work.

When drilling plastic it is usual to use a slow helix drill for a thermosetting plastic (one that has been hardened by heat during manufacture) and a quick helix one for thermoplastic (which softens when heated), but a normal one can be used with care. The work should be firmly clamped and the position of the hole carefully marked. The drill should not be forced through; thermosets tend to chip and thermoplastics will soften and tend to grip the drill. Soluble oil or even plain water can help prevent the latter happening, while thermosets are drilled dry.

**Counterbores** are used to make a recess for the head of a cheese head screw. The pilot which fits down the hole for the screw ensures that the two holes are concentric. Counterbores can also be used for spot facing, which is the machining of the rough surface of a casting to provide a flat seating for a washer.

If a counterbore is not available, the end of a normal drill can be ground flat and used for the operation. The main difficulty here is ensuring that the two holes are concentric.

**Countersink drills** are used to enlarge the beginning of a hole to take the head of a countersunk screw, and for countersinking prior to riveting. They are made with an included angle of 60° or 90°, the second being used for setting in screw heads. The rose countersink is usually made of high-carbon steel and is used for softer materials such as wood. It is made with a square or round shank. The machine countersink is made from high-speed steel and will withstand use on harder

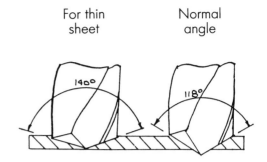

For thin sheet — Normal angle

Fig. 18 Drill point modified for sheet metal.

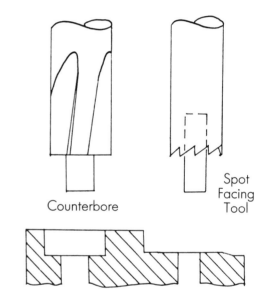

Counterbore — Spot Facing Tool

Fig. 19 A counterbore and spot facer.

materials. Care is needed in the use of both types, since they cannot normally be sharpened.

A **centre drill** is a twist drill and countersink combined. It is also known as a combination drill or slocombe drill. Its main use is for spotting the centre of a hole prior to drilling in the lathe, or preparing the work for mounting on a centre. These drills range in size from 3 mm diameter upwards, and the angle of their cutting edges is 60° to correspond to the 60° angle of a lathe centre. While they are mainly used for lathe work they can also be used to start off a small-diameter hole as their sturdy construction prevents the point wandering, which is always a possibility with small drills.

**Tank cutters** and **hole saws** are used for cutting out large washers or large holes in thin plate. The tank cutter is adjustable for size, the cutter being locked in position by means of a wing nut. Hole saws are not adjustable and, unlike the tank cutter, can be used in a power drill. Plenty of coolant is required when cutting metal, though they will cut through wood with ease. The more expensive types of hole saw will have blades of H.S.S., while the cheaper variety usually have low-carbon steel blades which will dull quickly on hard material.

**Flat drills** It is possible to make a flat drill as shown in Figure 20 for one-off or awkward sizes. The drill should be made from silver steel and the end heated and forged to shape. After filing or grinding to size it should be hardened and tempered to a dark straw colour. This type of drill does have the disadvantage of scraping rather than cutting and has a greater tendency to wander, but it is better than none at all.

Flat-bottomed drills and peg drills for counterboring can also be made from silver steel, hardened and tempered in the same way as the flat drill.

**Above right** *A tank cutter, held in a hand brace and used to cut holes in sheet metal.*

**Right** *A hole punch, available in a variety of sizes. Square punches can also be obtained.*

**Below** *Fig. 20 A flat drill.*

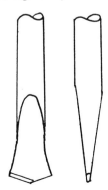

# Reamers and reaming

Reamers are used to produce a smooth, true-to-size hole; they are made from high-speed steel and should be looked after with care. The drill used before reaming should be sharpened correctly so as to produce as smooth a hole as possible and the hole should be drilled carefully. A reamer will follow the drilled hole, so it must be as accurate as possible.

The size of the hole is important; the amount of metal left to be removed must not be too much or

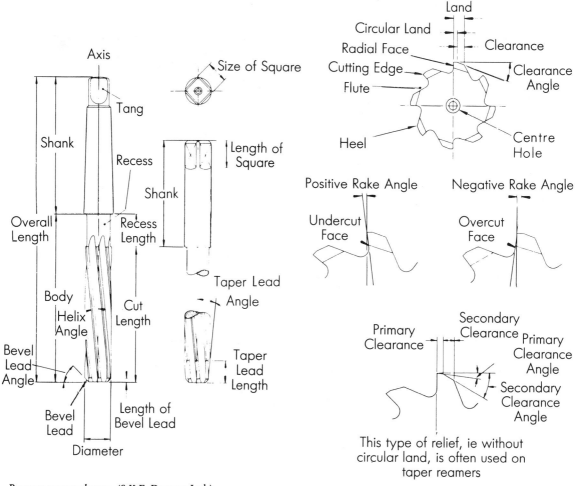

*Reamer nomenclature.* (S.K.F. Dormer Ltd.)

*Taper shank reamers for use in a machine.*

*Parallel shank reamers for use by hand or in a machine.*

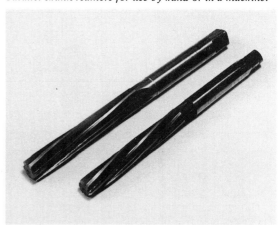

the reamer will have great difficulty in cutting, while too little metal left to remove will cause the reamer to rub rather than cut. The table in Figure 21 gives the amount of metal to be left for the reamer to cut.

Hand reamers are held in a tap wrench and should be used with some cutting lubricant such as 'Trefolex'. It is essential that the reamer is turned clockwise when cutting and while removing the tool from the hole. This prevents the cutting edges being dulled as they rub against the metal.

Machine and hand reamers can be used in a drilling machine providing the speed can be reduced to less than half that recommended for drilling.

Adjustable hand reamers have a two-fold advantage over normal reamers in that they can be adjusted slightly to match the hole being reamed to the shaft to give a perfect fit. They can also be dismantled and the blades sharpened easily.

If you have no reamer, a usable one can be made from a piece of silver steel of the correct diameter. The cutting portion should be filed or machined to exactly half the diameter of the rod, angled at the end and a slight lead filed on. The tools should be hardened and tempered to straw. See Figure 22.

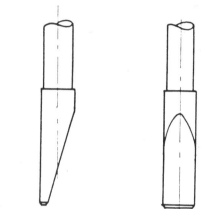

**Top** *An adjustable reamer.*

**Above** *Fig. 22 A hand-made reamer.*

**Overleaf** *Imperial and metric equivalents. These tables include the old gauge or number drills and letter drills.*

*Fig. 21 Stock removal.*

| SIZE OF REAMED HOLE: | WHEN PRE-DRILLED | WHEN PRE-CORE DRILLED |
|---|---|---|
| UP TO 10 INCLUSIVE | 0.30 | 0.20 |
| OVER 10 TO 14 INCLUSIVE | 0.40 | 0.25 |
| OVER 14 TO 18 INCLUSIVE | 0.50 | 0.25 |
| OVER 18 TO 30 INCLUSIVE | 0.50 | 0.30 |
| OVER 30 TO 50 INCLUSIVE | 1.00 | 0.40 |

| SIZE OF REAMED HOLE: | WHEN PRE-DRILLED | WHEN PRE-CORE DRILLED |
|---|---|---|
| UP TO $\frac{3}{8}$″ INCLUSIVE | .010 | .007 |
| OVER $\frac{3}{8}$″ TO $\frac{3}{4}$″ INCLUSIVE | $\frac{1}{64}$ | .010 |
| OVER $\frac{3}{4}$″ TO $1\frac{1}{4}$″ INCLUSIVE | .020 | .012 |
| OVER $1\frac{1}{4}$″ TO 2″ INCLUSIVE | $\frac{1}{32}$ | $\frac{1}{64}$ |

Above are listed general approximations of the amount of stock to be removed by a reamer. The second column shows stock removal when a two flute drill only has been used. The third, when a core drill has been used as a pre-finishing tool. Figures are in millimetres, except those shown in inches, and the derived drill diameters are all stocked sizes for whole millimetre reamers. It is essential to understand that parallel machine reamers only cut on the bevel lead, that parallel hand reamers which have both bevel and taper leads, may cut on both, but in neither case do the lands on the body do any cutting. Generally standard reamers are made right hand cutting with left hand spiral flutes, the spiral angle and number of flutes being at the manufacturer's discretion.

| Frac. | mm | Gauge | Inch | Frac. | mm | Gauge | Inch |
|---|---|---|---|---|---|---|---|
| 1/64 | .30 | | .0118 | | 1.45 | | .0571 |
| | .32 | | .0126 | | 1.50 | | .0591 |
| | .343 | 80 | .0135 | | 1.511 | 53 | .0595 |
| | .35 | | .0138 | | 1.55 | | .0610 |
| | .368 | 79 | .0145 | 1/16 | 1.588 | | .0625 |
| | .38 | | .0150 | | 1.60 | | .0630 |
| 1/64 | .397 | | .0156 | | 1.613 | 52 | .0635 |
| | .40 | | .0157 | | 1.65 | | .0650 |
| | .406 | 78 | .0160 | | 1.70 | | .0669 |
| | .42 | | .0165 | | 1.702 | 51 | .0670 |
| | .45 | | .0177 | | 1.75 | | .0689 |
| | .457 | 77 | .0180 | | 1.778 | 50 | .0700 |
| | .48 | | .0189 | | 1.80 | | .0709 |
| | .50 | | .0197 | | 1.85 | | .0728 |
| | .508 | 76 | .0200 | | 1.854 | 49 | .0730 |
| | .52 | | .0205 | | 1.90 | | .0748 |
| | .533 | 75 | .0210 | | 1.930 | 48 | .0760 |
| | .55 | | .0217 | | 1.95 | | .0768 |
| | .572 | 74 | .0225 | 5/64 | 1.984 | | .0781 |
| | .58 | | .0228 | | 1.994 | 47 | .0785 |
| | .60 | | .0236 | | 2.00 | | .0787 |
| | .610 | 73 | .0240 | | 2.05 | | .0807 |
| | .62 | | .0244 | | 2.057 | 46 | .0810 |
| | .635 | 72 | .0250 | | 2.083 | 45 | .0820 |
| | .65 | | .0256 | | 2.10 | | .0827 |
| | .660 | 71 | .0260 | | 2.15 | | .0846 |
| | .68 | | .0268 | | 2.184 | 44 | .0860 |
| | .70 | | .0276 | | 2.20 | | .0866 |
| | .711 | 70 | .0280 | | 2.25 | | .0886 |
| | .72 | | .0283 | | 2.261 | 43 | .0890 |
| | .742 | 69 | .0292 | | 2.30 | | .0906 |
| | .75 | | .0295 | | 2.35 | | .0925 |
| | .78 | | .0307 | | 2.375 | 42 | .0935 |
| | .787 | 68 | .0310 | 3/32 | 2.381 | | .0938 |
| 1/32 | .794 | | .0312 | | 2.40 | | .0945 |
| | .80 | | .0315 | | 2.438 | 41 | .0960 |
| | .813 | 67 | .0320 | | 2.45 | | .0965 |
| | .82 | | .0323 | | 2.489 | 40 | .0980 |
| | .838 | 66 | .0330 | | 2.50 | | .0984 |
| | .85 | | .0335 | | 2.527 | 39 | .0995 |
| | .88 | | .0346 | | 2.55 | | .1004 |
| | .889 | 65 | .0350 | | 2.578 | 38 | .1015 |
| | .90 | | .0354 | | 2.60 | | .1024 |
| | .914 | 64 | .0360 | | 2.642 | 37 | .1040 |
| | .92 | | .0362 | | 2.65 | | .1043 |
| | .940 | 63 | .0370 | | 2.70 | | .1063 |
| | .95 | | .0374 | | 2.705 | 36 | .1065 |
| | .965 | 62 | .0380 | | 2.75 | | .1083 |
| | .98 | | .0386 | 7/64 | 2.778 | | .1094 |
| | .991 | 61 | .0390 | | 2.794 | 35 | .1100 |
| | 1.00 | | .0394 | | 2.80 | | .1102 |
| | 1.016 | 60 | .0400 | | 2.819 | 34 | .1110 |
| | 1.041 | 59 | .0410 | | 2.85 | | .1122 |
| | 1.05 | | .0413 | | 2.870 | 33 | .1130 |
| | 1.067 | 58 | .0420 | | 2.90 | | .1142 |
| | 1.092 | 57 | .0430 | | 2.946 | 32 | .1160 |
| | 1.10 | | .0433 | | 2.95 | | .1161 |
| | 1.15 | | .0453 | | 3.00 | | .1181 |
| | 1.181 | 56 | .0465 | | 3.048 | 31 | .1200 |
| 3/64 | 1.191 | | .0469 | | 3.10 | | .1220 |
| | 1.20 | | .0472 | 1/8 | 3.175 | | .1250 |
| | 1.25 | | .0492 | | 3.20 | | .1260 |
| | 1.30 | | .0512 | | 3.25 | | .1280 |
| | 1.321 | 55 | .0520 | | 3.264 | 30 | .1285 |
| | 1.35 | | .0531 | | 3.30 | | .1299 |
| | 1.397 | 54 | .0550 | | 3.40 | | .1339 |
| | 1.40 | | .0551 | | | | |

| Frac. | mm | Gauge | Inch | Frac. | mm | Letter | Inch |
|---|---|---|---|---|---|---|---|
| | 3.454 | 29 | .1360 | | 6.045 | B | .2380 |
| | 3.50 | | .1378 | | 6.10 | | .2402 |
| | 3.569 | 28 | .1405 | | 6.147 | C | .2420 |
| 9/64 | 3.572 | | .1406 | | 6.20 | | .2441 |
| | 3.60 | | .1417 | | 6.248 | D | .2460 |
| | 3.658 | 27 | .1440 | | 6.25 | | .2461 |
| | 3.70 | | .1457 | | 6.30 | | .2480 |
| | 3.734 | 26 | .1470 | 1/4 | 6.350 | E | .2500 |
| | 3.75 | | .1476 | | 6.40 | | .2520 |
| | 3.797 | 25 | .1495 | | 6.50 | | .2559 |
| | 3.80 | | .1496 | | 6.528 | F | .2570 |
| | 3.861 | 24 | .1520 | | 6.60 | | .2598 |
| | 3.90 | | .1535 | | 6.629 | G | .2610 |
| | 3.912 | 23 | .1540 | | 6.70 | | .2638 |
| 5/32 | 3.969 | | .1562 | 17/64 | 6.747 | | .2656 |
| | 3.988 | 22 | .1570 | | 6.75 | | .2657 |
| | 4.00 | | .1575 | | 6.756 | H | .2660 |
| | 4.039 | 21 | .1590 | | 6.80 | | .2677 |
| | 4.089 | 20 | .1610 | | 6.90 | | .2717 |
| | 4.10 | | .1614 | | 6.909 | I | .2720 |
| | 4.20 | | .1654 | | 7.00 | | .2756 |
| | 4.216 | 19 | .1660 | | 7.036 | J | .2770 |
| | 4.25 | | .1673 | | 7.10 | | .2795 |
| | 4.30 | | .1693 | | 7.137 | K | .2810 |
| | 4.305 | 18 | .1695 | 9/32 | 7.144 | | .2812 |
| 11/64 | 4.366 | | .1719 | | 7.20 | | .2835 |
| | 4.394 | 17 | .1730 | | 7.25 | | .2854 |
| | 4.40 | | .1732 | | 7.30 | | .2874 |
| | 4.496 | 16 | .1770 | | 7.366 | L | .2900 |
| | 4.50 | | .1772 | | 7.40 | | .2913 |
| | 4.572 | 15 | .1800 | | 7.493 | M | .2950 |
| | 4.60 | | .1811 | | 7.50 | | .2953 |
| | 4.623 | 14 | .1820 | 19/64 | 7.541 | | .2969 |
| | 4.70 | 13 | .1850 | | 7.60 | | .2992 |
| | 4.75 | | .1870 | | 7.671 | N | .3020 |
| 3/16 | 4.762 | | .1875 | | 7.70 | | .3031 |
| | 4.80 | 12 | .1890 | | 7.75 | | .3051 |
| | 4.851 | 11 | .1910 | | 7.80 | | .3071 |
| | 4.90 | | .1929 | | 7.90 | | .3110 |
| | 4.915 | 10 | .1935 | 5/16 | 7.938 | | .3125 |
| | 4.978 | 9 | .1960 | | 8.00 | | .3150 |
| | 5.00 | | .1969 | | 8.026 | O | .3160 |
| | 5.055 | 8 | .1990 | | 8.10 | | .3189 |
| | 5.10 | | .2008 | | 8.20 | | .3228 |
| | 5.105 | 7 | .2010 | | 8.204 | P | .3230 |
| 13/64 | 5.159 | | .2031 | | 8.25 | | .3248 |
| | 5.182 | 6 | .2040 | | 8.30 | | .3268 |
| | 5.20 | | .2047 | 21/64 | 8.334 | | .3281 |
| | 5.220 | 5 | .2055 | | 8.40 | | .3307 |
| | 5.25 | | .2067 | | 8.433 | Q | .3320 |
| | 5.30 | | .2087 | | 8.50 | | .3346 |
| | 5.309 | 4 | .2090 | | 8.60 | | .3386 |
| | 5.40 | | .2126 | | 8.611 | R | .3390 |
| | 5.410 | 3 | .2130 | | 8.70 | | .3425 |
| | 5.50 | | .2165 | 11/32 | 8.731 | | .3438 |
| 7/32 | 5.556 | | .2188 | | 8.75 | | .3445 |
| | 5.60 | | .2205 | | 8.80 | | .3465 |
| | 5.613 | 2 | .2210 | | 8.839 | S | .3480 |
| | 5.70 | | .2244 | | 8.90 | | .3504 |
| | 5.75 | | .2264 | | 9.00 | | .3543 |
| | 5.791 | 1 | .2280 | | 9.093 | T | .3580 |
| | 5.80 | | .2283 | | 9.10 | | .3583 |
| | 5.90 | | .2323 | 23/64 | 9.128 | | .3594 |
| | 5.944 | A | .2340 | | 9.20 | | .3622 |
| 15/64 | 5.953 | | .2344 | | 9.25 | | .3642 |
| | 6.00 | | .2362 | | 9.30 | | .3661 |

| Frac. | mm | Letter | Inch | Frac. | mm | Inch |
|---|---|---|---|---|---|---|
| | 9.347 | U | .3680 | | 13.70 | .5394 |
| | 9.40 | | .3701 | | 13.75 | .5413 |
| | 9.50 | | .3740 | | 13.80 | .5433 |
| 3/8 | 9.525 | | .3750 | 35/64 | 13.891 | .5469 |
| | 9.576 | V | .3770 | | 13.90 | .5472 |
| | 9.60 | | .3780 | | 14.00 | .5512 |
| | 9.70 | | .3819 | | 14.25 | .5610 |
| | 9.75 | | .3839 | 9/16 | 14.288 | .5625 |
| | 9.80 | | .3858 | | 14.50 | .5709 |
| | 9.804 | W | .3860 | 37/64 | 14.684 | 5781 |
| | 9.90 | | .3898 | | 14.75 | .5807 |
| 25/64 | 9.922 | | .3906 | | 15.00 | .5906 |
| | 10.00 | | .3937 | 19/32 | 15.081 | .5938 |
| | 10.084 | X | .3970 | | 15.25 | .6004 |
| | 10.10 | | .3976 | 39/64 | 15.478 | .6094 |
| | 10.20 | | .4016 | | 15.50 | .6120 |
| | 10.25 | | .4035 | | 15.75 | .6201 |
| | 10.262 | Y | .4040 | 5/8 | 15.875 | .6250 |
| | 10.30 | | .4055 | | 16.00 | .6299 |
| 13/32 | 10.319 | | .4062 | | 16.25 | .6398 |
| | 10.40 | | .4094 | 41/64 | 16.272 | .6406 |
| | 10.490 | Z | .4130 | | 16.50 | .6496 |
| | 10.50 | | .4134 | 21/32 | 16.669 | .6562 |
| | 10.60 | | .4173 | | 16.75 | .6594 |
| | 10.70 | | .4213 | | 17.00 | .6693 |
| 27/64 | 10.716 | | .4219 | 43/64 | 17.066 | .6719 |
| | 10.75 | | .4232 | | 17.25 | .6791 |
| | 10.80 | | .4252 | 11/16 | 17.462 | .6875 |
| | 10.90 | | .4291 | | 17.50 | .6890 |
| | 11.00 | | .4331 | | 17.75 | .6988 |
| | 11.10 | | .4370 | 45/64 | 17.859 | .7031 |
| 7/16 | 11.112 | | .4375 | | 18.00 | .7087 |
| | 11.20 | | .4409 | | 18.25 | .7185 |
| | 11.25 | | .4429 | 23/32 | 18.256 | .7188 |
| | 11.30 | | .4449 | | 18.50 | .7283 |
| | 11.40 | | .4488 | 47/64 | 18.653 | .7344 |
| | 11.50 | | .4528 | | 18.75 | .7382 |
| 29/64 | 11.509 | | .4531 | | 19.00 | .7480 |
| | 11.60 | | .4567 | 3/4 | 19.050 | .7500 |
| | 11.70 | | .4606 | | 19.25 | .7579 |
| | 11.75 | | .4626 | 49/64 | 19.447 | .7656 |
| | 11.80 | | .4646 | | 19.50 | .7677 |
| | 11.90 | | .4685 | | 19.75 | .7776 |
| 15/32 | 11.906 | | .4688 | 25/32 | 19.844 | .7812 |
| | 12.00 | | .4724 | | 20.00 | .7874 |
| | 12.10 | | .4764 | 51/64 | 20.241 | 7969 |
| | 12.20 | | .4803 | | 20.25 | .7972 |
| | 12.25 | | .4823 | | 20.422 | .8040 |
| | 12.30 | | .4843 | | 20.50 | .8071 |
| 31/64 | 12.303 | | .4844 | 13/16 | 20.638 | .8125 |
| | 12.40 | | .4882 | | 20.75 | .8619 |
| | 12.50 | | .4921 | | 21.00 | .8268 |
| | 12.60 | | .4961 | 53/64 | 21.034 | .8281 |
| 1/2 | 12.70 | | .5000 | | 21.25 | .8366 |
| | 12.75 | | .5020 | 27/32 | 21.431 | .8438 |
| | 12.80 | | .5039 | | 21.50 | .3465 |
| | 12.90 | | .5079 | | 21.75 | .8563 |
| | 13.00 | | .5118 | 55/64 | 21.828 | .8594 |
| 33/64 | 13.097 | | .5156 | | 22.00 | .8661 |
| | 13.10 | | .5157 | 7/8 | 22.225 | .8750 |
| | 13.20 | | .5197 | | 22.25 | .8760 |
| | 13.25 | | .5217 | | 22.50 | .8858 |
| | 13.30 | | .5236 | 57/64 | 22.622 | .8906 |
| | 13.40 | | .5276 | | 22.75 | .8957 |
| 17/32 | 13.494 | | .5312 | | 23.00 | .9055 |
| | 13.50 | | .5315 | 29/32 | 23.019 | .9062 |
| | 13.60 | | .5354 | | 23.25 | .9154 |

| Frac. | mm | Inch | Frac. | mm | Inch |
|---|---|---|---|---|---|
| 59/64 | 23.416 | .9219 | | 34.50 | 1.3583 |
| | 23.50 | .9252 | 1,23/64 | 34.528 | 1.3594 |
| | 23.75 | .9350 | 1, 3/8 | 34.925 | 1.3750 |
| 15/16 | 23.812 | .9375 | | 35.00 | 1.3780 |
| | 24.00 | .9449 | 1,25/64 | 35.322 | 1.3906 |
| 61/64 | 24.209 | .9531 | | 35.50 | 1.3976 |
| | 24.25 | .9547 | 1,13/32 | 35.719 | 1.4062 |
| | 24.50 | .9646 | | 36.00 | 1.4173 |
| 31/32 | 24.606 | .9688 | 1,27/64 | 36.116 | 1.4219 |
| | 24.75 | .9744 | | 36.50 | 1.4370 |
| | 25.00 | .9843 | 1, 7/16 | 36.512 | 1.4375 |
| 63/64 | 25.003 | .9844 | 1,29/64 | 36.909 | 1.4531 |
| | 25.25 | .9941 | | 37.00 | 1.4567 |
| 1 | 25.400 | 1.0000 | 1,15/32 | 37.306 | 1.4688 |
| | 25.50 | 1.0039 | | 37.50 | 1.4764 |
| | 25.75 | 1.0138 | 1,31/64 | 37.703 | 1.4844 |
| 1, 1/64 | 25.797 | 1.0156 | | 38.00 | 1.4961 |
| | 26.00 | 1.0236 | 1, 1/2 | 38.100 | 1.5000 |
| 1, 1/32 | 26.194 | 1.0312 | 1,33/64 | 38.497 | 1.5156 |
| | 26.25 | 1.0335 | | 38.50 | 1.5157 |
| | 26.50 | 1.0433 | 1,17/32 | 38.894 | 1.5312 |
| 1, 3/64 | 26.591 | 1.0469 | | 39.00 | 1.5354 |
| | 26.75 | 1.0531 | 1,35/64 | 39.291 | 1.5469 |
| 1, 1/16 | 26.988 | 1.0625 | | 39.50 | 1.5551 |
| | 27.00 | 1.0630 | 1, 9/16 | 39.688 | 1.5625 |
| | 27.25 | 1.0728 | | 40.00 | 1.5748 |
| 1, 5/64 | 27.384 | 1.0781 | 1.37 64 | 40.084 | 1.5781 |
| | 27.50 | 1.0827 | 1,19 32 | 40.481 | 1.5938 |
| | 27.75 | 1.0925 | | 40.50 | 1.5945 |
| 1, 3/32 | 27.781 | 1.0938 | 1,39 64 | 40.878 | 1.6094 |
| | 28.00 | 1.1024 | | 41.00 | 1.6142 |
| 1, 7/64 | 28.178 | 1.1094 | 1, 5 8 | 41.275 | 1.6250 |
| | 28.25 | 1.1122 | | 41.50 | 1.6339 |
| | 28.50 | 1.1220 | 1,41 64 | 41.672 | 1.6406 |
| 1, 1/8 | 28.575 | 1.1250 | | 42.00 | 1.6535 |
| | 28.75 | 1.1319 | 1,21 32 | 42.069 | 1.6562 |
| 1, 9/64 | 28.972 | 1.1406 | 1,43 64 | 42.466 | 1.6719 |
| | 29.00 | 1.1417 | | 42.50 | 1.6732 |
| | 29.25 | 1.1516 | 1,11 16 | 42.862 | 1.6875 |
| 1, 5/32 | 29.369 | 1.1562 | | 43.00 | 1.6929 |
| | 29.50 | 1.1614 | 1,45 64 | 43.259 | 1.7031 |
| | 29.75 | 1.1713 | | 43.50 | 1.7126 |
| 1,11/64 | 29.766 | 1.1719 | 1,23 32 | 43.656 | 1.7188 |
| | 30.00 | 1.1811 | | 44.00 | 1.7323 |
| 1, 3/16 | 30.162 | 1.1875 | 1,47 64 | 44.053 | 1.7344 |
| | 30.25 | 1.1909 | 1, 3 4 | 44.450 | 1.7500 |
| | 30.50 | 1.2008 | | 44.50 | 1.7520 |
| 1,13/64 | 30.559 | 1.2031 | 1,49 64 | 44.847 | 1.7656 |
| | 30.75 | 1.2106 | | 45.00 | 1.7717 |
| 1, 7/32 | 30.956 | 1.2188 | 1,25 32 | 45.244 | 1.7812 |
| | 31.00 | 1.2205 | | 45.50 | 1.7913 |
| | 31.25 | 1.2303 | 1,51 64 | 45.641 | 1.7969 |
| 1,15/64 | 31.353 | 1.2344 | | 46.00 | 1.8110 |
| | 31.50 | 1.2402 | 1,13 16 | 46.038 | 1.8125 |
| 1, 1/4 | 31.75 | 1.2500 | 1,53 64 | 46.434 | 1.8281 |
| | 32.00 | 1.2598 | | 46.50 | 1.8307 |
| 1,17/64 | 32.147 | 1.2656 | 1,27 32 | 46.831 | 1.8438 |
| | 32.50 | 1.2795 | | 47.00 | 1.8504 |
| 1, 9/32 | 32.544 | 1.2812 | 1,55 64 | 47.228 | 1.8594 |
| | 32.766 | 1.2900 | | 47.50 | 1.8701 |
| 1,19/64 | 32.941 | 1.2969 | 1, 7 8 | 47.625 | 1.8750 |
| | 33.00 | 1.2992 | | 48.00 | 1.8898 |
| 1.5/16 | 33.338 | 1.3125 | 1,57 64 | 48.022 | 1.8906 |
| | 33.50 | 1.3189 | 1,29 32 | 48.419 | 1.9062 |
| 1,21/64 | 33.734 | 1.3281 | | 48.50 | 1.9094 |
| | 34.00 | 1.3386 | 1,59 64 | 48.816 | 1.9219 |
| 1, 11/32 | 34.131 | 1.3438 | | 49.00 | 1.9291 |

| Frac. | mm | Inch | Frac. | mm | Inch |
|---|---|---|---|---|---|
| 1.15/16 | 49.212 | 1.9375 | 2, 3/8 | 60.325 | 2.3750 |
| | 49.50 | 1.9488 | | 61.00 | 2.4016 |
| 1,61/64 | 49.609 | 1.9531 | 2,13/32 | 61.119 | 2.4062 |
| | 50.00 | 1.9685 | 2, 7/16 | 61.912 | 2.4375 |
| 1,31/32 | 50.006 | 1.9688 | | 62.00 | 2.4409 |
| 1,63/64 | 50.403 | 1.9844 | 2,15/32 | 62.706 | 2.4688 |
| | 50.50 | 1.9882 | | 63.00 | 2.4803 |
| 2 | 50.800 | 2.0000 | 2, 1/2 | 63.500 | 2.5000 |
| | 51.000 | 2.0079 | | 64.00 | 2.5197 |
| 2, 1/32 | 51.594 | 2.0312 | 2,17/32 | 64.294 | 2.5312 |
| | 52.00 | 2.0472 | | 65.00 | 2.5591 |
| 2, 1/16 | 52.388 | 2.0625 | 2, 9/16 | 65.088 | 2.5625 |
| | 53.00 | 2.0866 | 2,19/32 | 65.881 | 2.5938 |
| 2, 3/32 | 53.181 | 2.0938 | | 66.00 | 2.5984 |
| 2, 1/8 | 53.975 | 2.1250 | 2, 5/8 | 66.675 | 2.6250 |
| | 54.00 | 2.1260 | | 67.00 | 2.6378 |
| 2, 5/32 | 54.769 | 2.1562 | 2,21/32 | 67.469 | 2.6562 |
| | 55.00 | 2.1654 | | 68.00 | 2.6772 |
| 2, 3/16 | 55.562 | 2.1875 | 2,11/16 | 68.262 | 2.6875 |
| | 56.000 | 2.2047 | | 69.00 | 2.7165 |
| 2, 7/32 | 56.356 | 2.2188 | 2,23/32 | 69.056 | 2.7188 |
| | 57.00 | 2.2441 | 2, 3/4 | 69.850 | 2.7500 |
| 2, 1/4 | 57.150 | 2.2500 | | 70.00 | 2.7559 |
| 2, 9/32 | 57.944 | 2.2812 | 2,25/32 | 70.644 | 2.7812 |
| | 58.00 | 2.2835 | | 71.00 | 2.7953 |
| 2, 5/16 | 58.738 | 2.3125 | 2,13/16 | 71.438 | 2.8125 |
| | 59.00 | 2.3228 | | 72.00 | 2.8346 |
| 2, 11/32 | 59.531 | 2.3438 | 2,27/32 | 72.231 | 2.8438 |
| | 60.00 | 2.3622 | | 73.00 | 2.8740 |

| Frac. | mm | Inch | Frac. | mm | Inch |
|---|---|---|---|---|---|
| 2, 7/8 | 73.025 | 2.8750 | 3, 3/8 | 85.725 | 3.3750 |
| 2,29/32 | 73.819 | 2.9062 | | 86.00 | 3.3858 |
| | 74.00 | 2.9134 | 3,13/32 | 86.519 | 3.4062 |
| 2,15/16 | 74.612 | 2.9375 | | 87.00 | 3.4252 |
| | 75.00 | 2.9528 | 3, 7/16 | 87.312 | 3.4375 |
| 2,31/32 | 75.406 | 2.9688 | | 88.00 | 3.4646 |
| | 76.00 | 2.9921 | 3,15/32 | 88.106 | 3.4688 |
| 3 | 76.200 | 3.0000 | 3, 1/2 | 88.900 | 3.5000 |
| 3, 1/32 | 76.994 | 3.0312 | | 89.00 | 3.5039 |
| | 77.00 | 3.0315 | | 90.00 | 3.5433 |
| 3, 1/16 | 77.788 | 3.0625 | 3, 9/16 | 90.488 | 3.5625 |
| | 78.00 | 3.0709 | | 91.00 | 3.5827 |
| 3, 3/32 | 78.581 | 3.0938 | | 92.00 | 3.6220 |
| | 79.00 | 3.1102 | 3, 5/8 | 92.075 | 3.6250 |
| 3, 1/8 | 79.375 | 3.1250 | | 93.00 | 3.6614 |
| | 80.00 | 3.1496 | 3,11/16 | 93.662 | 3.6875 |
| 3, 5/32 | 80.169 | 3.1562 | | 94.00 | 3.7008 |
| 3, 3/16 | 80.962 | 3.1875 | | 95.00 | 3.7402 |
| 3, 7/32 | 81.756 | 3.2188 | 3, 3/4 | 95.250 | 3.7500 |
| | 82.00 | 3.2283 | | 96.00 | 3.7795 |
| 3, 1/4 | 82.550 | 3.2500 | 3,13/16 | 96.838 | 3.8125 |
| | 83.00 | 3.2677 | | 97.00 | 3.8189 |
| 3, 9/32 | 83.344 | 3.2812 | | 98.00 | 3.8583 |
| | 84.00 | 3.3071 | 3, 7/8 | 98.425 | 3.8750 |
| 3, 5/16 | 84.138 | 3.3125 | | 99.00 | 3.8976 |
| 3,11/32 | 84.931 | 3.3438 | | 100.00 | 3.9370 |
| | 85.00 | 3.3465 | 3,15/16 | 100.012 | 3.9375 |
| | | | 4 | 101.600 | 4.0000 |

# CHAPTER 7

# Screwthreads and screwcutting

In an ideal world the numerous nuts and bolts that hold most of a motor cycle together would be interchangeable with any machine whatever its age and country of origin. Unfortunately this is not the case and there have been a variety of different types of screwthreads used throughout the life of the industry.

In the very early days, around the turn of the century, there was no accepted standardised thread for motor cycles. Companies that graduated from bicycle manufacture used the same system for their motor cycles as push bikes. Other manufacturers used the British Standard Whitworth (B.S.W.) series; its coarse pitch was useful in cast iron or aluminium where it provided more strength than a fine pitch. To this was added in 1908 the British Standard Fine (B.S.F.)); the finer thread was less likely to be affected by vibration. The British Association (B.A.) thread was also used for electrical fittings and components as well as some other applications where small diameters were required. Other manufacturers who imported the engines for their machines from the Continent used the metric system. There were even some who decided to add to the confusion by using a thread system of their own design.

In an effort to reduce this confusion the Cycle Engineers' Institute (C.E.I.) thread was formulated in 1902 and many motor cycle manufacturers standardised on this. However, there still continued to be companies that used B.S.W., metric or a combination of threads on their products.

It was not just the British who indulged in this confusion; even though the Zurich Congress of 1898 decided on an International System for the Continent, some countries produced slight variations for their own purposes.

The British Standard Cycle (B.S.C.) thread was introduced to rationalise the C.E.I. thread. This used the same thread form as the C.E.I. but reduced the number of available sizes.

The Americans rationalised their own threads in 1918 when the National Fine (N.F.) and the National Coarse (N.C.) threads were agreed on by the Society of Automotive Engineers (S.A.E.) and the American Society of Mechanical Engineers (A.S.M.E.). After the Second World War Britain, Canada and the U.S.A. agreed on this common thread form and it was renamed Unified National Fine (U.N.F.) and Unified National Coarse (U.N.C.). British car manufacturers began to use this thread in preference to the B.S.F. and B.S.W. series, but rarely did they appear on British motor cycles, manufacturers continuing to use the B.S.C., B.S.F., B.S.W. and B.A. threads.

When Britain joined the E.E.C. this prompted another change, albeit slow, to the I.S.O. metric system of metric fine and metric coarse which was and is standard on Continental and Japanese motor bikes.

It can be seen from this that it is difficult to be precise and say that motor bikes from any particular era will have this or that thread series holding them together. Indeed, motor bikes of any age that have had a number of owners could have been fitted with non-standard threads, particularly where separate nuts and bolts are concerned.

Fortunately it is possible, with the correct tools, to identify threads of any type that may be fitted to your bike. You will need a micrometer or vernier

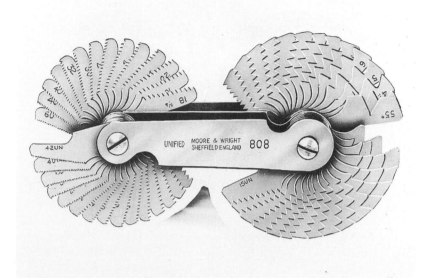

**Left** *Screw pitch gauge for checking screw threads.* (James Neill Ltd.)

**Right** *Fig. 23 Thread details.*

**Far right** *Fig. 24 Cross-section view of a set of taps.*

**Below right** *Tap wrenches.*

callipers and a screw pitch gauge. First you measure the outside diameter of the thread—this will tell you whether it is an imperial size ¼ inch, ⅜ inch, etc., or a metric size, 6 mm, 8 mm, etc. Then select the blade from the screw pitch gauge which corresponds with this.

If, for example, the outside diameter was ¼ inch (·250) it could be ¼ inch B.S.C., ¼ inch B.S.F., ¼ inch B.S.W., ¼ U.N.F., or ¼ inch U.N.C. Each of these threads has a different pitch; in addition B.S.F. and B.S.W. have a 55° thread form, while B.S.C., U.N.F. and U.N.C. have a 60° thread form. Try each of the blades in turn until one matches exactly with the thread of the bolt. Though this sounds complicated it is surprising how quickly you will be able to distinguish visually the different pitches, cutting down on the amount of checking needed.

Always take great care that the nuts and bolts you use match each other; a 10 mm nut will turn onto a ⅜ inch B.S.W. bolt easily and will tighten fairly well, but the difference in size and the angles of the thread, 55° for the B.S.W. and 60° for the metric, will mean that the strength of the resulting combination will be far less than if the correct nut had been used, and the threads could fail with disastrous results. Metric nuts and bolts can be identified by two circles stamped into the face of the nut and the head of the bolt.

# Cutting screwthreads

Figure 23 shows a diagram of a thread and the names of the various parts.

**Internal threads**

To cut an internal screwthread the first thing to do is to drill a hole slightly larger than the core diameter of the thread. The correct size can be found by referring to the tables at the end of this chapter; this will give the correct depth of thread.

If the correct size of drill is not available, it is possible to use one very slightly larger, up to 0·1 mm or 0·004 inch on sizes between ¼ inch (6 mm) and ½ inch (12 mm) diameter. Any larger will reduce the strength of the thread considerably. On no account should a smaller-sized drill be used as this will make the thread difficult to cut and may cause the tap to bind and perhaps break off in the hole.

The tool used to cut an internal thread is called a tap. There are three of each size in a set: they are the taper tap, which is used first; the second or intermediate tap, used, as its name implies, second; and the plug or bottoming tap, which is used last, mainly in blind holes where the thread must reach to the bottom of the hole. They are made of either high-speed or carbon steel. See Figure 24.

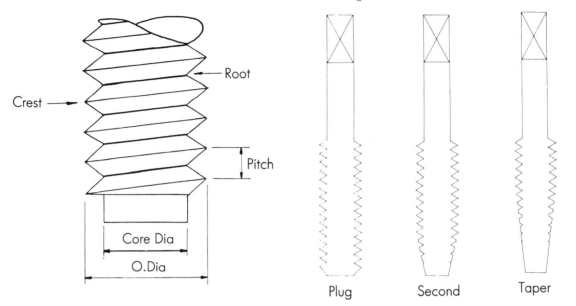

Crest

Root

Pitch

Core Dia

O. Dia

Plug          Second          Taper

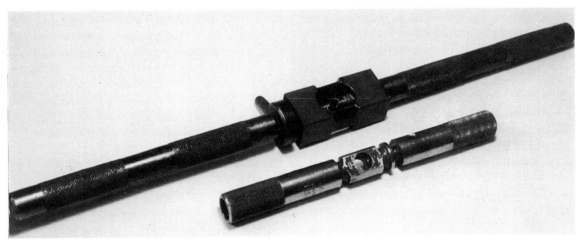

The taper tap should be held in the tap wrench and a small amount of lubricant applied to the edges. There are special cutting compounds such as 'Trefolux' that can be bought, but any oil or grease will be better than nothing for steel. Paraffin is best for aluminium and brass, while cast iron should be cut dry. It is very important for the tap to enter the hole true, otherwise a drunken thread will result. The tap should be started in the hole turning clockwise for a right-hand thread; as soon as the tap begins to bite into the metal, it should be checked for squareness in two directions; if it is out of square, this can easily be seen as one handle of the tap wrench will be higher than the other.

As soon as the tap is started square, the thread can be cut. Turn the tap wrench one full turn forward, followed by half a turn back. This turning back is important as it breaks off the chip of metal being formed by the cutting edge of the tap. Failure to turn the tap backwards will result in swarf collecting in the flutes of the tap and finally jamming the whole thing solid; the usual consequence of this is the tap breaking. When the tap is cutting it will not need any downward pressure on the tap wrench; the shape of the teeth will pull it down into the hole. Indeed, any pressure that is

*A tap guide for starting taps at 90°.*

applied is likely to produce a drunken thread.

If your taps have a shank of the same diameter or larger than the teeth, a simple guide (see illustration) can be made to help achieve a square start to the thread. This should preferably be made of metal, though a good hard wood will suffice. Obviously the top and bottom faces must be parallel to each other and at right angles to the hole and the hole should be the same size as the shank of the tap. The thickness of the block should allow the tap to reach the metal and be supported by the shank, but leave enough clearance at the top to enable the tap to cut several threads into the metal. The guide is held in one hand and the tap started with the other. This cannot be used in all circumstances, but it will help in many situations.

If the metal you are tapping is not too thick, it is possible to cut a full thread with the taper tap, but where a blind hole is being tapped, the second and plug taps will have to be used. As soon as the tap reaches the bottom of the hole, stop turning, as the tap can easily break or the bottom teeth chip. Before using the second tap, and also between using the second and plug taps, any swarf that has collected at the bottom of the hole must be removed, otherwise it will be impossible to thread the hole to the bottom.

Should you be unfortunate enough to break off a tap inside the hole you have problems. If the tap has broken leaving some of the shank above the surface, it may be possible to use a pair of mole grips or a similar tool to turn the tap out, having removed as much of the swarf as possible from the hole. If the tap remains below the surface your options are limited; it is impossible to drill out the tap, as it is harder than the drill.

One method of removing a broken tap is to use a tap extractor. This tool has three fingers which fit down the flutes of the tap once the swarf has been removed. The extractor is then turned, unscrewing the tap from the hole.

If this method does not work, then spark erosion is the only suitable method open to you. This involves using an electric spark to burn out, or erode, the tap, turning it into a powder. Obviously this requires specialised equipment which may be available at your local engineering works or from other engineers who work with special steels and die-making.

**External threads**

External threads are cut with a tool called a die, which is held in a die-stock. The type of die most commonly used is called a circular split die. The die should be placed into the die-stock with the engraved side showing; this is because that side of the die has a slight taper on the teeth to help the die to start cutting. The centre screw of the die-stock should be tightened first, to expand the die — again this will help the die to start cutting — and the two outer screws need to be 'nipped' in to hold the die firm.

The end of the metal bar should be chamfered to ease the work of the die and a small amount of lubricant applied to it. The die and stock should now be placed on the work with the writing on the die downwards. The die should be held square to the work, pressure applied, and the die stock turned clockwise.

When the die has started cutting it should be checked to see if it is square to the bar; if it is, turn the stock through 90° and check again. If it is still square, start cutting the thread. Should the die stock be out of true, which can be seen from one handle of the stock being higher than the other, pressure should be applied to the handle that is higher and the die stock turned through 90° and checked again; this should be done until both are level.

The cutting operation is the same for the internal thread: one turn forward, followed by half

**Right** *A circular split die and die stock.*

**Below right** *Die nuts.*

**Bottom** *A re-threading file.*

a turn backwards to break off the swarf. Again it is important that, once the die is cutting a true thread, no pressure is applied to the diestock as this will almost certainly produce a drunken thread.

Having cut the thread to the correct length, the die and die stock should be removed and the thread tested with a nut or in the hole into which it is to be fitted. Should the thread feel tight, it can be eased by running the die down it again. This time the centre screw of the die stock should be loosened slightly and the outer screws tightened, squeezing the die closer. It can then be run down the thread again to remove a small amount of metal and the fit of the thread tested again. When cutting both parts of a thread, the internal one should be cut first, then the external one cut to suit with the adjustable dies.

Die nuts (see the illustration on the previous page) are similar in appearance to a normal nut, though larger for any given size and with teeth like a die inside. They are not designed to cut threads but to clean up damaged ones. Their hexagonal shape enables them to be turned with a spanner or socket in a confined space.

Re-threading files are also used for repairing damaged or rusty threads; they are double ended, and each face has teeth cut to suit a thread of different teeth-per-inch or pitch. This means that one file has the capacity for cleaning up eight different threads.

## Removing broken studs

To remove a stud from its hole, a stud remover can be used; if not, two nuts should be run onto the thread, then tightened together so that they are locked onto the stud. The lower nut is then turned and, if all goes well, the stud will unscrew from its hole. Should the stud refuse to move, easing oil left to soak may do the trick. If the stud is set in aluminium, heat may be the answer, as the aluminium will expand quicker than the steel stud, but be careful with the amount of heat you apply.

If the stud has broken flush with the surface, a stud extractor will have to be used. First the broken end of the stud is filed flat, then the centre of the stud is centre punched and the correct sized hole drilled into it. The extractor is then screwed into the hole anticlockwise and as it tightens it should unscrew the stud. Great care should be taken during this operation; the cheaper types of stud extractor are very brittle and will snap easily if they are bent or forced in any way. The type of extractor with four flutes is much better.

Should it prove necessary to drill out the whole of the stud, care must be taken in accurately centre punching the centre of the stud and drilling carefully with a pilot drill first. Do not let the drill

*Fitting a thread insert.* (Hurley Engine Services Ltd.)

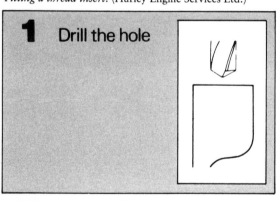

**1 Drill the hole**

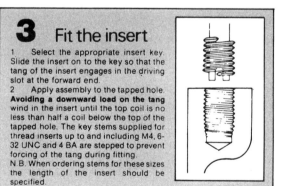

**3 Fit the insert**

1   Select the appropriate insert key. Slide the insert on to the key so that the tang of the insert engages in the driving slot at the forward end.
2   Apply assembly to the tapped hole. **Avoiding a downward load on the tang** wind in the insert until the top coil is no less than half a coil below the top of the tapped hole. The key stems supplied for thread inserts up to and including M4, 6-32 UNC and 4 BA are stepped to prevent forcing of the tang during fitting.
N.B. When ordering stems for these sizes the length of the insert should be specified.

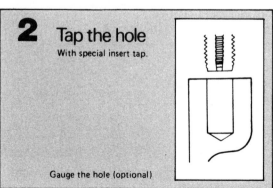

**2 Tap the hole**

With special insert tap.

Gauge the hole (optional)

**4 Break off tang**

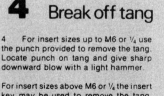

½ PITCH (MIN) BELOW SURFACE

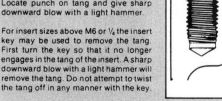

4   For insert sizes up to M6 or ¼ use the punch provided to remove the tang. Locate punch on tang and give sharp downward blow with a light hammer.

For insert sizes above M6 or ¼ the insert key may be used to remove the tang. First turn the key so that it no longer engages in the tang of the insert. A sharp downward blow with a light hammer will remove the tang. Do not attempt to twist the tang off in any manner with the key.

wander away from the centre of the stud, especially if it is set in aluminium. The drill will find the aluminium easier to cut than the stud, and will be forced into the aluminium by the steel of the stud even if the work is clamped down.

If the broken stud is one of a set, e.g. a timing case stud, it will help to centre punch the broken stud accurately if the timing cover is bolted up and a transfer centre punch used. Alternatively, a punch made from a piece of silver steel of the right diameter can be used.

**Thread inserts**

Where a thread has stripped inside a hole, it is not always possible to re-drill the hole to take a larger sized thread, e.g. in the case of a sparking plug thread or the thin wall of a timing case. In these cases a thread insert may be the answer.

The damaged thread is first drilled out using the correct oversized drill, then a special tap is used to cut a new thread inside the hole. The insert, which is a coil of diamond section steel, phosphor bronze or heat-resisting alloy wire, should be screwed into the thread that has been cut using a special tool. When it is fully home, the tool is removed and the insert is ready to accept the original bolt or stud. The illustration (left) shows the process in detail. The kit of parts to undertake this process is not cheap for one-off applications, but most engineering firms and many motor cycle repair shops will undertake the work or hire out the equipment.

Countersunk Head

Raised Countersunk Head

Pan Head

Flange Head

Hexagon Head

*Fig. 25 Self-tapping screws.*

# Self-tapping screws

Another type of screw is the self-tapping screw, made of hardened steel, which is able to cut its own thread in metal or plastics. They are available in the following head shapes, which have either a plain or cross slot for a screwdriver: pan, hexagonal, countersunk, or raised countersunk.

For best results it is important that the correct sized hole is drilled to match the size of screw and the thickness and type of material. The tables at the end of this chapter give an accurate guide for the majority of installations.

*Fig. 26 Self-tapping screws: suggested hole and drill sizes in thermopliable plastics.*

| SCREW SIZE | NORMAL PENETRATION | | | MINIMUM PENETRATION IN BLIND HOLES |
|---|---|---|---|---|
| NO. AND NOMINAL DIAMETER | HOLE DIAMETER REQUIRED IN. | DRILL SIZE MM | ALTERNATIVES | |
| 2 (0.086″) | 0.070 | 1.80 | 50 | $\frac{1}{4}$″ |
| 4 (0.112″) | 0.093 | 2.35 | 42 | $\frac{1}{4}$″ |
| 6 (0.138″) | 0.114 | 2.90 | 32 | $\frac{1}{4}$″ |
| 8 (0.164″) | 0.135 | 3.40 | 29 | $\frac{5}{16}$″ |
| 10 (0.186″) | 0.154 | 3.90 | 23 | $\frac{5}{16}$″ |
| 12 (0.212″) | 0.180 | 4.60 | 15 | $\frac{3}{8}$″ |
| 14 (0.242″) | 0.210 | 5.30 | 4 | $\frac{3}{8}$″ |

*Fig. 27 Self-tapping screws: suggested hole and drill sizes in mild steel, brass, aluminium alloy, stainless steel and monel metal sheet.*

**Note:** It is important that the correct hole size is used and the recommendations below should be followed, but a slightly larger hole may have to be used in very hard material, and a smaller one in very soft material.

| SCREW SIZE | MATERIAL THICKNESS | | | PIERCED OR EXTRUDED HOLE DIA IN. | DRILLED OR CLEAN-PUNCHED HOLES | | |
|---|---|---|---|---|---|---|---|
| NO. AND NOMINAL DIA. | IN. | MM | SWG OR FRACTION | | HOLE DIA. REQUIRED IN. | DRILL SIZE | |
| | | | | | | MM | ALTERNATIVES |
| 2 (0.086″) | 0.018 | 0.45 | 26 | – | 0.063 | 1.60 | 52 |
| | 0.036 | 0.91 | 20 | – | 0.073 | 1.85 | 49 |
| | 0.064 | 1.62 | 16 | – | 0.077 | 1.95 | 48 |
| 4 (0.112″) | 0.018 | 0.45 | 26 | – | 0.081 | 2.05 | 46 |
| | 0.036 | 0.91 | 20 | 0.098 | 0.091 | 2.30 | 42 |
| | 0.064 | 1.62 | 16 | – | 0.095 | 2.40 | 41 |
| | 0.080 | 2.03 | 14 | – | 0.102 | 2.60 | 38 |
| 6 (0.138″) | 0.018 | 0.45 | 26 | – | 0.092 | 2.35 | 42 |
| | 0.036 | 0.91 | 20 | 0.111 | 0.110 | 2.80 | 35 |
| | 0.064 | 1.62 | 16 | – | 0.116 | 2.95 | 32 |
| | 0.080 | 2.03 | 14 | – | 0.122 | 3.10 | 31 |
| | 0.104 | 2.64 | 12 | – | 0.126 | 3.20 | 30 |
| 8 (0.164″) | 0.028 | 0.71 | 22 | – | 0.114 | 2.90 | 33 |
| | 0.036 | 0.91 | 20 | 0.136 | 0.122 | 3.10 | $\frac{1}{8}″$ |
| | 0.048 | 1.22 | 18 | – | 0.126 | 3.20 | 30 |
| | 0.064 | 1.62 | 16 | – | 0.134 | 3.40 | 29 |
| | 0.104 | 2.64 | 12 | – | 0.146 | 3.70 | 26 |
| | 0.125 | 3.18 | $\frac{1}{8}″$ | – | 0.150 | 3.80 | 25 |
| 10 (0.186″) | 0.028 | 0.71 | 22 | – | 0.134 | 3.40 | 29 |
| | 0.048 | 1.22 | 18 | – | 0.142 | 3.60 | 28 |
| | 0.064 | 1.62 | 16 | – | 0.150 | 3.80 | 25 |
| | 0.104 | 2.64 | 12 | – | 0.161 | 4.10 | 20 |
| | 0.125 | 3.18 | $\frac{1}{8}″$ | – | 0.169 | 4.30 | 18 |
| | 0.187 | 4.75 | $\frac{3}{16}″$ | – | 0.177 | 4.50 | 16 |
| 12 (0.212″) | 0.028 | 0.71 | 22 | – | 0.161 | 4.10 | 20 |
| | 0.048 | 1.22 | 18 | – | 0.169 | 4.30 | 18 |
| | 0.064 | 1.62 | 16 | – | 0.177 | 4.50 | 16 |
| | 0.104 | 2.64 | 12 | – | 0.189 | 4.80 | 12 |
| | 0.125 | 3.18 | $\frac{1}{8}″$ | – | 0.193 | 4.90 | 10 |
| | 0.187 | 4.75 | $\frac{3}{16}″$ | – | 0.201 | 5.10 | 7 |
| 14 (0.242″) | 0.048 | 1.22 | 18 | – | 0.189 | 4.80 | 12 |
| | 0.064 | 1.62 | 16 | – | 0.205 | 5.20 | 6 |
| | 0.080 | 2.03 | 14 | – | 0.213 | 5.40 | 3 |
| | 0.125 | 3.18 | $\frac{1}{8}″$ | – | 0.224 | 5.70 | 1 |
| | 0.187 | 4.75 | $\frac{3}{16}″$ | – | 0.232 | 5.90 | A |
| | 0.250 | 6.35 | $\frac{1}{4}″$ | – | 0.236 | 6.00 | B |

*Fig. 28 Nuts, bolts and washers.*

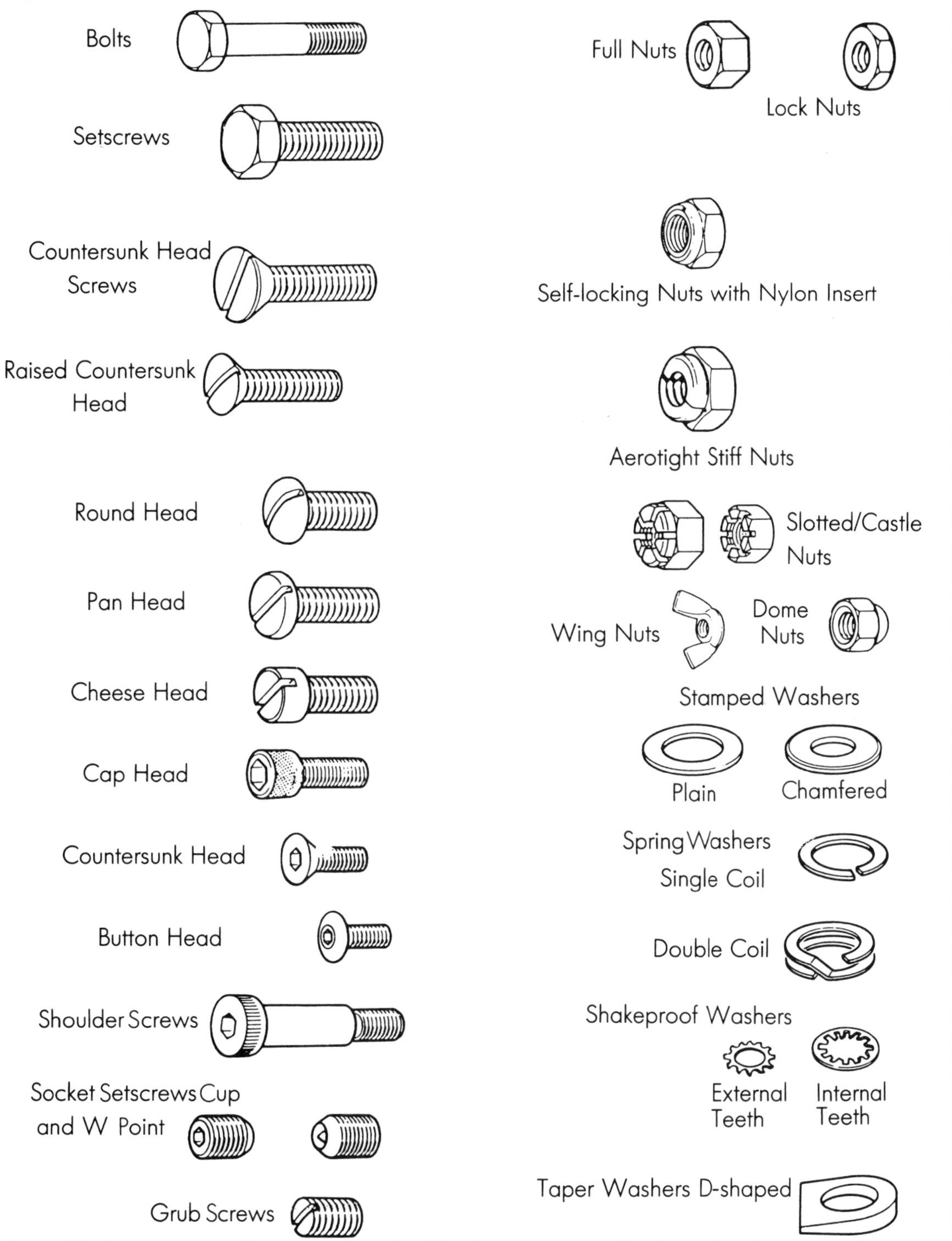

Bolts

Setscrews

Countersunk Head Screws

Raised Countersunk Head

Round Head

Pan Head

Cheese Head

Cap Head

Countersunk Head

Button Head

Shoulder Screws

Socket Setscrews Cup and W Point

Grub Screws

Full Nuts

Lock Nuts

Self-locking Nuts with Nylon Insert

Aerotight Stiff Nuts

Slotted/Castle Nuts

Wing Nuts    Dome Nuts

Stamped Washers

Plain    Chamfered

Spring Washers Single Coil

Double Coil

Shakeproof Washers

External Teeth    Internal Teeth

Taper Washers D-shaped

*Thread information tables*
(S.K.F. Dormer)

### I.S.O. METRIC COARSE

THREAD FORM

r = Basic Radius = ·1443 p

hn = Basic Height of Internal
Thread & Depth of
Thread Engagement
= ·54127 p

hs = Basic Height of External
Thread = **·61344** p

p = Pitch

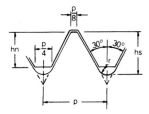

| nom. dia. | pitch | basic major diameter | basic effective diameter | basic minor diameter of external threads | basic minor diameter of internal threads | recommended tapping drill size | clearance drill size |
|---|---|---|---|---|---|---|---|
| mm | mm | mm | mm | mm | mm | mm | mm |
| 1 | 0.25 | 1.000 | 0.838 | 0.693 | 0.729 | 0.75 | 1.05 |
| 1.1 | 0.25 | 1.100 | 0.938 | 0.793 | 0.829 | 0.85 | 1.15 |
| 1.2 | 0.25 | 1.200 | 1.038 | 0.893 | 0.929 | 0.95 | 1.25 |
| 1.4 | 0.30 | 1.400 | 1.205 | 1.032 | 1.075 | 1.10 | 1.45 |
| 1.6 | 0.35 | 1.600 | 1.373 | 1.170 | 1.221 | 1.25 | 1.65 |
| 1.8 | 0.35 | 1.800 | 1.573 | 1.370 | 1.421 | 1.45 | 1.85 |
| 2 | 0.40 | 2.000 | 1.740 | 1.509 | 1.567 | 1.60 | 2.05 |
| 2.2 | 0.45 | 2.200 | 1.908 | 1.648 | 1.713 | 1.75 | 2.25 |
| 2.5 | 0.45 | 2.500 | 2.208 | 1.948 | 2.013 | 2.05 | 2.60 |
| 3 | 0.50 | 3.000 | 2.675 | 2.387 | 2.459 | 2.50 | 3.10 |
| 3.5 | 0.60 | 3.500 | 3.110 | 2.764 | 2.850 | 2.90 | 3.60 |
| 4 | 0.70 | 4.000 | 3.545 | 3.141 | 3.242 | 3.30 | 4.10 |
| 4.5 | 0.75 | 4.500 | 4.013 | 3.580 | 3.688 | 3.70 | 4.60 |
| 5 | 0.80 | 5.000 | 4.480 | 4.019 | 4.134 | 4.20 | 5.10 |
| 6 | 1.00 | 6.000 | 5.350 | 4.773 | 4.917 | 5.00 | 6.10 |
| 7 | 1.00 | 7.000 | 6.350 | 5.773 | 5.917 | 6.00 | 7.20 |
| 8 | 1.25 | 8.000 | 7.188 | 6.466 | 6.647 | 6.80 | 8.20 |
| 9 | 1.25 | 9.000 | 8.188 | 7.466 | 7.647 | 7.80 | 9.20 |
| 10 | 1.50 | 10.000 | 9.026 | 8.160 | 8.376 | 8.50 | 10.20 |
| 11 | 1.50 | 11.000 | 10.026 | 9.160 | 9.376 | 9.50 | 11.20 |
| 12 | 1.75 | 12.000 | 10.863 | 9.853 | 10.106 | 10.20 | 12.20 |
| 14 | 2.00 | 14.000 | 12.701 | 11.546 | 11.835 | 12.00 | 14.25 |
| 16 | 2.00 | 16.000 | 14.701 | 13.546 | 13.835 | 14.00 | 16.25 |
| 18 | 2.50 | 18.000 | 16.376 | 14.933 | 15.294 | 15.50 | 18.25 |
| 20 | 2.50 | 20.000 | 18.376 | 16.933 | 17.294 | 17.50 | 20.25 |
| 22 | 2.50 | 22.000 | 20.376 | 18.933 | 19.294 | 19.50 | 22.25 |
| 24 | 3.00 | 24.000 | 22.051 | 20.319 | 20.752 | 21.00 | 24.25 |
| 27 | 3.00 | 27.000 | 25.051 | 23.319 | 23.752 | 24.00 | 27.25 |
| 30 | 3.50 | 30.000 | 27.727 | 25.706 | 26.211 | 26.50 | 30.50 |
| 33 | 3.50 | 33.000 | 30.727 | 28.706 | 29.211 | 29.50 | 33.50 |
| 36 | 4.00 | 36.000 | 33.402 | 31.093 | 31.670 | 32.00 | 36.50 |
| 39 | 4.00 | 39.000 | 36.402 | 34.093 | 34.670 | 35.00 | 39.50 |
| 42 | 4.50 | 42.000 | 39.077 | 36.479 | 37.129 | 37.50 | 42.50 |
| 45 | 4.50 | 45.000 | 42.077 | 39.479 | 40.129 | 40.50 | 45.50 |
| 48 | 5.00 | 48.000 | 44.752 | 41.866 | 42.587 | 43.00 | 48.50 |
| 52 | 5.00 | 52.000 | 48.752 | 45.866 | 46.587 | 47.00 | 53.00 |
| 56 | 5.50 | 56.000 | 52.428 | 49.252 | 50.046 | 50.50 | 57.00 |

## I.S.O. METRIC SPECIAL PITCHES

THREAD FORM

r = Basic Radius = ·1443 p

hn = Basic Height of Internal Thread & Depth of Thread Engagement = ·54127 p

hs = Basic Height of External Thread = ·61344 p

p = Pitch

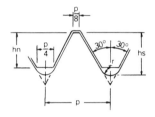

| nom. dia. | pitch | basic major diameter | basic effective diameter | basic minor diameter of external threads | basic minor diameter of internal threads | recom-mended tapping drill size | clearance drill size |
|---|---|---|---|---|---|---|---|
| mm | mm | mm | mm | mm | mm | mm | mm |
| 1.7 | 0.35 | 1.700 | 1.473 | 1.270 | 1.321 | 1.35 | 1.80 |
| 2.0 | 0.45 | 2.000 | 1.708 | 1.448 | 1.513 | 1.55 | 2.10 |
| 2.3 | 0.40 | 2.300 | 2.040 | 1.809 | 1.867 | 1.90 | 2.40 |
| 2.6 | 0.45 | 2.600 | 2.308 | 2.048 | 2.113 | 2.15 | 2.70 |
| 3.0 | 0.60 | 3.000 | 2.610 | 2.264 | 2.350 | 2.40 | 3.10 |
| 4.0. | 0.75 | 4.000 | 3.513 | 3.080 | 3.188 | 3.20 | 4.10 |
| 5.0 | 0.90 | 5.000 | 4.415 | 3.896 | 4.026 | 4.10 | 5.10 |
| 5.5 | 0.90 | 5.500 | 4.915 | 4.396 | 4.526 | 4.60 | 5.60 |
| 8.0 | 0.75 | 8.000 | 7.513 | 7.080 | 7.188 | 7.20 | 8.20 |
| 9.0 | 1.00 | 9.000 | 8.350 | 7.773 | 7.917 | 8.00 | 9.20 |
| 10.0 | 0.75 | 10.000 | 9.513 | 9.080 | 9.188 | 9.20 | 10.20 |
| 10.0 | 1.00† | 10.000 | 9.350 | 8.773 | 8.917 | 9.00 | 10.20 |
| 12.0 | 1.00 | 12.000 | 11.350 | 10.773 | 10.917 | 11.00 | 12.20 |
| 12.0 | 1.50 | 12.000 | 11.026 | 10.160 | 10.376 | 10.50 | 12.20 |
| 14.0 | 1.50 | 14.000 | 13.026 | 12.160 | 12.376 | 12.50 | 14.25 |
| 16.0 | 1.00 | 16.000 | 15.350 | 14.773 | 14.917 | 15.00 | 16.25 |
| 20.0 | 1.00 | 20.000 | 19.350 | 18.773 | 18.917 | 19.00 | 20.25 |
| 20.0 | 2.00 | 20.000 | 10.701 | 17.546 | 17.835 | 18.00 | 20.25 |
| 24.0 | 1.00 | 24.000 | 23.350 | 22.773 | 22.917 | 23.00 | 24.25 |
| 24.0 | 1.50 | 24.000 | 23.026 | 22.160 | 22.376 | 22.50 | 24.25 |
| 25.0 | 1.50* | 25.000 | 24.026 | 23.160 | 23.376 | 23.50 | 25.25 |
| 32.0 | 1.50* | 32.000 | 31.026 | 30.160 | 30.376 | 30.50 | 32.50 |

## I.S.O. METRIC FINE

THREAD FORM

r = Basic Radius = ·1443 p

hn = Basic Height of Internal Thread & Depth of Thread Engagement = ·54127 p

hs = Basic Height of External Thread = ·61344 p

p = Pitch

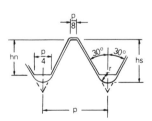

| nom. dia. | pitch | basic major diameter | basic effective diameter | basic minor diameter of external threads | basic minor diameter of internal threads | recom-mended tapping drill size | clearance drill size |
|---|---|---|---|---|---|---|---|
| mm | mm | mm | mm | mm | mm | mm | mm |
| 3.0 | 0.35 | 3.000 | 2.773 | 2.570 | 2.621 | 2.65 | 3.10 |
| 4.0 | 0.50 | 4.000 | 3.675 | 3.387 | 3.459 | 3.50 | 4.10 |
| 5.0 | 0.50 | 5.000 | 4.675 | 4.387 | 4.459 | 4.50 | 5.10 |
| 6.0 | 0.75 | 6.000 | 5.513 | 5.080 | 5.188 | 5.20 | 6.10 |
| 7.0 | 0.75 | 7.000 | 6.513 | 6.080 | 6.188 | 6.20 | 7.20 |
| 8.0 | 1.00 | 8.000 | 7.350 | 6.773 | 6.917 | 7.00 | 8.20 |
| 10.0 | 1.25 | 10.000 | 9.188 | 8.466 | 8.647 | 8.80 | 10.20 |
| 12.0 | 1.25† | 12.000 | 11.188 | 10.466 | 10.647 | 10.80 | 12.20 |
| 14.0 | 1.25† | 14.000 | 13.188 | 12.466 | 12.647 | 12.80 | 14.25 |
| 16.0 | 1.50* | 16.000 | 15.026 | 14.160 | 14.376 | 14.50 | 16.25 |
| 18.0 | 1.50† | 18.000 | 17.026 | 16.160 | 16.376 | 16.50 | 18.25 |
| 20.0 | 1.50* | 20.000 | 19.026 | 18.160 | 18.376 | 18.50 | 20.25 |
| 22.0 | 1.50 | 22.000 | 21.026 | 20.160 | 20.376 | 20.50 | 22.25 |
| 24.0 | 2.00 | 24.000 | 22.701 | 21.546 | 21.835 | 22.00 | 24.25 |
| 27.0 | 2.00 | 27.000 | 25.701 | 24.546 | 24.835 | 25.00 | 27.25 |
| 30.0 | 2.00 | 30.000 | 28.701 | 27.546 | 27.835 | 28.00 | 30.50 |

NOTES: Pitch/Diameter combinations marked thus(*) are Metric Spark Plug.
Pitch/Diameter combinations marked thus (†) are Metric Conduit.

## UNIFIED COARSE

(U.N.C.)

THREAD FORM

r – Basic Radius = ·1443 p

hn – Basic Height of Internal Thread & Depth of Thread Engagement = ·54127 p

hs – Basic Height of External Thread = ·**61344** p

$$p = \text{Pitch} = \frac{1}{\text{t.p.i.}}$$

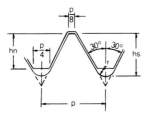

| nom. size | t.p.i. | basic major diameter inches | basic effective diameter inches | basic minor dia. of ext. threads inches | basic minor dia. of int. threads inches | recommended tapping drill size mm | clearance drill size mm |
|---|---|---|---|---|---|---|---|
| No. 1 | 64 | 0.0730 | 0.0629 | 0.0538 | 0.0561 | 1.55 | 1.95 |
| No. 2 | 56 | 0.0860 | 0.0744 | 0.0641 | 0.0667 | 1.85 | 2.30 |
| No. 3 | 48 | 0.0990 | 0.0855 | 0.0734 | 0.0764 | 2.10 | 2.65 |
| No. 4 | 40 | 0.1120 | 0.0958 | 0.0813 | 0.0849 | 2.35 | 2.95 |
| No. 5 | 40 | 0.1250 | 0.1088 | 0.0943 | 0.0979 | 2.65 | 3.30 |
| No. 6 | 32 | 0.1380 | 0.1177 | 0.0997 | 0.1042 | 2.85 | 3.60 |
| No. 8 | 32 | 0.1640 | 0.1437 | 0.1257 | 0.1302 | 3.50 | 4.30 |
| No. 10 | 24 | 0.1900 | 0.1629 | 0.1389 | 0.1449 | 3.90 | 4.90 |
| No. 12 | 24 | 0.2160 | 0.1889 | 0.1649 | 0.1709 | 4.50 | 5.60 |
| 1/4 | 20 | 0.2500 | 0.2175 | 0.1887 | 0.1959 | 5.10 | 6.50 |
| 5/16 | 18 | 0.3125 | 0.2764 | 0.2443 | 0.2524 | 6.60 | 8.10 |
| 3/8 | 16 | 0.3750 | 0.3344 | 0.2983 | 0.3073 | 8.00 | 9.70 |
| 7/16 | 14 | 0.4375 | 0.3911 | 0.3499 | 0.3602 | 9.40 | 11.30 |
| 1/2 | 13 | 0.5000 | 0.4500 | 0.4056 | 0.4167 | 10.80 | 13.00 |
| 9/16 | 12 | 0.5625 | 0.5084 | 0.4603 | 0.4723 | 12.20 | 14.50 |
| 5/8 | 11 | 0.6250 | 0.5660 | 0.5135 | 0.5266 | 13.50 | 16.25 |
| 3/4 | 10 | 0.7500 | 0.6850 | 0.6273 | 0.6417 | 16.50 | 19.25 |
| 7/8 | 9 | 0.8750 | 0.8028 | 0.7387 | 0.7547 | 19.50 | 22.50 |
| 1 | 8 | 1.0000 | 0.9188 | 0.8466 | 0.8647 | 22.25 | 25.75 |
| 1, 1/8 | 7 | 1.1250 | 1.0322 | 0.9497 | 0.9704 | 25.00 | 29.00 |
| 1, 1/4 | 7 | 1.2500 | 1.1572 | 1.0747 | 1.0954 | 28.00 | 32.00 |
| 1, 3/8 | 6 | 1.3750 | 1.2667 | 1.1705 | 1.1946 | 30.75 | 35.50 |
| 1, 1/2 | 6 | 1.5000 | 1.3917 | 1.2955 | 1.3196 | 34.00 | 38.50 |
| 1, 3/4 | 5 | 1.7500 | 1.6201 | 1.5046 | 1.5335 | 39.50 | 45.00 |
| 2 | 4, 1/2 | 2.0000 | 1.8557 | 1.7274 | 1.7594 | 45.00 | 51.00 |
| 2, 1/4 | 4, 1/2 | 2.2500 | 2.1057 | 1.9774 | 2.0094 | 52.00 | 58.00 |

## UNIFIED FINE

(U.N.F.)

THREAD FORM

r = Basic Radius = ·1443 p

hn = Basic Height of Internal Thread & Depth of Thread Engagement = ·54127 p

hs = Basic Height of External Thread = ·61344 p

p = Pitch = $\dfrac{1}{\text{t.p.i.}}$

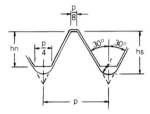

| nom. size | t.p.i. | basic major diameter inches | basic effective diameter inches | basic minor dia. of ext. threads inches | basic minor dia. of int. threads inches | recommend- ed tapping drill size mm | clearance drill size mm |
|---|---|---|---|---|---|---|---|
| No. 0 | 80 | 0.0600 | 0.0519 | 0.0447 | 0.0465 | 1.25 | 1.60 |
| No. 1 | 72 | 0.0730 | 0.0640 | 0.0560 | 0.0580 | 1.55 | 1.95 |
| No. 2 | 64 | 0.0860 | 0.0759 | 0.0668 | 0.0691 | 1.90 | 2.30 |
| No. 3 | 56 | 0.0990 | 0.0874 | 0.0771 | 0.0797 | 2.15 | 2.65 |
| No. 4 | 48 | 0.1120 | 0.0985 | 0.0864 | 0.0894 | 2.40 | 2.95 |
| No. 5 | 44 | 0.1250 | 0.1102 | 0.0971 | 0.1004 | 2.70 | 3.30 |
| No. 6 | 40 | 0.1380 | 0.1218 | 0.1073 | 0.1109 | 2.95 | 3.60 |
| No. 8 | 36 | 0.1640 | 0.1460 | 0.1299 | 0.1339 | 3.50 | 4.30 |
| No. 10 | 32 | 0.1900 | 0.1697 | 0.1517 | 0.1562 | 4.10 | 4.90 |
| No. 12 | 28 | 0.2160 | 0.1928 | 0.1722 | 0.1773 | 4.70 | 5.60 |
| 1/4 | 28 | 0.2500 | 0.2268 | 0.2062 | 0.2113 | 5.50 | 6.50 |
| 5/16 | 24 | 0.3125 | 0.2854 | 0.2614 | 0.2674 | 6.90 | 8.10 |
| 3/8 | 24 | 0.3750 | 0.3479 | 0.3239 | 0.3299 | 8.50 | 9.70 |
| 7/16 | 20 | 0.4375 | 0.4050 | 0.3762 | 0.3834 | 9.90 | 11.30 |
| 1/2 | 20 | 0.5000 | 0.4675 | 0.4387 | 0.4459 | 11.50 | 13.00 |
| 9/16 | 18 | 0.5625 | 0.5264 | 0.4943 | 0.5024 | 12.90 | 14.50 |
| 5/8 | 18 | 0.6250 | 0.5889 | 0.5568 | 0.5649 | 14.50 | 16.25 |
| 3/4 | 16 | 0.7500 | 0.7094 | 0.6733 | 0.6823 | 17.50 | 19.25 |
| 7/8 | 14 | 0.8750 | 0.8286 | 0.7874 | 0.7977 | 20.40 | 22.50 |
| 1 | 12 | 1.0000 | 0.9459 | 0.8978 | 0.9098 | 23.25 | 25.75 |
| 1, 1/8 | 12 | 1.1250 | 1.0709 | 1.0228 | 1.0348 | 26.50 | 29.00 |
| 1, 1/4 | 12 | 1.2500 | 1.1959 | 1.1478 | 1.1598 | 29.50 | 32.00 |
| 1, 3/8 | 12 | 1.3750 | 1.3209 | 1.2728 | 1.2848 | 32.75 | 35.50 |
| 1, 1/2 | 12 | 1.5000 | 1.4459 | 1.3978 | 1.4098 | 36.00 | 38.50 |

## BRITISH ASSOCIATION

(B.A.)

THREAD FORM

r = Basic Radius = ·1808346 p

h = Basic Depth of Thread = ·6 p

p = Pitch

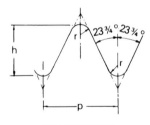

NON-PREFERRED THREAD SERIES

| B.A. no. | pitch inches | basic depth of thread inches | basic major diameter inches | basic effective diameter inches | basic minor diameter inches | recom- mended tapping drill size mm | clearance drill size mm |
|---|---|---|---|---|---|---|---|
| 0 | 0.0394 | 0.0236 | 0.2362 | 0.2126 | 0.1890 | 5.10 | 6.10 |
| 1 | 0.0354 | 0.0213 | 0.2087 | 0.1874 | 0.1661 | 4.50 | 5.40 |
| 2 | 0.0319 | 0.0191 | 0.1850 | 0.1659 | 0.1468 | 4.00 | 4.80 |
| 3 | 0.0287 | 0.0172 | 0.1614 | 0.1441 | 0.1268 | 3.40 | 4.20 |
| 4 | 0.0260 | 0.0156 | 0.1417 | 0.1262 | 0.1106 | 3.00 | 3.70 |
| 5 | 0.0232 | 0.0139 | 0.1260 | 0.1120 | 0.0980 | 2.65 | 3.30 |
| 6 | 0.0209 | 0.0125 | 0.1102 | 0.0976 | 0.0850 | 2.30 | 2.90 |
| 7 | 0.0189 | 0.0113 | 0.0984 | 0.0870 | 0.0756 | 2.05 | 2.60 |
| 8 | 0.0169 | 0.0102 | 0.0866 | 0.0764 | 0.0661 | 1.80 | 2.25 |
| 9 | 0.0154 | 0.0092 | 0.0748 | 0.0656 | 0.0563 | 1.55 | 1.95 |
| 10 | 0.0138 | 0.0083 | 0.0669 | 0.0587 | 0.0504 | 1.40 | 1.75 |
| 11 | 0.0122 | 0.0073 | 0.0591 | 0.0518 | 0.0445 | 1.20 | 1.60 |
| 12 | 0.0110 | 0.0066 | 0.0512 | 0.0445 | 0.0378 | 1.05 | 1.40 |
| 13 | 0.0098 | 0.0059 | 0.0472 | 0.0413 | 0.0354 | 0.98 | 1.30 |
| 14 | 0.0091 | 0.0054 | 0.0394 | 0.0339 | 0.0283 | 0.80 | 1.10 |
| 15 | 0.0083 | 0.0050 | 0.0354 | 0.0305 | 0.0256 | 0.70 | 0.98 |
| 16 | 0.0075 | 0.0045 | 0.0311 | 0.0266 | 0.0220 | 0.60 | 0.88 |

## BRITISH STANDARD WHITWORTH

(B.S.W.)

THREAD FORM

r = Basic Radius = ·137329 p

h = Basic Depth of Thread = ·640327 p

p = Pitch = $\dfrac{1}{t.p.i.}$

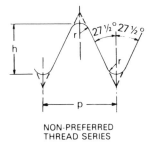

NON-PREFERRED THREAD SERIES

| nom. dia. inches | t.p.i. | basic depth of thread inches | basic major diameter inches | basic effective diameter inches | basic minor diameter inches | recommended tapping drill size mm | clearance drill size mm |
|---|---|---|---|---|---|---|---|
| 1/16 | 60 | 0.0107 | 0.0625 | 0.0518 | 0.0411 | 1.20 | 1.65 |
| 3/32 | 48 | 0.0133 | 0.0938 | 0.0805 | 0.0672 | 1.85 | 2.50 |
| 1/8 | 40 | 0.0160 | 0.1250 | 0.1090 | 0.0930 | 2.55 | 3.30 |
| 5/32 | 32 | 0.0200 | 0.1562 | 0.1362 | 0.1162 | 3.20 | 4.10 |
| 3/16 | 24 | 0.0267 | 0.1875 | 0.1608 | 0.1341 | 3.70 | 4.90 |
| 7/32 | 24 | 0.0267 | 0.2188 | 0.1921 | 0.1654 | 4.50 | 5.70 |
| 1/4 | 20 | 0.0320 | 0.2500 | 0.2180 | 0.1860 | 5.10 | 6.50 |
| 5/16 | 18 | 0.0356 | 0.3125 | 0.2769 | 0.2413 | 6.50 | 8.10 |
| 3/8 | 16 | 0.0400 | 0.3750 | 0.3350 | 0.2950 | 7.90 | 9.70 |
| 7/16 | 14 | 0.0457 | 0.4375 | 0.3918 | 0.3461 | 9.30 | 11.30 |
| 1/2 | 12 | 0.0534 | 0.5000 | 0.4466 | 0.3932 | 10.50 | 13.00 |
| 9/16 | 12 | 0.0534 | 0.5625 | 0.5091 | 0.4557 | 12.10 | 14.50 |
| 5/8 | 11 | 0.0582 | 0.6250 | 0.5668 | 0.5086 | 13.50 | 16.25 |
| 11/16 | 11 | 0.0582 | 0.6875 | 0.6293 | 0.5711 | 15.00 | 17.75 |
| 3/4 | 10 | 0.0640 | 0.7500 | 0.6860 | 0.6220 | 16.25 | 19.25 |
| 13/16 | 10 | 0.0640 | 0.8125 | 0.7485 | 0.6845 | 18.00 | 21.00 |
| 7/8 | 9 | 0.0711 | 0.8750 | 0.8039 | 0.7328 | 19.25 | 22.50 |
| 15/16 | 9 | 0.0711 | 0.9375 | 0.8664 | 0.7953 | 20.75 | 24.00 |
| 1 | 8 | 0.0800 | 1.0000 | 0.9200 | 0.8400 | 22.00 | 25.75 |
| 1, 1/8 | 7 | 0.0915 | 1.1250 | 1.0335 | 0.9420 | 24.75 | 29.00 |
| 1, 1/4 | 7 | 0.0915 | 1.2500 | 1.1585 | 1.0670 | 28.00 | 32.00 |
| 1, 3/8 | 6 | 0.1067 | 1.3750 | 1.2683 | 1.1616 | 30.25 | 35.50 |
| 1, 1/2 | 6 | 0.1067 | 1.5000 | 1.3933 | 1.2866 | 33.50 | 38.50 |
| 1, 5/8 | 5 | 0.1281 | 1.6250 | 1.4969 | 1.3688 | 35.50 | 41.50 |
| 1, 3/4 | 5 | 0.1281 | 1.7500 | 1.6219 | 1.4938 | 39.00 | 45.00 |
| 1, 7/8 | 4, 1/2 | 0.1423 | 1.8750 | 1.7327 | 1.5904 | 41.50 | 48.00 |
| 2 | 4, 1/2 | 0.1423 | 2.0000 | 1.8577 | 1.7154 | 44.50 | 51.00 |
| 2, 1/4 | 4 | 0.1601 | 2.2500 | 2.0899 | 1.9298 | 51.00 | 58.00 |
| 2, 1/2 | 4 | 0.1601 | 2.5000 | 2.3399 | 2.1798 | 57.00 | 64.00 |

## BRITISH STANDARD TAPER PIPE

(Rc Series)

THREAD FORM

r = Basic Radius = ·137278 p

h = Basic Depth of Thread = ·640327 p

p = Pitch = $\dfrac{1}{t.p.i.}$

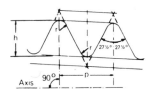

Taper 1 in 16 on dia. (shown exaggerated in diagram)

| nom. size inches | t.p.i. | basic depth of thread inches | basic diameters at gauge plane* major diameter inches | effective diameter inches | minor diameter inches | recommended tapping drill size mm |
|---|---|---|---|---|---|---|
| 1/16 | 28 | 0.0229 | 0.304 | 0.2812 | 0.2583 | 6.40 |
| 1/8 | 28 | 0.0229 | 0.383 | 0.3601 | 0.3372 | 8.40 |
| 1/4 | 19 | 0.0337 | 0.518 | 0.4843 | 0.4506 | 11.20 |
| 3/8 | 19 | 0.0337 | 0.656 | 0.6223 | 0.5886 | 14.75 |
| 1/2 | 14 | 0.0457 | 0.825 | 0.7793 | 0.7336 | 18.25 |
| 3/4 | 14 | 0.0457 | 1.041 | 0.9953 | 0.9496 | 23.75 |
| 1 | 11 | 0.0582 | 1.309 | 1.2508 | 1.1926 | 30.00 |
| 1, 1/4 | 11 | 0.0582 | 1.650 | 1.5918 | 1.5336 | 38.50 |
| 1, 1/2 | 11 | 0.0582 | 1.882 | 1.8238 | 1.7656 | 44.50 |
| 2 | 11 | 0.0582 | 2.347 | 2.2888 | 2.2306 | 56.00 |
| 2, 1/2 | 11 | 0.0582 | 2.960 | 2.9018 | 2.8436 | 71.00 |

*'Gauge plane' – The plane, perpendicular to the axis, at which the major cone has the gauge diameter.

NOTE: The gauge plane is theoretically located at the face of the internal thread or at a distance equal to the basic gauge length from the small end of the external thread.

## BRITISH STANDARD FINE

(B.S.F.)

THREAD FORM

r = Basic Radius = ·137329 p

h = Basic Depth of Thread = ·640327 p

$$p = Pitch = \frac{1}{t.p.i.}$$

NON-PREFERRED THREAD SERIES

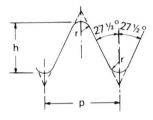

| nom. dia. | t.p.i. | basic depth of thread | basic major diameter | basic effective diameter | basic minor diameter | recommended tapping drill size | clearance drill size |
|---|---|---|---|---|---|---|---|
| inches | | inches | inches | inches | inches | mm | mm |
| 3/16 | 32 | 0.0200 | 0.1875 | 0.1675 | 0.1475 | 4.00 | 4.90 |
| 7/32 | 28 | 0.0229 | 0.2188 | 0.1959 | 0.1730 | 4.60 | 5.70 |
| 1/4 | 26 | 0.0246 | 0.2500 | 0.2254 | 0.2008 | 5.30 | 6.50 |
| 5/16 | 22 | 0.0291 | 0.3125 | 0.2834 | 0.2543 | 6.80 | 8.10 |
| 3/8 | 20 | 0.0320 | 0.3750 | 0.3430 | 0.3110 | 8.30 | 9.70 |
| 7/16 | 18 | 0.0356 | 0.4375 | 0.4019 | 0.3663 | 9.70 | 11.30 |
| 1/2 | 16 | 0.0400 | 0.5000 | 0.4600 | 0.4200 | 11.10 | 13.00 |
| 9/16 | 16 | 0.0400 | 0.5625 | 0.5225 | 0.4825 | 12.70 | 14.50 |
| 5/8 | 14 | 0.0457 | 0.6250 | 0.5793 | 0.5336 | 14.00 | 16.25 |
| 11/16 | 14 | 0.0457 | 0.6875 | 0.6418 | 0.5961 | 15.50 | 17.75 |
| 3/4 | 12 | 0.0534 | 0.7500 | 0.6966 | 0.6432 | 16.75 | 19.25 |
| 7/8 | 11 | 0.0582 | 0.8750 | 0.8168 | 0.7586 | 19.75 | 22.50 |
| 1 | 10 | 0.0640 | 1.0000 | 0.9360 | 0.8720 | 22.75 | 25.75 |
| 1, 1/8 | 9 | 0.0711 | 1.1250 | 1.0539 | 0.9828 | 25.50 | 29.00 |
| 1, 1/4 | 9 | 0.0711 | 1.2500 | 1.1789 | 1.1078 | 28.50 | 32.00 |
| 1, 3/8 | 8 | 0.0800 | 1.3750 | 1.2950 | 1.2150 | 31.50 | 35.50 |
| 1, 1/2 | 8 | 0.0800 | 1.5000 | 1.4200 | 1.3400 | 34.50 | 38.50 |
| 1, 3/4 | 7 | 0.0915 | 1.7500 | 1.6585 | 1.5670 | 41.00 | 45.00 |
| 2 | 7 | 0.0915 | 2.0000 | 1.9085 | 1.8170 | 47.00 | 52.00 |
| 2, 1/4 | 6 | 0.1067 | 2.2500 | 2.1433 | 2.0366 | 53.00 | 58.00 |
| 2, 1/2 | 6 | 0.1067 | 2.5000 | 2.3933 | 2.2866 | 58.00 | 64.00 |

## BRITISH STANDARD PIPE

THREAD FORM

r = Basic Radius = ·137329 p

h = Basic Depth of Thread = ·640327 p

$$p = Pitch = \frac{1}{t.p.i.}$$

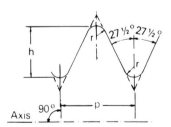

| nom. size | t.p.i. | basic depth of thread | basic major diameter | basic effective diameter | basic minor diameter | recommended tapping drill size | |
|---|---|---|---|---|---|---|---|
| inches | | inches | inches | inches | inches | Rp mm | G mm |
| 1/16 | 28 | 0.0229 | 0.304 | 0.2812 | 0.2583. | 6.60 | 6.80 |
| 1/8 | 28 | 0.0229 | 0.383 | 0.3601 | 0.3372 | 8.60 | 8.80 |
| 1/4 | 19 | 0.0337 | 0.518 | 0.4843 | 0.4506 | 11.50 | 11.80 |
| 3/8 | 19 | 0.0337 | 0.656 | 0.6223 | 0.5886 | 15.00 | 15.25 |
| 1/2 | 14 | 0.0457 | 0.825 | 0.7793 | 0.7336 | 18.50 | 19.00 |
| 5/8 | 14 | 0.0457 | 0.902 | 0.8563 | 0.8106 | | 21.00 |
| 3/4 | 14 | 0.0457 | 1.041 | 0.9953 | 0.9496 | 24.00 | 24.50 |
| 7/8 | 14 | 0.0457 | 1.189 | 1.1433 | 1.0976 | | 28.25 |
| 1 | 11 | 0.0582 | 1.309 | 1.2508 | 1.1926 | 30.25 | 30.75 |
| 1, 1/4 | 11 | 0.0582 | 1.650 | 1.5918 | 1.5336 | 39.00 | 39.50 |
| 1, 1/2 | 11 | 0.0582 | 1.882 | 1.8238 | 1.7656 | 45.00 | 45.00 |
| 1, 3/4 | 11 | 0.0582 | 2.116 | 2.0578 | 1.9996 | | 51.00 |
| 2 | 11 | 0.0582 | 2.347 | 2.2888 | 2.2306 | 56.50 | 57.00 |
| 2, 1/4 | 11 | 0.0582 | 2.587 | 2.5288 | 2.4706 | | |
| 2, 1/2 | 11 | 0.0582 | 2.960 | 2.9018 | 2.8436 | NO SIZES OF | |
| 2, 3/4 | 11 | 0.0582 | 3.210 | 3.1518 | 3.0936 | B.S. DRILLS ARE | |
| 3 | 11 | 0.0582 | 3.460 | 3.4018 | 3.3436 | RECOMMENDED | |
| 3, 1/4 | 11 | 0.0582 | 3.700 | 3.6418 | 3.5836 | IN B.S. 1157:1975 | |
| 3, 1/2 | 11 | 0.0582 | 3.950 | 3.8918 | 3.8336 | FOR THIS RANGE | |
| 3, 3/4 | 11 | 0.0582 | 4.200 | 4.1418 | 4.0836 | | |
| 4 | 11 | 0.0582 | 4.450 | 4.3918 | 4.3336 | | |

**BRITISH STANDARD
CYCLE THREAD**

| size inches | t.p.i. | tapping drill size | clearance drill size mm |
|---|---|---|---|
| 1/8 | 40 | 39 | 3.3 |
| 5/32 | 32 | 30 | 4.1 |
| 3/16 | 32 | 5/32 | 4.9 |
| 1/4 | 26 | No. 3 | 6.5 |
| 9/32 | 26 | Letter D | 7.5 |
| 5/16 | 26 | Letter J | 8.1 |
| 3/8 | 26 | Letter R | 9.7 |
| 9/16 | 26 | 33/64 | 13.20 |
| 1 | 26 | 31/32 | 1, 1/64 in. |
| 1.290 | 24 | 1 1/4 | 32 |
| 1.370 | 24 | 1, 21/64 | 34 |
| 1, 7/16 | 24 | 1, 13/32 | 37 |
| 1, 1/2 | 24 | 1, 15/32 | 37.50 |

*Fig. 29 Other fixings.*

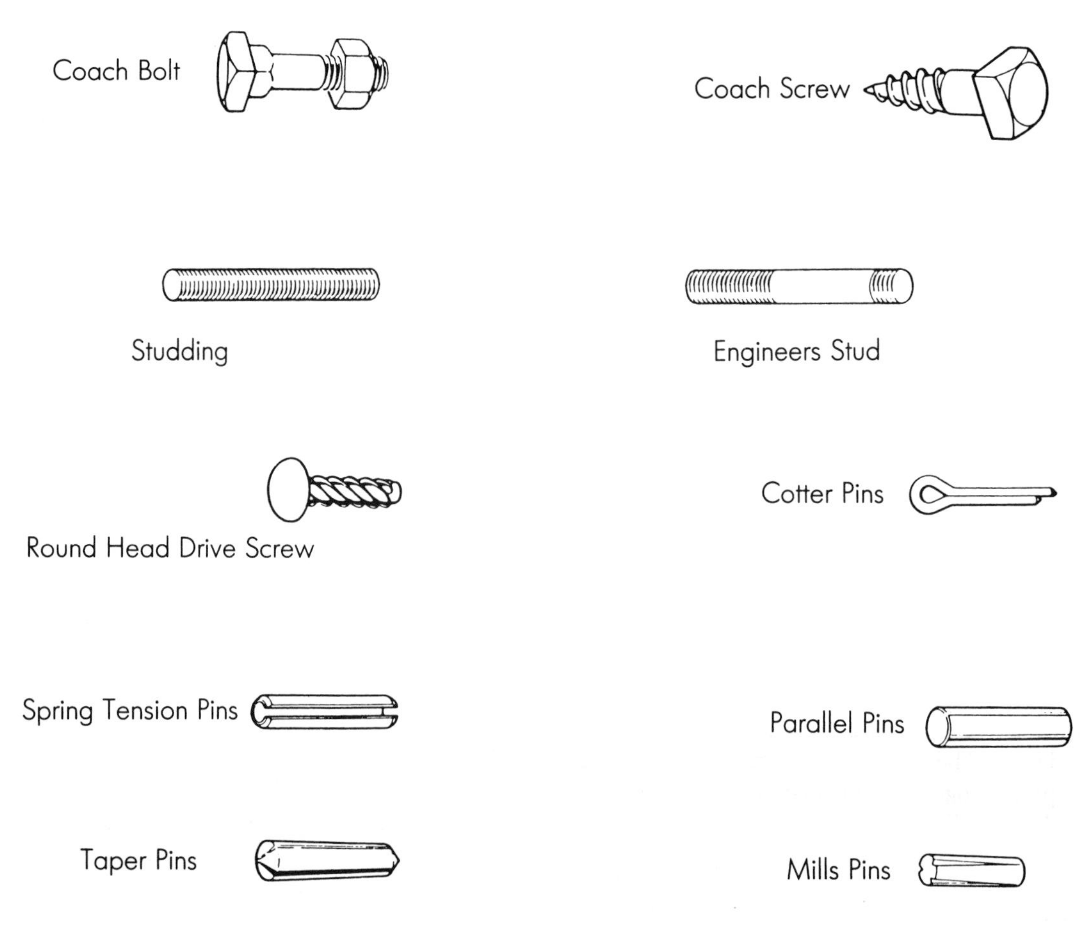

Coach Bolt

Coach Screw

Studding

Engineers Stud

Round Head Drive Screw

Cotter Pins

Spring Tension Pins

Parallel Pins

Taper Pins

Mills Pins

# CHAPTER 8

# Riveting

Riveting is a means of joining metals together in a permanent fashion. Rivets fall into two main groups: solid rivets and blind or 'pop' rivets. Solid rivets are stronger and have to be worked from both sides and closed by hand; 'pop' rivets, on the other hand, can be worked from one side using special riveting pliers.

## Solid rivets

Solid rivets are normally made from mild steel, aluminium, copper or brass, and should be used in similar metal to prevent problems of electrolytic corrosion, particularly between steel and aluminium. They are available with the shaped heads shown in Figure 30.

Before starting to rivet metal together it should be decided what head shape is going to be used and the diameter of the shank. For the best results the diameter of the shank should not exceed three times the thickness of the plates being joined, and should not be less than the thickness of the plates.

When riveting two pieces together, the position of the holes should be marked and centre punched on one piece of metal. If possible, clamp the pieces together and drill *one* hole through the pieces. It is important that the drill is the correct size; if it is too large the rivet will not grip the sides of the hole but bend in it. Where it is not possible to drill through the pieces together, the first hole in each piece should be drilled, any burrs removed and the hole countersunk, if necessary. The size of the countersink should be twice the diameter of the rivet; any larger and it would be difficult to fill; smaller and it would remove some of the strength of the rivet.

The first rivet should be placed through the hole and the plates closed together with the rivet set. With a snap head rivet, the head should be supported with the rivet snap while the tail is formed with the ball pein head of the hammer to either a round head, finished with a rivet snap, or the countersink filled.

The head of the countersunk rivet should be supported on a flat surface—an anvil or heavy block of metal is best. Do not use the vice for hammering on; the casting may crack unless the vice has been designed for this purpose. Once the rivet is closed do not continue to hammer it because it may work harden and crack. Before clenching the rivet, the tail must be cut to the right length. If a countersunk rivet is being formed, then three-quarters of the diameter of the shank should be left; for a snap head rivet, the allowance is one and a half times the diameter of the shank.

Once the first rivet has been clenched, the remaining holes can be drilled. Do not attempt to drill more than one hole in each piece of metal while they are separated because the holes will not line up accurately enough, no matter how carefully you mark out and drill. When riveting thin sheets to thicker material it is better not to countersink the thin material as this would weaken it, but to countersink the thicker material so that the thin sheet is forced into the countersink by the rivet.

Loose rivets for sidecar hood frames and other movable parts should be assembled with a washer between the two parts, preferably of brass, to prevent rusting. The rivet should be greased lightly and then clenched until the joint is firm.

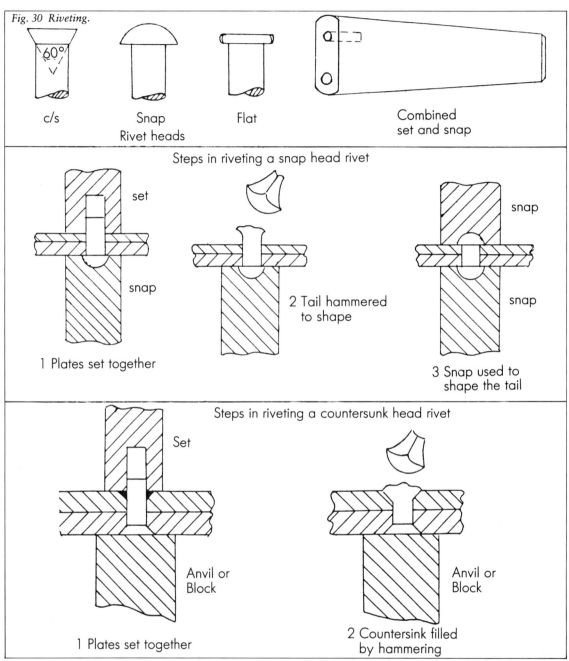

*Fig. 30 Riveting.*

60°

c/s

Snap

Rivet heads

Flat

Combined
set and snap

Steps in riveting a snap head rivet

set

snap

1 Plates set together

2 Tail hammered
to shape

snap

snap

3 Snap used to
shape the tail

Steps in riveting a countersunk head rivet

Set

Anvil or
Block

1 Plates set together

Anvil or
Block

2 Countersink filled
by hammering

## Removing solid rivets

To remove a snap head rivet, the head should be ground or filed off. If you intend using a cold chisel to remove the head, cut across the centre of the head in two directions so that it looks like a hot cross bun; it will then chisel away more easily. Do not attempt to drill right through the rivet as it is almost impossible to ensure that the drill will line up perfectly with the original hole and this will only cause more problems. Once the head has been removed, the shank of the rivet can be driven out using a pin punch. Do not use a sharp punch as this will merely swell the end of the shank into the hole.

Countersunk rivets should be carefully centre punched and the countersunk portion of the rivet drilled out. The rest of the rivet can then be punched out.

Where rivets have been used to join any items under stress and they are showing signs of coming loose, do not try to tighten them. It is much better to remove them all, even those that appear sound, and use high tensile bolts instead. The holes must be a good fit on the bolts and it may be necessary to enlarge the holes to the next size up. Self-locking nuts should be used, or plain nuts with the end of the bolts peined over to lock the nut onto the thread.

Ensure that the joint is clean and rust-free before bolting up. It is not advisable to paint the surfaces of the joint because the layer of paint could flake away, leaving the joint slightly loose, which will lead to further trouble. This also applies to riveted joints.

## 'Pop' or blind rivets

The advantage of 'pop' or blind rivets is that they can be used when access is restricted to one side of the work. Their main disadvantage is that they are not as strong as solid rivets.

There are two head shapes, pan or dome and countersunk, and they are available in steel, monel, aluminium and, in certain applications, copper, cupro-nickel and stainless steel. The rivets are normally available in three diameters with each size having three different lengths, though aluminium rivets are available in a longer size. Retail outlets usually sell the three sizes as short, medium and long, and it is important that the rivets are matched to the correct thickness of material being riveted. If the rivet is too short it will 'pop' before it has gripped the work sufficiently; too long and it will also 'pop' before it has begun to compress the work. Rivets that are too long can have washers put under the head or the tail to increase the thickness of the material being riveted. Washers can also be used to spread the clamping pressure when riveting soft or brittle materials such as plastics, leather, hardboard, etc.

The 'King Klik' Metro range of aluminium rivets are available in three different diameters that have a much wider range of lengths, giving a grip range from 0·5 mm (0·020 inch) to 36 mm (1·5 inch). Tables showing the complete range of these and standard blind rivets are shown Figures 31 and 32 overleaf.

For marking out and drilling the holes for the rivets, the procedure for 'pop' rivets is the same as that for solid rivets. Once the first pair of holes has been drilled the rivet is placed through the hole. The riveting tool should now be placed over the mandrel of the rivet, after checking that the nozzle of the tool is the correct size for the rivet. The handles of the tool must be held apart so that the tail of the rivet will pass through the gripping jaws of the riveting tool. When the nozzle is in contact with the head of the rivet, the handles of the riveting tool must be squeezed together while applying pressure to the head of the rivet to keep it in place. The mandrel will be pulled through the tail of the rivet, compressing the end of it and expanding the part of the tail inside the work. When the tail has been compressed, the mandrel will break with the characteristic 'pop' and the rivet will be fixed in place.

Until recently bolting together sheet metal where only one side was accessible meant the use of captive nuts resistance welded to the underside of the sheet. If these became loose or broken off, or the sheet to which they were attached had to be replaced, the amateur restorer was in difficulties with their replacement. Now there is a system of rivet nuts that can be used for a wide range of applications where access to a loose nut is impossible or time consuming. These rivet nuts — there are three basic types, T, X and J — can be installed with the same riveting tool as used for 'pop' rivets. The correct sized hole is drilled and the rivet nut placed into the hole. A threaded mandrel is screwed into the rivet nut and this mandrel is pulled by the riveting tool until the rivet nut is firmly anchored to the sheet. The mandrel is then unscrewed and the rivet nut is ready to accept a screw. The charts in Figures 33, 34 and 35 show a cross-sectional view of each type of rivet nut together with a table of sizes and data.

Fig. 31 Standard pop rivets. (Riveting Systems Ltd.)

**DOME HEAD RIVETS OF ALUMINIUM ALLOY, STEEL OR MONEL. ALL MANDRELS ARE STEEL. RIVET DIAMETERS ARE FRACTIONAL INCH. OTHER DIMENSIONS ARE DECIMAL INCH.**

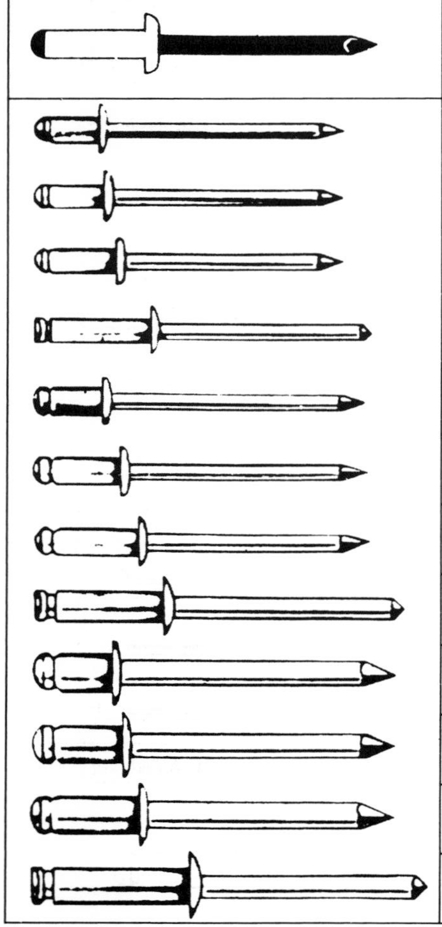

| LIFE SIZE ILLUSTRATIONS | DIAMETER | LENGTH | HOLE SIZE | HEAD DIAM. | MIN. GRIP | MAX. GRIP |
|---|---|---|---|---|---|---|
| | 1/8" | 0.23 | 0.13 | 0.23 | 0.04 | 0.10 |
| | 1/8" | 0.29 | 0.13 | 0.23 | 0.10 | 0.16 |
| | 1/8" | 0.35 | 0.13 | 0.23 | 0.16 | 0.22 |
| | 1/8" ALUMINIUM ALLOY ONLY | 0.53 | 0.13 | 0.25 | 0.22 | 0.38 |
| | 5/32" | 0.27 | 0.16 | 0.28 | 0.05 | 0.12 |
| | 5/32" | 0.35 | 0.16 | 0.28 | 0.12 | 0.20 |
| | 5/32" | 0.41 | 0.16 | 0.28 | 0.20 | 0.27 |
| | 5/32" ALUMINIUM ALLOY ONLY | 0.56 | 0.16 | 0.31 | 0.27 | 0.38 |
| | 3/16" | 0.31 | 0.19 | 0.34 | 0.07 | 0.15 |
| | 3/16" | 0.39 | 0.19 | 0.34 | 0.15 | 0.20 |
| | 3/16" | 0.47 | 0.19 | 0.34 | 0.20 | 0.27 |
| | 3/16" ALUMINIUM ALLOY ONLY | 0.72 | 0.19 | 0.37 | 0.27 | 0.50 |

*Fig. 32 'King Klik' metro range of blind rivets.* (Riveting Systems Ltd.)

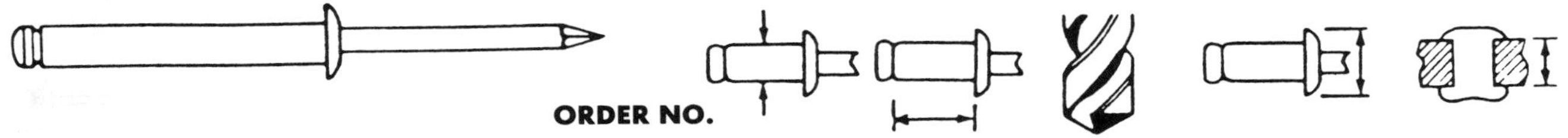

DIMENSIONS IN MILLIMETRES

**ALLUMINIUM ALLOY**

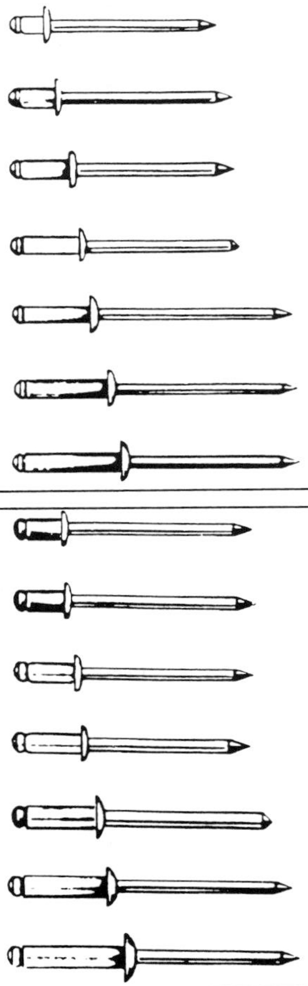

| ORDER NO. | DIAMETER | LENGTH | HOLE SIZE | DOME HEAD | GRIP RANGE |
|---|---|---|---|---|---|
| TA2904 | 2.9 | 4 | 3 | 5.9 | 0.5–2.5 |
| TA2906 | 2.9 | 6 | 3 | 5.9 | 2.6–4.0 |
| TA2908 | 2.9 | 8 | 3 | 5.9 | 4.1–6.0 |
| TA2910 | 2.9 | 10 | 3 | 5.9 | 6.1–8.0 |
| TA2912 | 2.9 | 12 | 3 | 5.9 | 8.1–10.0 |
| TA2915 | 2.9 | 15 | 3 | 5.9 | 10.1–12.0 |
| TA2918 | 2.9 | 18 | 3 | 5.9 | 12.1–15.0 |
| TA3906 | 3.9 | 6 | 4 | 7.5 | 1.5–3.5 |
| TA3907 | 3.9 | 7 | 4 | 7.5 | 3.6–4.5 |
| TA3908 | 3.9 | 8 | 4 | 7.5 | 4.6–6.5 |
| TA3910 | 3.9 | 10 | 4 | 7.5 | 6.6–7.5 |
| TA3912 | 3.9 | 12 | 4 | 7.5 | 7.6–9.5 |
| TA3915 | 3.9 | 15 | 4 | 7.5 | 9.6–12.0 |
| TA3918 | 3.9 | 18 | 4 | 7.5 | 12.1–15.0 |

*Fig. 32 continued*

| | | | | | |
|---|---|---|---|---|---|
| TA4906 | 4.9 | 6 | 5 | 9.5 | 1.5–3.5 |
| TA4908 | 4.9 | 8 | 5 | 9.5 | 3.6–5.0 |
| TA4910 | 4.9 | 10 | 5 | 9.5 | 5.1–7.0 |
| TA4912 | 4.9 | 12 | 5 | 9.5 | 7.1–9.5 |
| TA4914 | 4.9 | 14 | 5 | 9.5 | 9.6–11.5 |
| TA4916 | 4.9 | 16 | 5 | 9.5 | 11.6–13.0 |
| TA4918 | 4.9 | 18 | 5 | 9.5 | 13.1–15.0 |
| TA4921 | 4.9 | 21 | 5 | 9.5 | 15.1–18.0 |
| TA4924 | 4.9 | 24 | 5 | 9.5 | 18.1–21.0 |
| TA4927 | 4.9 | 27 | 5 | 9.5 | 21.1–24.0 |
| TA4930 | 4.9 | 30 | 5 | 9.5 | 24.1–27.0 |
| TA4932 | 4.9 | 32 | 5 | 9.5 | 27.1–29.0 |
| TA4935 | 4.9 | 35 | 5 | 9.5 | 29.1–31.0 |
| TA4940 | 4.9 | 40 | 5 | 9.5 | 31.1–36.0 |

STEEL WASHERS—To spread the clamping force when rivets are used in soft materials. Finish–Bright Zinc Plated.

| | |
|---|---|
| W2.9 | WASHERS FOR 2.9 MM RIVETS |
| W3.9 | WASHERS FOR 3.9 MM RIVETS |
| W4.9 | WASHERS FOR 4.9 MM RIVETS |

*Fig. 33 The T-rivet nut.* (Riveting Systems Ltd.)

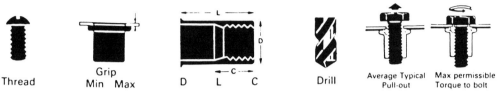

| | | | | |
|---|---|---|---|---|
| Thread | Grip<br>Min    Max | D    L    C | Drill | Average Typical<br>Pull-out    Max permissible<br>Torque to bolt |

| STEEL ZINC PLATED<br>(EXCEPT M3 WHICH IS BRASS, ZINC PLATED) | | METRIC | | | DIMENSIONS IN<br>MILLIMETRES | | |
|---|---|---|---|---|---|---|---|
| M3† | 0.51–1.27 | 4.72 | 9.02 | 5.21 | 4.8 | – | 13 lbf |
| M4 | 0.51–1.27 | 6.32 | 10.41 | 6.35 | 6.4 | 920 lbf | 45 |
| M5 | 0.51–1.27 | 7.11 | 11.81 | 6.10 | 7.2 | 1,280 | 70 |
| M6 | 0.76–3.25 | 9.5 | 15.5 | 8.51 | 9.6 | 1,520 | 110 |
| M8 | 0.91–3.25 | 10.57 | 16.0 | 9.27 | 10.6 | – | 145 |

| STEEL ZINC PLATED | | IMPERIAL, UNIFIED,<br>B.A. | | | DIMENSIONS IN INCHES | | |
|---|---|---|---|---|---|---|---|
| 6 UNC<br>6 UNF<br>4 BA | .020–.050 | .249 | .410 | .250 | $\frac{1}{4}$ | 920 lbf | 45 lbf |
| 8 UNC<br>8 UNF | .020–.050 | .249 | .410 | .250 | $\frac{1}{4}$ | 920 | 45 |
| 10 UNC<br>10 UNF<br>$\frac{3}{16}$ BSW<br>2 BA | .020–.050 | .280 | .465 | .240 | $\frac{9}{32}$ | 1,280 | 70 |
| $\frac{1}{4}$ UNC<br>$\frac{1}{4}$ UNF<br>$\frac{1}{4}$ BSW<br>0 BA | .030–.128 | .374 | .610 | .335 | $\frac{3}{8}$ | 1,520 | 110 |

† Except M3 which is brass, zinc plated.
Hole dimensions may have to be varied according to hardness, brittleness and thickness. Generally, holes in hard or thick materials should be larger than in soft or thin. The T system can be used in thicker material if installation and function are proved suitable.

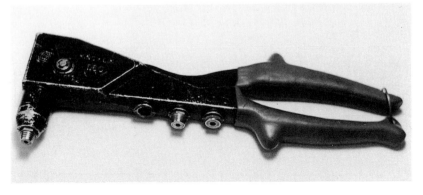

*Pop rivet pliers.*

*Fig. 34 The X-rivet nut.* (Riveting Systems Ltd.)

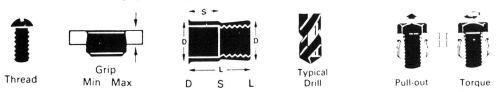

Thread | Grip Min Max | D S L | Typical Drill | Pull-out Torque

| STEEL, ZINC PLATED | | | METRIC | | | | DIMENSIONS IN MILLIMETRES |
|---|---|---|---|---|---|---|---|
| M3 | | | 4.74 | 4.91 | 9.66 | 4.8 | |
| M4 | | | 6.33 | 4.91 | 6.4 | | |
| M5 | 0.85 | NO MAX | 7.12 | 4.91 | 9.66 | 7.2 | SEE TABLE BELOW |
| M6 | | | 9.50 | 6.69 | 13.21 | 9.6 | |
| M8 | | | 12.68 | 7.96 | 15.75 | 12.7 | |
| M10 | | | 14.27 | 9.48 | 18.80 | 14.3 | |

| STEEL, ZINC PLATED | | | IMPERIAL, UNIFIED, BA | | | | DIMENSIONS IN INCHES |
|---|---|---|---|---|---|---|---|
| 4 UNC | 0.034 | NO MAX | .186 | .193 | .380 | $\frac{3}{16}$ | |
| 6 UNC<br>6 UNF<br>4 BA | 0.034 | NO MAX | .218 | .193 | .380 | $\frac{7}{32}$ | The pull-out and torque of the X-rivet system depend very much on the nature and thickness of the |
| 8 UNC<br>8 UNF | 0.034 | NO MAX | .249 | .193 | .380 | $\frac{1}{4}$ | work material and on the hole size. |
| 10 UNC<br>10 UNF<br>$\frac{3}{16}$ BSW<br>2 BA | 0.034 | NO MAX. | .280 | .193 | .380 | $\frac{9}{32}$ | |
| $\frac{1}{4}$ UNF<br>$\frac{1}{4}$ UNC<br>$\frac{1}{4}$ BSW<br>$\frac{1}{4}$ BSF<br>0 BA | 0.034 | NO MAX | .374 | .263 | .520 | $\frac{3}{8}$ | Pull out (tensile) strength is very high. The average test force to pull |
| $\frac{5}{16}$ UNC<br>$\frac{5}{16}$ UNF<br>$\frac{5}{16}$ BSW<br>$\frac{5}{16}$ BSF | 0.034 | NO MAX. | .499 | .313 | .620 | $\frac{1}{2}$ | a 10 mm ⅜" rivet nut out of 6 mm steel was 4,480 lbf, 2,032 Kp. |
| $\frac{3}{8}$ UNC<br>$\frac{3}{8}$ UNF<br>$\frac{3}{8}$ BSW<br>$\frac{3}{8}$ BSF | 0.034 | NO MAX. | .562 | .373 | .740 | $\frac{9}{16}$ | |

Hole dimensions given in the table are typical for general, non-critical sheet metal applications. Generally, holes in hard or thick material should be larger than in soft or thin materials.

*Fig. 35 The J-rivet nut.* (Riveting Systems Ltd.)

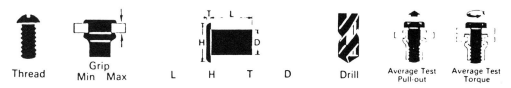

Hole sizes in the table for the J-rivet system below apply to drilling or piercing. The general oversize tolerance is +0,10mm, +0.004″. Stricter tolerances are needed for high stress situations.

The table is continued over the page.

| ALUMINIUM ALLOY | | | | IMPERIAL, UNIFIED, BA | | | | DIMENSIONS IN INCHES | |
|---|---|---|---|---|---|---|---|---|---|
| 4 BA | .076<br>.141<br>.181 | .100<br>.160<br>.200 | .375<br>.437<br>.500 | .320 | .035 | .187 | .190 | 770 lbf | 23 lbf in |
| 6-32 UNC | .076<br>.141<br>.181 | .100<br>.160<br>.200 | .438<br>.500<br>.562 | .330 | .035 | .187 | .190 | 770 | 23 |
| 8-32 UNC | .076<br>.141<br>.181 | .100<br>.160<br>.200 | .438<br>.500<br>.625 | .362 | .035 | .219 | .220 | 900 | 32 |
| 10-32 UNF<br>$\frac{3}{16}$ BSW<br>2 BA | .076<br>.121<br>.161<br>.201 | .120<br>.160<br>.200<br>.240 | .500<br>.500<br>.562<br>.625 | .382 | .035 | .250 | .252 | 1130 | 45 |
| $\frac{1}{4}$ UNC<br>$\frac{1}{4}$ UNF<br>$\frac{1}{4}$ BSW<br>$\frac{1}{4}$ BSF<br>0 BA | .010<br>.101<br>.161 | .100<br>.160<br>.220 | .562<br>.625<br>.687 | .520 | .063 | .344 | .347 | 2400 | 150 |
| $\frac{5}{16}$ UNC<br>$\frac{5}{16}$ UNF<br>$\frac{5}{16}$″ BSW<br>$\frac{5}{16}$ BSF | .010<br>.101<br>.161 | .100<br>.160<br>.220 | .625<br>.687<br>.750 | .615 | .063 | .406 | .409 | 3100 | 220 |
| $\frac{3}{8}$ UNC<br>$\frac{3}{8}$ UNF<br>$\frac{3}{8}$ BSW<br>$\frac{3}{8}$ BSF | .010<br>.101<br>.161 | .100<br>.160<br>.220 | .625<br>.687<br>.750 | .692 | .063 | .469 | .472 | 3700 | 320 |

*The J-rivet nut continued.*

| ALUMINIUM ALLOY | | | METRIC | | | | DIMENSIONS IN MILLIMETRES | | |
|---|---|---|---|---|---|---|---|---|---|
| M3 | 1.0 3.0 5.0 | 2.0 4.0 6.0 | 8.5 10.5 12.5 | 6.8 | 0.9 | 4.5 | 4.55 | 350 kp | 2.6Nm |
| M4 | 1.0 3.0 5.0 | 2.0 4.0 6.0 | 12.0 14.0 16.0 | 8.3 | 0.9 | 5.5 | 5.55 | 400 | 3.6 |
| M5 | 0.25 3.0 5.0 | 2.0 4.0 6.0 | 13.0 15.0 17.0 | 9.8 | 0.9 | 6.5 | 6.55 | 500 | 5.0 |
| M6 | 0.25 1.5 4.5 | 1.5 3.0 6.0 | 15.0 16.5 19.5 | 12.5 | 1.5 | 8.5 | 8.6 | 1100 | 17.0 |
| M8 | 0.25 4.0 5.5 | 2.5 5.5 7.0 | 16.5 19.5 21.0 | 15.6 | 1.5 | 10.5 | 10.6 | 1400 | 23.0 |
| M10 | 0.25 4.0 5.5 | 2.5 5.5 7.0 | 18.5 21.5 23.0 | 18.5 | 1.5 | 12.5 | 12.6 | 1700 | 36.0 |
| **STEEL AND BRASS** | | | **METRIC** | | | | **DIMENSIONS IN MILLIMETRES** | | |
| M3 | 1.0 3.0 5.0 | 2.0 4.0 6.0 | 8.5 10.5 12.5 | 8.00 | 0.75 | 5.0 | 5.1 | 550 kp | 5.3 Nm |
| M4 | 1.0 3.0 5.0 | 2.0 4.0 6.0 | 9.75 11.75 13.75 | 10.00 | 0.75 | 6.0 | 6.1 | 1000 | 7.4 |
| M5 | 1.0 3.0 5.0 | 2.0 4.0 6.0 | 11.00 13.00 16.00 | 11.00 | 1.0 | 7.0 | 7.1 | 1500 | 10.5 |
| M6 | 0.25 3.0 4.5 | 1.5 4.5 6.0 | 13.00 16.00 17.50 | 13.00 | 1.5 | 9.0 | 9.1 | 2000 | 35.0 |
| M8 | 0.25 3.0 4.5 | 1.5 4.5 6.0 | 14.50 17.50 19.00 | 16.00 | 1.5 | 11.0 | 11.1 | 3200 | 48.0 |
| M10 | 0.25 3.0 4.5 | 1.5 4.5 6.0 | 15.00 18.00 19.50 | 18.00 | 1.5 | 12.0 | 12.1 | 4000 | 75.0 |

## SYSTEM T

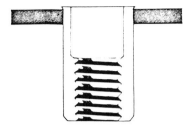  

1 The rivet nut is placed into the hole drilled in the workpiece.

2 The installation tool pulls the threaded part of the rivet nut shank upwards. The plain, unthreaded part of the shank is compressed and bulges outwards. The flange is forced against the surface of the work.

3 The bulge is completely expanded. The flange has buried itself into the work along the hole edge. The rivet nut is securely anchored and presents a flush surface.

## SYSTEM X

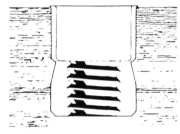 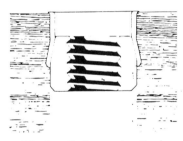 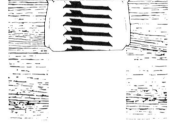

1 The rivet nut is placed into the hole. The shell of the fastener is connected by a thin wall of material to the internally threaded core.

2 The installation tool pulls the core upwards, breaking the thin wall between core and shell. The core enters the shell which starts to expand outwards into the work.

3 The shell is expanded into the work. In work thicknesses less than the depth of the shell, the shell is also bulged at the back of the work. The flange is seated in the work surface.

## SYSTEM J

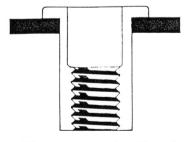 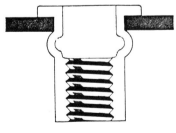 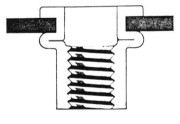

1 The rivet nut is placed into the hole drilled in the workpiece.

2 The installation tool pulls the threaded part of the rivet nut shank upwards. The plain part is compressed and bulges outwards. The flange is forced against the surface of the work.

3 The fully expanded bulge and the flange securely clamp the rivet nut to the work, ready to take a screw.

# CHAPTER 9

# Joining metals with heat

## Soldering

### Soft soldering

Soft soldering is a low-temperature method of joining metals together using a suitable alloy. Soft solder is an alloy of tin and lead with a small addition of antimony or bismuth to improve its properties.

The table shows the four main types of soft solder available. Of these, the tinman's and the plumber's solder will serve all the common needs of the motor cycle restorer.

There are two types of flux used in soft soldering — passive and active. Passive fluxes are usually supplied in paste form and are resin or tallow based; they will protect the cleaned surface of the joint from oxidation. However, they will not remove any grease or dirt, even from apparently clean hands. Active fluxes are usually liquid, 'Bakers Fluid' perhaps being one of the best known. These fluxes will remove a limited amount of grease and will corrode the metal if left for any length of time. For this reason they should not be used for electrical wiring work as some of the flux will be drawn up under the insulation of the wire and will resist all attempts at removal. It will gradually eat through the wire, which will then fail, usually at the most inconvenient time. Wherever active fluxes are used they should be washed off thoroughly afterwards.

Soldering irons come in different shapes and sizes, and can be heated either by gas stove or electrically.

### How to soft solder

1. Clean the joint thoroughly and ensure that it is as good a fit as possible, as solder should not be used to fill gaps, and if it does the joint will be weak. Apply the flux to the joint.
2. Heat the soldering iron; one with a copper bit heated in a flame will have reached the correct temperature when the flame turns green.
3. The iron should be quickly dipped into the flux to clean it and then held onto, or rubbed with, the stick of solder, until the bit is covered.
4. The iron is held onto the joint until the metal has reached the same temperature as the solder. The iron is then drawn slowly along the joint. As soon as the iron begins to cool it should be reheated.

*Soft solders.*

| COMPOSITION OF SOFT SOLDERS | | | | | | |
|---|---|---|---|---|---|---|
| SOLDER | | | | | | USES |
| BLOW PIPE OR FINE | 345 | 65 | | 0.5 | 183°C | COMPONENTS NEEDING A FREE RUNNING SOLDER |
| TINMAN'S | 48 | 50 | | 2 | 205°C | GENERAL PURPOSE WORK |
| PLUMBER'S | 66 | 34 | | | 250°C | WIPED JOINTS LEAD LOADING |
| PEWTERER'S | 25 | 25 | 50 | | 96°C | SOLDER FOR TIN AND LEAD ALLOYS |

Solder can be applied direct to the work by using a gas blowtorch to heat the work and by rubbing the solder along the joint. Care must be taken to ensure that the work is not overheated; oxides will be formed on the surface which will prevent the solder adhering to the joint. An alternative method is to cut off small pieces of solder and place them along the joint; as the blowtorch is moved along the joint the solder will melt as the metal reaches the correct temperature.

Sweating is a method of soldering where the two parts are coated with solder before they are put together. They are then placed together and heat applied until the solder melts and joins the parts. A good example of this is soldering a pipe inside a fitting; if the parts were assembled first, only a ring of solder would be holding the parts together at the top of the fitting. Coating the end of the pipe with solder before assembly and then heating the joint results in a much stronger join. Solder paint, which is a mixture of powdered solder and flux, can be painted onto the parts before assembly and then the work heated.

### Rules for successful soldering

1. The joint must be clean.
2. The joint must be close fitting.
3. The correct flux must be used.
4. The soldering iron must be in good condition and properly tinned.
5. The work must be heated to the temperature of the molten solder. On small work or thin sheet, the heat of the iron is sufficient to do this. On thicker work it is sometimes necessary to heat the whole job; this can be done by placing the work in a domestic oven or by the use of a blowtorch. It is important not to overheat the work.
6. The work should be cleaned after soldering to remove any residue of flux.

### Leading

Leading, or body solder, is used to fill small dents in steel components such as mudguards or petrol tanks after the damage has been rectified as much as possible with a hammer or other means. This method of filling dents is much better than using paste body filler as it will not crack with vib-

rations, nor is it porous to water.

The solder used has a high lead content and because of its composition it becomes pasty before it finally melts to a liquid. This property enables it to be spread over the surface of the metal providing the heat is carefully controlled.

Solder with a high lead content does not adhere easily to steel and the metal must first be tinned with normal soft solder. Naturally the area must be cleaned to bare rust-free metal and the tinning kept as thin as possible. The body solder is applied by heating the end of the stick of solder with a blowtorch and, as it becomes pasty, pressing it onto the steel and twisting off a small piece of it. This is done all over the area to be filled. Next the body solder is carefully heated until it becomes pasty, allowing it to be spread with a spatula made from either stainless steel or a hardwood such as beech. It is important that the tinning on the panel is melted as the body solder is spread, otherwise it will not adhere properly to the steel. The spatula should be rubbed in resin flux or tallow occasionally to help produce a smooth surface on the solder. The advantage of the wooden spatula, or 'bat' as it is sometimes called, over a stainless steel one is that it can be easily shaped to suit the area being filled, particularly if there are many concave curves involved.

It is important to make sure that the area is properly filled before using a 'Surform' or millenicut file to shape the lead. If, after shaping the lead, there are some small pin holes in the surface and you are loth to use the blowtorch and perhaps ruin the shape you have achieved, they can be filled with tinman's or fine solder and a soldering iron, though this is tricky on a vertical panel. Perhaps it would be best to stop while you are ahead and use body filler for the final touch.

If you are intending to use body solder on a petrol tank it is essential to make sure that there is no petrol or petrol vapour still in the tank. Wash out the tank with a strong detergent and rinse it thoroughly, then dry it out using a hair drier. *Do not* attempt to use a blowtorch near the tank until you are certain it is safe. If the area to be filled is not too large then it is possible to work on the tank with it filled with water for extra safety.

| TYPE | COMPOSITION | FLUX | MELTING POINT |
|------|-------------|------|---------------|
| ENAMELLING | 81% SILVER PLUS COPPER & ZINC | BORAX | 800°C |
| HARD | 78% SILVER | BORAX | 775°C |
| MEDIUM | 74% SILVER | BORAX | 750°C |
| EASY | 67% SILVER | BORAX | 720°C |
| EASY-FLO | 50% SILVER | EASY-FLO | 625°C |

*Silver solders.*

### Silver soldering

Where a stronger joint is required than can be obtained with soft solder, silver or hard solder can provide the answer; in some cases the only answer. As its name suggests, it contains a high percentage of silver which accounts for its high price.

The accompanying table shows the range of silver solders and their melting points. The reason for having a range of solders is quite simple. Where an article has to be built up of several different pieces, e.g. a coffee pot with soldered-on base, handle, spout and lid hinge, it would be very difficult, if not impossible, to do this with one type of solder. However, the silversmith can start with the highest melting point solder and work down the range without disturbing the pieces already in position.

Silver solder is ideal for copper and copper alloys since brazing (see below) uses a brass filler rod which melts at the same temperature as these alloys, causing great difficulty in joining them together without reducing the parts being joined to a molten blob, especially if the parts are small and they are being heated with a blowtorch. Because of the extra heat required for silver soldering and brazing, a small hearth built up from firebricks can be very useful. Old electric night storage heaters provide a good source of firebricks.

### How to silver solder

1. The joint must be clean and close fitting, wired together if necessary.
2. Mix the flux to a smooth paste with water and apply to the joint.
3. Heat the joint; the flux will first dry and then be seen to melt. At this point the joint is near to the correct temperature.
4. Apply the solder. When it melts capillary action should make it flow along the joint. It is important that the solder is heated by the heat of the metal rather than the flame.
5. Remove the heat and allow the work to cool before moving.

Sometimes it is easier or more convenient to cut small pieces of solder and lay them along the joint prior to heating. This will avoid overheating the joint, which will lead to the formation of scale, preventing the solder from joining the parts together.

## Brazing

Next up the temperature scale is brazing or bronze welding, depending on the filler rod used. This process requires a temperature of 950-1,000°C to achieve a good joint so a powerful blowtorch, an oxy-acetylene or oxy-propane set or a carbon arc torch fitted to an arc welder is needed. Where heavy sections are involved or fine control is needed, an oxy-acetylene set will prove the most versatile.

The actual process of brazing is very similar to hard soldering; the joint should be prepared in the same way. Although brazing flux is capable of cleaning a certain amount of rust from the joint, it is easier if you can make the joint as clean as possible. The flux should be mixed with water and applied to the joint, which should then be heated to bright cherry red. The end of the brazing rod, or spelter, as it is correctly named, should be heated, dipped into the dry powder flux and held onto the joint. It is important that the spelter is melted by the heat of the metal rather than the torch, otherwise the molten spelter could well sit on the join and prevent the metal heating up. Once the spelter has melted and run into the join, the work should be left to cool before being moved. It is not advisable to quench the joint in water as this can lead to the joint becoming brittle and cracking under load. A simple brazing hearth can be made using refractory bricks on an angle iron stand.

# Welding

Welding is a method of joining metals together whereby the metals being joined are actually melted at the joint face. In most cases a filler rod of similar metal is melted into the joint to complete the weld.

The source of heat can either be electricity or a combustible gas mixed with oxygen. Electric welding can be one of several types.

### Manual metallic arc (M.M.A.) welding

This is perhaps the most common form of arc welding used in home workshops. It consists of a transformer with an adjustable output of amperes. One of the leads from the transformer should be clamped to the workpiece; this is called the earth lead. The other has an insulated clamp for holding the consumable electrode. When the electrode is brought into contact with the workpiece, the circuit is complete and an arc is formed between the electrode and the work, the heat generated being sufficient to melt both the work and the electrode.

Because the welding current is induced by magnetic action between the windings, there is no direct connection between the mains supply and the output cables. Should the circuit be completed by a person touching both the electrode and the earthed workpiece, only a very small current will flow. The degree to which this may be felt will depend on the individual and the prevailing conditions. For instance, dampness will always increase conductivity but the current can never reach above a level of complete safety on the output side of the transformer.

Correct protection for the eyes is also essential — a heat-resisting face mask fitted with the correct grade of darkened glass must be used. Sunglasses or gas welding goggles are not good enough and their use could result in serious eye damage. It is also important that people or pets in the vicinity are not able to look at the arc since they will also be affected.

The amperage setting on the welder must be altered to suit both the thickness of the work and the diameter of the electrode. The thicker the work, the higher the setting must be to produce sufficient heat to melt the metal of the work and the electrode. The accompanying table shows the relationship between electrode size, amps and work thickness. This is only a guide, as several factors can influence the selection of the amperes; for example, Sunday lunch being cooked on a domestic electric cooker can have an effect on a welder operating off the domestic ring main!

The correct way is to test the setting on a scrap piece of metal of the same size as your work and adjust the welder until the right setting is found. I would recommend that this is done every time you begin welding, even if the welder has been left at a setting that proved suitable for the same gauge metal you are intending to weld. This applies

*Electrode-amperes chart.* (S.I.P. Products Ltd.)

| DIAMETER OF ROD | | RECOMMENDED CURRENT RANGE | APPROXIMATE MATERIAL THICKNESS TO BE WELDED |
|---|---|---|---|
| (MM) | (S.W.G.) | (AMPS) | |
| 1.6 | 16 | 25– 50 | 20–16 S.W.G. |
| 2.0 | 16 | 50– 75 | 16–12 S.W.G. |
| 2.5 | 12 | 75–105 | 12– 8 S.W.G. |
| 3.25 | 10 | 105–135 | $\frac{1}{8}'' - \frac{3}{16}''$ |
| 4 | 8 | 135–190 | $\frac{3}{16}'' - \frac{1}{4}''$ |
| 5 | 6 | 190–240 | $\frac{1}{4}'' - \frac{3}{8}''$ |
| 6 | 4 | 240–290 | $\frac{3}{8}'' - \frac{1}{2}''$ |

There are no hard and fast rules by which a particular gauge of electrode is selected. This is usually determined by the type of weld required in relation to the thickness of the workpiece. The above table is meant for guidance purposes only and should not be taken as an authority on the selection of any combination of the variables in question.

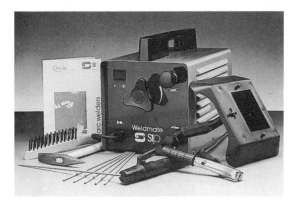

*Weldmate 140 arc welder.* (S.I.P. Products Ltd.)

particularly when welding thin metal, as a slight variation in output can burn through the metal.

The metal core of the electrode should be coated with flux, which melts as the weld progresses. The molten flux forms a fluid coating over the weld, which protects the molten weld pool from the oxidising effect of the atmosphere. Some of the ingredients of the flux form a gas shield around the arc, which helps to stabilise it. The fumes given off by the flux should not be inhaled for any period of time and it is advisable to ensure adequate ventilation to remove these.

The metal core of the electrode should also be matched to the metal being welded; low-carbon rods for low-carbon steels, alloy steel rods for alloy steels, nickel-rich or monel for cast iron. Non-ferrous metals are welded with electrodes having a similar composition to the metal being welded.

Successful arc welding is very much a question of 'practice makes perfect' and plenty of time should be devoted to practising the techniques required to produce a satisfactory weld before attempting to weld something important. The first technique to be learned is striking the arc between the electrode and the work. One method is to scratch the tip of the rod on the surface and then lift the rod sharply to create a gap of between $\frac{1}{16}$ inch (1·6–3 mm). Another method is to tap the end of the rod onto the work and lift it quickly to produce the arc. If the rod is not 'bounced' quickly off the metal it may stick, resulting in a direct short circuit welding the rod to the metal. The trans-

former should then be switched off and the rod loosened by bending it from side to side. Should there be difficulty in striking the arc, the earth clamp should be checked for a proper connection with the work and the welding current also checked, as this may be too low for the electrode selected.

To produce a satisfactory weld bead, only two movements are required, a steady movement in the direction of the weld and a slow downward movement to maintain the correct arc length as the electrode melts (see Figure 36). It is important to maintain the arc length and correct rate of travel at all times. If the rate of travel is too slow, the slag formed will flow in front of the weld pool and become trapped in the weld, weakening it with impurities and gas pockets. A correctly made weld is the same width throughout its length, has good penetration, and is uniformly rippled.

If the current setting is too low, a thin bead will be deposited, having little or no penetration into the metal. The sound the arc makes will be an intermittent crackling with irregular spluttering. Too high a current will provide plenty of penetration but the bead will be undercut and the electrode will burn away very fiercely, and there is the possibility of burning through the work, especially if it is fairly thin.

When the travel is too fast, a very small bead will be formed; too slow will produce a wide bead and the overheating caused could lead to distortion of the work. When the electrode is held too far away from the work, producing a long arc, the rod will shoot off in globules, with scarcely any

*Fig. 36 Electrode angle for M.M.A. welding.* (S.I.P. Products Ltd.)

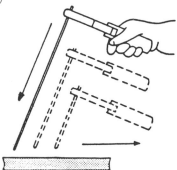

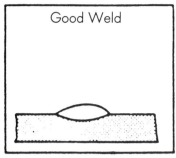

**NORMAL CONDITIONS**
Uniform ripples on surface of weld. Arc makes steady crackling sound.

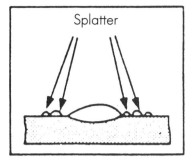

**ARC TOO LONG**
Surface of weld rough. Rod melts off in globules. Arc makes hissing sound.

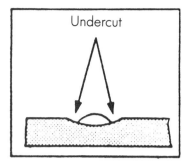

**TRAVEL TOO FAST**
Small bead undercut in some places. Rough surface and little penetration.

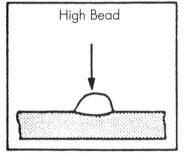

**CURRENT TOO LOW**
Arc is difficult to maintain. Very little penetration.

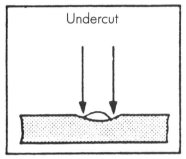

**CURRENT TOO HIGH**
Wide thick bead, undercut. Crater pointed and long. Rod burns away very quickly.

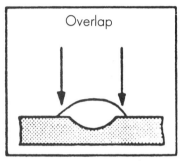

**TRAVEL TOO SLOW**
Metal builds up producing a wide heavy bead which noticeably overlaps at sides.

*Fig. 37 Cross-sections of different welds.* (S.I.P. Products Ltd.)

penetration and producing an irregular surface. The arc itself will make a hissing sound and may peter out from time to time. Figure 37 shows cross-sections through different types of weld.

**Metal inert gas (M.I.G.) welding**
This type of arc welding has gained in popularity in recent years with the introduction of smaller units and the appreciation of its qualities. The consumable electrode is in the form of a thin wire which is fed automatically into the weld pool from the welding torch assembly. At the same time an inert gas is passed through the torch assembly to form a shield around the weld pool and the electrode. It is this shield which gives M.I.G. welding its great advantage over M.M.A. welding.

Because the gas protects the weld from the oxidising effects of the atmosphere, the electrode does not have to be covered with flux. This in turn means that the welding wire can be supplied from a reel on the equipment, obviating the need to stop welding every few minutes when an electrode is used up.

The second advantage is that the gas shield also helps to cool the welded metal down, which reduces distortion and the spread of heat, so making it possible to weld much closer to inflammable materials such as seat covers without removing them. This does not, of course, apply to petrol tanks, which should always be emptied and removed from the bike before any welding is done, unless you wish to meet an untimely end in a very impressive explosion!

There are two gases that can be used, either argon or carbon dioxide. These can be used in the

## IDEAL 150

| WIRE DIAMETER | 0.6MM | | | | | |
|---|---|---|---|---|---|---|
| VOLTAGE SETTING | MIN. 1 | MIN. 3 | MIN. 5 | MAX. 1 | MAX. 3 | MAX. 6 |
| MATERIAL THICKNESS | 22.20SWG 0.7–0.9MM | 20–18SWG 0.9–1.2MM | 18–16SWG 1.2–1.6MM | 14SWG 2MM | 1/8″ 3.2MM | 3/16″ 4.8MM |
| WIRE SPEED SETTING | 2 | 3–3.5 | 4–5 | 5–6 | 5.5–7 | 7–8.5 |
| WIRE DIAMETER | 0.8MM | | | | | |
| VOLTAGE SETTING | MIN. 1 | MIN. 3 | MIN. 5 | MAX. 1 | MAX. 3 | MAX. 6 |
| MATERIAL THICKNESS | 22.20SWG 0.7–0.9MM | 20–18SWG 0.9–1.2MM | 18–16SWG 1.2–1.6MM | 14SWG 2MM | 1/8″ 3.2MM | 3/16″ 4.8MM |
| WIRE SPEED SETTING | 1.5–2 | 2–2.5 | 3–4 | 3.5–4.5 | 4.5–5.5 | 5.5–7 |

## IDEAL 180

| WIRE DIAMETER | 0.6MM | | | | | |
|---|---|---|---|---|---|---|
| VOLTAGE SETTING | MIN. 1 | MIN. 3 | MIN. 5 | MAX. 1 | MAX. 3 | MAX. 6 |
| MATERIAL THICKNESS | 22.20SWG 0.7–0.9MM | 20–18SWG 0.9–1.2MM | 18–16SWG 1.2–1.6MM | 14SWG–1/8″ 2–3.2MM | 1/8–3/16″ 3.2–4.8MM | 3/16–1/4″ 4.8–6.4MM |
| WIRE SPEED SETTING | 0.5–2 | 1.5–2.5 | 1.5–3 | 5–6 | 3–5.5 | 4.5–8 |
| WIRE DIAMETER | 0.8MM | | | | | |
| VOLTAGE SETTING | MIN. 1 | MIN. 3 | MIN. 5 | MAX. 1 | MAX. 3 | MAX. 6 |
| MATERIAL THICKNESS | 22.20SWG 0.7–0.9MM | 20–18SWG 0.9–1.2MM | 18–16SWG 1.2–1.6MM | 14SWG–1/8″ 2–3.2MM | 1/8–3/16″ 3.2–4.8MM | 3/16–1/4″ 4.8–6.4MM |
| WIRE SPEED SETTING | 0.5–1.5 | 1–2 | 1.5–2.5 | 2–3 | 2.5–4 | 3–6 |

**Above** *Settings for M.I.G. welders.* (S.I.P. Products Ltd.)

**Left** *S.I.P. Ideal M.I.G. welders.* (S.I.P. Products Ltd.)

**Right** *The S.I.P. Handymig, which can be used with or without gas.* (S.I.P. Products Ltd.)

pure state, though argon is usually mixed with 5% $CO_2$ and 2% oxygen. This is sold as 'Argoshield 5' by the British Oxygen Company or 'Cougar 95/5' by Air Products Ltd. For welding steel, carbon dioxide is the cheaper of the two but, because it is a cooler gas, the welder will need higher settings to cope with the cooling effects. Aluminium has to be welded with pure argon while stainless steel requires argon mixed with 1% or 2% oxygen. Naturally the correct welding wire must also be used.

The rate at which the wire is fed through the torch assembly, the current setting and the gas flow will all depend on the thickness and type of material being welded; full instructions for this should be in the booklet that accompanies the welder.

The tables opposite show the settings used for the S.I.P. 150 and 180 M.I.G. welders. These should be used as a basic guide and fine adjustment on either side of these settings will find the best results. A steady purr from the torch with little spatter is the indication that all is correct.

It is possible to produce a type of spot welding with an M.I.G. torch. Most sets have a spot welding nozzle which has two legs protruding from the end. When these legs are placed onto the metal, the nozzle is held stationary and when the welding wire strikes the metal it passes through the top layer into the one below. To aid the process, it is a good idea to drill a small hole in the top piece of metal and to ensure that the two plates are clamped close together. The power required to weld successfully in this situation is greater than that for seam welding and the settings required should be in the user's handbook for your machine. A similar process can be undertaken with an M.M.A. welder providing the hole is drilled through the top piece of metal, but here it is very easy to burn right through the metal unless you are very careful.

Larger machines usually have a timer incorporated in them for this type of welding (and once set will produce a weld of consistent quality each time). This timer can also be used to 'stitch' a joint by giving a 'weld on' time followed by a 'weld off' time.

On smaller machines your own judgement has to be used for the length of time for the spot weld. Too little time will produce a weak weld with little penetration; too long a time will produce a large build-up of weld or a complete burn through of the plates.

**Gasless M.I.G. welding** One of the disadvantages of M.I.G. welding is the difficulty of using the equipment outside, where any slight breeze can easily blow the shielding gas away from the weld pool making welding impossible. To overcome this difficulty a continuous cored welding wire has been developed that requires no external gas to shield the arc. The gas shield is formed by the chemicals making up the core burning in the heat of the arc.

A new range of welding machines has been developed to use this cored wire, including dual-purpose machines that can be switched from gas to gasless by simply reversing the polarity of the machine and changing the reel of wire. This new development makes M.I.G. welding for the amateur a much more versatile and practical proposition.

**Welding problems with an M.I.G.**
**Fault 1**
Arc unstable, excessive spatter and weld porosity.
**Causes**
1)   Insufficient shielding gas.
2)   Torch held too far from metal being welded.
3)   Grease, rust or paint on the metal.

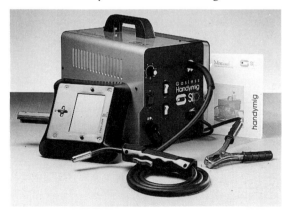

Set wire speed initially to the wire speed setting suggested below for the selected voltage setting. Fine adjustment of the wire speed control can then be made to give a smooth crackling sound to the arc.

## MILD STEEL

**GAS:** ARGON $CO_2$ MIXTURE
**WIRE:** 0.6 mm/0.024″ MILD STEEL

| VOLTAGE SETTING | WIRE SPEED SETTING | MATERIAL THICKNESS | | |
|---|---|---|---|---|
| RANGE 1 Min. | 3 | 20/22 SWG | 1.0 mm/0.7 mm | 0.039″/0.027″ |
| Max. | 4 | 16/18 SWG | 1.5 mm/1.2 mm | 0.058″/0.047″ |
| RANGE 2 Min. | 4.5 | 16 SWG | 1.5 mm | 0·058″ |
| Max. | 6.5 | 14 SWG/$\frac{1}{8}$″ | 3.0 mm/2.0 mm | 0.078″ |

**GAS:** $CO_2$
**WIRE:** 0.6 mm/0.024″ MILD STEEL

| VOLTAGE SETTING | WIRE SPEED SETTING | MATERIAL THICKNESS | | |
|---|---|---|---|---|
| RANGE 1 Min. | 2 | 20/22 SWG | 1.0 mm/0.7 mm | 0.039″/0.027″ |
| RANGE 2 Min. | 3 | 16/18 SWG | 1.5 mm/1.2 mm | 0·058″/0·047″ |
| Max. | 5 | 14 SWG/$\frac{1}{8}$″ | 2.0 mm | 0.078″ |

## STAINLESS STEEL

**GAS:** ARGON/OXYGEN OR ARGON $CO_2$
**WIRE:** 0.8 mm/0.030″ STAINLESS STEEL

| VOLTAGE SETTING | WIRE SPEED SETTING | MATERIAL THICKNESS | | |
|---|---|---|---|---|
| RANGE 1 Min. | 3.0 | 20/22 SWG | 1.0 mm/0.7 mm | 0.039″/0.027″ |
| Max. | 4.0 | 16/18 SWG | 1.5 mm/1.2 mm | 0.058″/0.047″ |
| RANGE 2 Min. | 4.5 | 16 SWG | 1.5 mm | 0·058″ |
| Max. | 6.5 | 14 SWG/$\frac{1}{8}$″ | 3.0 mm/2.0 mm | 0·125″/0.078″ |

## ALUMINIUM

**GAS:** PURE ARGON
**WIRE:** 0.8 mm/0.024″ ALUMINIUM 5% SILICON ALLOY

| VOLTAGE SETTING | WIRE SPEED SETTING | MATERIAL THICKNESS | | |
|---|---|---|---|---|
| RANGE 2 Min. | 9.0 | 16 SWG | 1.5 mm | 0.058″ |
| Max. | 10.0 | 14 SWG$\frac{1}{8}$″ | 3.0 mm/2.0 mm | 0.078″ |

Note: Always start with maximum wire speed when using Aluminium.

## MILD STEEL – CORED WIRE & TORCH NEGATIVE

**WIRE:** 0.8 mm/0.030″ SELF SHIELDING WIRE

| VOLTAGE SETTING | WIRE SPEED SETTING | MATERIAL THICKNESS | | |
|---|---|---|---|---|
| RANGE 1 Min. | 1.5–2.5 | 20/22 SWG | 1.0 mm/0.7 mm | 0.039″/0.027″ |
| Max. | 1.5–2.5 | 16/18 SWG | 1.5 mm/1.2 mm | 0.058″/0.047″ |
| RANGE 2 Min. | 1.5–2.5 | 16 SWG | 1.5 mm | 0·058″ |
| Max. | 1.5/3.0 | 14 SWG/$\frac{1}{8}$″ | 3.0 mm/2.0 mm | 0·125″/0.078″ |

*Settings for use with Handymig. With and without gas. (S.I.P. Products Ltd.)*

## Solutions

1) Check contents gauge of gas bottle, setting of regulator, and pipes for kinks.
   Don't weld in a strong draught either indoors or outside.
2) Don't hold the torch more than 10 mm ($\frac{3}{8}$) inch) away from the work.
3) Clean work off thoroughly.

## Fault 2
Weld deposit too thick.
### Causes
1) Welding voltage too low.
2) Moving torch too slowly over metal being welded.
### Solutions
1) Turn up power until welder 'purrs' correctly.
2) Move torch more quickly.

## Fault 3
Weld deposit stringy.
### Causes
1) Gas flow incorrect.
2) Moving torch too quickly.
### Solutions
1) See Fault 1.1.
2) Slow movement of torch—always move in one direction, don't back track.

## Fault 4
Lack of penetration.
### Causes
1) Moving torch too quickly.
2) Wire feed speed too low.
3) Welding volts too low.
### Solutions
1) Slow down.
2) Turn up power one setting at a time.
3) As above. If $CO_2$ is being used, the low temperature of the gas could make welding difficult with thicker metals.

## Fault 5
Burning through the metal.
### Causes
1) Wire feed speed too high.
2) Welding volts too high.
3) Torch moved too slowly.

## Solutions
1) Step power setting down one step at a time.
2) As 1.
3) Keep torch moving continuously and smoothly.

## Fault 6
Wire repeatedly burns back.
### Causes
1) Torch too close to work.
2) Wire speed too slow.
3) Gas coverage poor.
4) Intermittent break in welding circuit. Possible causes:
   a) Welding wire corroded.
   b) Contact tip damaged or loose.
5) Wire feed slipping. Possible causes:
   a) Pressure wire roll adjustment incorrect.
   b) Worn feed rolls.
   c) Corrosion or blockage in liner.
   d) Faulty contact tip.
### Solutions
1) Hold torch 10 mm ($\frac{3}{8}$ in) away from work.
2) Adjust wire feed.
3) Check nozzle is not filled with spatter, see Fault 1.1.
4) a) Replace wire.
   b) Check and replace tip if necessary.
5) a) Adjust pressure.
   b) Replace feed rolls.
   c) Check and replace liner if necessary.
   d) Check and replace tip if necessary.

## Gas welding
The heat source used in the most common form of gas welding is a mixture of oxygen and acetylene known universally as oxy-acetylene. Propane and oxygen can also be used; the techniques of welding are the same with either gas.

The gas is stored under pressure in cylinders colour-coded black for oxygen and maroon for acetylene. The rubber hoses connecting the cylinders to the torch are also coloured in the same way and the regulators that screw into the cylinders are threaded differently—a right-hand thread for oxygen, left-hand thread for acetylene.

The left-hand threads can be identified by small cuts on the corners of all the relevant nuts.

The regulators have two dials — the right-hand one indicates the cylinder contents, the left reads the outlet pressure. The regulators also have a pressure-regulating screw which is operated once the main cylinder valve has been opened.

Before the regulators are fitted, the cylinders must be 'vented', the term used to describe the method of making sure that the threads and valve at the top of the cylinder are clean. The cylinder valve should be opened very briefly, allowing a short, sharp release of gas which will blow out any particles of dirt.

It is important when fixing the regulators to the cylinders that no cross-threading occurs and that the correct spanner is used; do not over-tighten as this could strain the brass of the fittings. The hoses and the torch should be fitted next, and the main cylinder valves opened.

The torch is basically a mixing chamber for the two gases; the amount of gas allowed into the torch is controlled by a knob, blue for oxygen, red for acetylene. The combined gases leave the torch via the nozzle to be burned at the nozzle tip.

The nozzle of the torch is removable and nozzles are available with different hole diameters at the tip; it is this size that determines the thickness of metal that can be welded. The most common sizes are 1, 2, 3, 4, 5, 7, 10, 13, 16, 25 and 35. The larger the number, the larger the hole in the tip. For thin sheet metalwork, the number 1 nozzle is the most suitable. For metal over 1·0 mm (20 S.W.G.) thick a number 2 or 3 will be required. Commercially available sets of nozzles usually incorporate a chart, matching nozzle size to metal size, but this should only be regarded as a guide rather than a hard and fast rule, because the flame adjustment and the material can also affect the tip size.

For most welds a filler rod will be needed and should be of the same composition as the metal being welded. Mild steel rods are copper-coated to help reduce oxidation; the most common size is 1·6 mm diameter, and they are generally sold by weight.

When everything is ready, the main cylinder valves should be turned on and the pressure regulated to the required setting. Once set, the torch valves can be opened and the pressure levels re-adjusted if necessary. After closing the valves the torch is ready for lighting.

The acetylene control should be opened slightly and the torch lit. The flame should then be increased in size until it begins to smoke. Then the acetylene control should be gradually closed until the flame just ceases to smoke. The oxygen control can now be opened gradually. As the amount of oxygen is increased, a white cone will become visible in the centre of the flame. The oxygen control on the torch should be adjusted until this cone is only a few millimetres long with a rounded tip. This type of flame is called a neutral flame. There are two other types of flame that can be produced by adjusting the proportion of oxygen to acetylene: an oxidising flame is produced by reducing the flow of acetylene, which will reduce the overall size of the cone and flame; and a reducing or carburising flame is achieved by increasing the flow of acetylene until a feather-like haze appears around the central cone.

These different types of flame are required for welding different types of metal. An oxidising flame is used for welding brass and bronze; the excess oxygen helps to prevent the zinc in the brass from vapourising out. The reducing flame is used for welding cast iron, while the neutral flame is ideal for mild steel, copper and aluminium.

There are two main methods of welding with a gas torch, known as leftward and rightward welding (see Figure 38). For thinner metal below 5 mm ($\frac{3}{16}$ inch) thick, leftward welding is used with the filler rod introduced in front of the flame. The flame should be kept moving forward all the time coupled with a slight zig-zag movement to ensure that both sides of the joint are kept molten. The filler rod is fed into the centre of the weld pool to produce a satisfactory joint.

Rightward welding is used on work that is over 5 mm thick; in this instance the torch is moved to the right in a circular movement and the filler rod is fed into the weld pool behind the torch. This method enables the torch to pre-heat the metal and ensure a fluid weld pool that joins the two parts together. One of the main problems with gas

*Fig. 38 Leftward and rightward welding.*

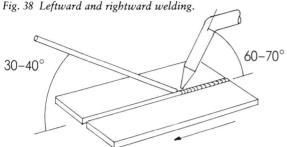

30–40°    60–70°

Direction of welding (leftward)

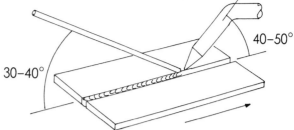

40–50°    30–40°

Direction of welding (rightward)

welding is heat distortion; the thinner the metal being welded, the greater the distortion. The main precaution used to overcome this is to tack weld the joint prior to the final weld; the thinner the metal, the closer the tacks should be. They should be kept as small as practicable to prevent obstructions when completing the joint.

The metal for gas welding does not have to be completely clean as the torch will weld through a small amount of debris, but it can cause spitting and spluttering which can be disconcerting when you are concentrating on producing a sound joint.

### Tungsten inert gas (T.I.G.) welding

T.I.G. welding is not a method of welding available to the amateur but a brief description of the process will at least remove the confusion that often exists in people's minds over the different forms of welding. In the T.I.G. process, the heat is supplied by an electric arc from a tungsten electrode which will withstand the high temperature without melting. The electrode is surrounded by a nozzle which conducts the shielding gas to the weld area; the gases used are either argon or helium. A filler rod is fed into the weld area by hand or, in an automated set-up, by machine.

T.I.G. welding is used extensively in the aircraft and atomic energy industries because it will produce high-quality welds in light alloys and other difficult metals. It is also very versatile, using current from as little as 0.5 amp to as high as 750 amps. Very small currents used with specialised air-cooled torches can weld metals as little as 0·05 mm thick.

### Spot welding

Most motor bikes with pressed steel frames have the seams of the frame spot welded together. A spot weld is achieved by clamping the parts to be joined firmly between a pair of heavy electrodes which are connected to the secondary circuit of a step-down transformer. The maximum resistance in the circuit is at the point of contact between the two parts being joined and localised heating occurs. The rise in temperature is sufficient for the metal to fuse together, forming a rigid joint. Figure 39 shows, in diagrammatic form, a section through a spot weld being formed. Spot welders are usually rated at 25 amps and if run from a domestic 13 amp ring main could blow the fuses — an uprated circuit is needed to cope with the extra load — and they can only work when access is possible to both sides of the metal. This in turn gives rise to the need for interchangeable arms to allow the welder to reach into awkward places and over longer distances.

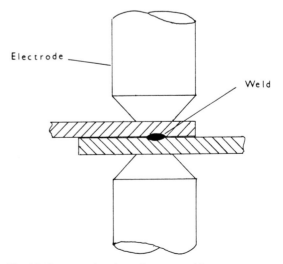

Electrode

Weld

*Fig. 39 Cross-section through a spot weld.*

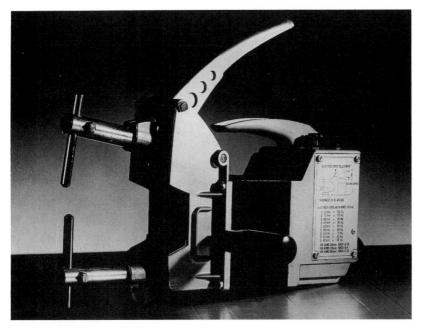

*The Pulsamatic spot welder.*
*(S.I.P. Products Ltd.)*

To produce satisfactory spot welds, the metal must be clean and the joints close fitting. The parts should be clamped together in several places to ensure that the panel cannot move out of alignment during welding. The position of the welds should be marked out along the join to give an even spacing. If you are not sure of the spacing, measure those on a similar area of welding and use that as a guide.

The faces of the electrodes should be clean and smooth to achieve a good contact between them and the metal. The electrodes are brought into contact with the work and pressure applied before the current is allowed to flow. Once the joint is formed, the current is switched off and the joint allowed to cool sufficiently to prevent movement before the pressure is removed. The more expensive spot welders incorporate a timer which can be set to switch off the current when the weld is complete, depending on the thickness of the metal being welded. This makes the process easier and the welds more uniform in quality.

## Spot welding problems
### Fault 1
Holes burned through work.

**Causes**
1) Weld time too long.
2) Weld settings too high.
3) Distance between metals being joined too wide.
4) Weld too close to the edge.

**Solutions**
1) Reduce weld time.
2) Reduce settings.
3) Clamp close together, ensure plates are flat, use self-tapping screws if necessary.
4) Use a seam weld if the spot weld position cannot be moved away from the edge.

### Fault 2
Insufficient penetration
**Causes**
1) Weld time too short.
2) Weld settings too low.
3) Distance between metals too wide.

**Solutions**
1) Increase time.
2) Increase setting.
3) See Solution 1.3.

## Carbon arc torch
A useful addition to an ordinary welder is a carbon arc torch. This consists of an insulated handle

which has two metal rods passing through it, at the end of one of which there is a clamp for holding a copper-coated carbon electrode. The other rod, which can slide in and out of the handle, has a clamp for holding the other electrode. The two rods are connected by electric cable to the positive and negative clamps of the welder, which is set to a low amperage; when the sliding electrode is brought into close contact with the fixed electrode, an arc flame is formed between the two. It must be emphasised that a full head shield is necessary plus gloves and long sleeves for this operation. The arc gives off strong ultra-violet radiation which can burn the skin in the same way as a long session of sunbathing.

The actual process of brazing with the carbon arc torch is the same as that when using an ordinary blowtorch; the metal to be joined must be clean, the joint close fitting, and flux must be used to prevent the metal oxidising in the flame.

The main disadvantage of using the carbon arc torch is the difficulty of seeing when the metal has reached the correct temperature (cherry red) because of the dark glass of the headshield. It is possible to burn through thin metal without realising how hot it is becoming. This can be avoided by cutting off small pieces of brazing spelter and placing them on the joint. When the metal reaches the right temperature, the pieces of spelter will melt and run along the joint. A second disadvantage is the large amount of distortion that can be caused by the flame. This can be minimised by careful clamping of the work, or by the use of self-tapping screws where possible to hold the parts together.

The latest types of carbon arc torch can be used for a form of spot welding using only one carbon rod. One of the arms is replaced with a different carbon holder that holds the carbon rod parallel to the torch arms. The torch is connected to the welder in the normal way and the lowest setting selected. The fixed arm of the torch with no rod fitted is held on the workpiece, while the carbon rod in the other holder is slid forward until it reaches the metal. When contact is made, slide the carbon back slightly to create the full arc. The weld will be achieved in a few seconds and it is easy

*A carbon arc brazing kit.* (S.I.P. Products Ltd.)

to see when it is complete; the exact time taken will depend on the thickness of the metal being welded. Galvanised and other coated steel needs to have a small amount of brazing spelter fed into the joint.

## Types of welding

**Flat welding** includes all joints in which the weld is laid horizontally and the electrode or filler rod is fed downwards into the joint. Flat welding is the easiest form of welding since there is no tendency for the molten pool to run under the force of gravity which can make other forms of welding difficult. Therefore it is preferable wherever possible to arrange the work so that the joint is flat. However, it is not always easy to achieve a flat position and welding vertically and overhead should be practised.

**Vertical welding** can be done vertical-up or vertical-down. The basic problem is the sag of the weld pool; for this reason vertical-down is preferable as the cold metal below the weld prevents the pool sagging too easily. Fine control is necessary whichever type of welding you are using, and practice is essential on similar thickness material until you are satisfied that the weld can be accomplished correctly.

**Overhead welding** is probably the most difficult to achieve successfully. Avoid trying to lay too much weld at one time as this leads to a larger weld pool which is likely to drop. You may find it easier to weld the join with a series of tacks, gradually filling in the gaps. A head screen, leather apron and gauntlet gloves should be worn as protection against splatter and molten metal dropping from the joint.

### Welding joints

No matter what type of welder you use, apart from a pure spot welder, the different types of joints are given the same names (see Figure 40). Before trying any new type of joint it is best to practise on some scrap metal first.

Before welding butt joints together the edges of the metal must be prepared to achieve adequate penetration of the weld into the joint (see Figure 41).

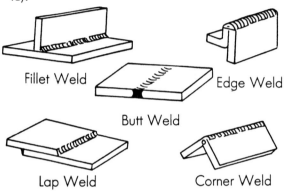

*Fig. 40 Different welds.* (S.I.P. Products Ltd.)

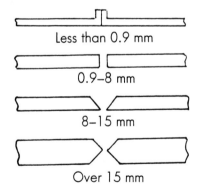

Less than 0.9 mm

0.9–8 mm

8–15 mm

Over 15 mm

*Fig. 41 Edge preparation.*

### Welding safety

It is important to remember that whichever type of welding is used, there are some important safety precautions that must be taken.

● Suitable clothing must be worn; a cotton boiler suit that secures at the neck and wrists is ideal. Do not use nylon because any hot sparks or molten slag will melt through it, increasing the danger of burns. A strong leather apron and gloves will also give added protection; metal that has been welded retains the heat for some time and gloves can save many painful burns.

● Eye protection is essential and it is important that the correct grade of dark glass is used for the type of welding being undertaken. Ensure that onlookers are protected from the flash of arc welding and the glare from carbon arc brazing. If you are using an extension lead connected to an arc welder, make sure all the lead is unwound from the drum; the high current passing through the cable can cause overheating if it is left coiled.

● Gas bottles should be used upright and checked carefully for leaks before lighting the torch.

● When welding direct onto a motor bike, check carefully that there is nothing inflammable near the weld, such as electrical wiring, hydraulic brake pipes, petrol pipes or tanks, and disconnect the battery. Always have a suitable fire extinguisher handy in case the worst happens.

● Never weld in a confined space where you could be trapped in the event of fire. If you have to weld in such a position, have someone standing by to help you in an emergency.

● Always provide adequate ventilation when welding. It is not healthy to breathe the fumes produced by welding fluxes, and some metals, particularly galvanised steel, can produce fumes that cause temporary breathing problems and uncontrolled tremors of the hands. If you have to weld galvanised steel and you do not have adequate ventilation or extraction equipment, restrict your welding to very short periods, allowing plenty of time between to let the fumes disperse.

# CHAPTER 10

# Sheet metal and tube work

Though there is not much sheet metal used in the construction of a solo motor cycle, what there is can be very easily seen and needs to look its best. If mudguards, legshields, petrol tanks, headlights, etc., are dented or damaged in any way it detracts from the rest of the machine.

One advantage the motor cycle restorer has over the car restorer is that all the metalwork can be removed and is much easier to handle because of its size. Given time and careful working most of the sheet metal repairs needed on a motor cycle can be accomplished with a few basic tools and a little practice.

Sheet metal working can be broken down into three stages: marking and cutting out, shaping, and joining. The joining of sheet metal has already been dealt with in other sections of this book, so I shall concentrate here on the other two.

## Marking and cutting out sheet metal

Normal marking out tools are required for sheet metal and the only point to remember is that when

marking out soft metals or coated steel — e.g. tinplate, etc. — a soft pencil should be used unless the metal is going to be cut along the marked line. Soft metals scratch very easily and the blemish is difficult to remove, while cutting through the protective coating on sheet steel will encourage rust to spread under the coating and lift it off.

The most commonly used thickness of sheet metal for such items as mudguards, legshields, etc., is either 16 or 18 S.W.G., although some manufacturers used 20 S.W.G. for engine covers on motor scooters and similar lightweight machines. When making replacement parts, do not use a thicker gauge material than the original. It is not necessary from a strength point of view, and the thicker the gauge, the harder it is to work.

Hand-held tin snips for cutting sheet metal are usually adequate up to 18 S.W.G. in steel or 16 S.W.G. in copper or aluminium. Beyond this it is very hard work and accuracy is very difficult.

A pair of bench shears will cope with thicker sections, but as with the tin snips they distort the metal that is being cut off. In many instances this does not matter, but where both pieces are needed the distortion can cause problems. A hand tool such as the 'Monodex' cutter will cut without

*Tin snips.*

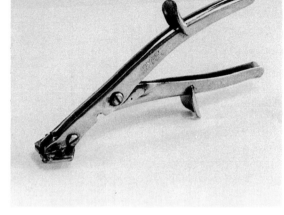

distortion, as will bench shears that are designed to remove a strip of metal as they cut. A 'nibbler' fitted to an electric drill will cut through metal easily, reducing the effort required enormously.

### Forming panel edges
There are various hammers and mallets available for working on sheet metal but you do not need to buy more than one or two. Hammers for sheet metal work should not be used for nailing or other normal hammer work; if the faces become damaged, they will transfer the marks to the metal every time they are used. For general shaping of the metal, a mallet made from hide, wood or rubber is the best tool to use; it will not bruise the metal in the same way as a hammer, yet will have sufficient weight to form the metal.

Dollies are shaped lumps of steel with polished

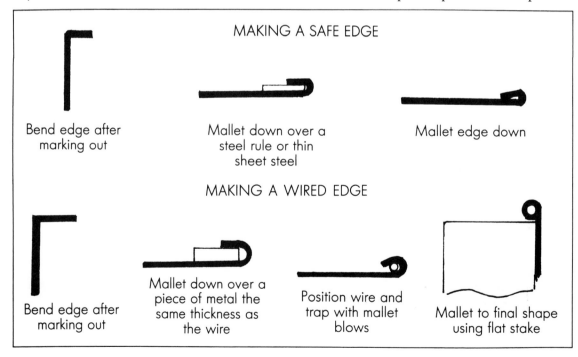

MAKING A SAFE EDGE

Bend edge after marking out

Mallet down over a steel rule or thin sheet steel

Mallet edge down

MAKING A WIRED EDGE

Bend edge after marking out

Mallet down over a piece of metal the same thickness as the wire

Position wire and trap with mallet blows

Mallet to final shape using flat stake

faces; they are available in different shapes and sizes and are used to support the metal on the opposite side to the hammer blows.

After the metal has been cut, the raw edge is often sharp and jagged. Leather gloves are invaluable when handling sheet metal and save many an annoying and painful cut or snag on the hands. It is not often that the edge of a piece of sheet is left raw on a finished piece of work. Usually it is treated in such a way as to increase the strength of the component or to provide a decorative finish. The simplest method of treating the edge of the metal is to produce a 'safe edge' by bending the edge of the metal back over itself and malleting it down flat.

Mark a line $\frac{1}{4}$ inch (6 mm) from the edge and first bend the metal at right-angles for the length of

Above far left *A bench guillotine.*

Above left *A 'Monodex' cutter.*

Below left *Fig. 42 Edge treatment of sheet metal.*

Below *A legshield from a 1926 500cc Matchless. Note the wired edge.*

Below right *Bending sheet metal using the bench edge, G-cramps and a bar. (See also photo overleaf.)*

the component. Then, working from one end, mallet down the edge. Do not bend the edge right over in one place before you move on but gradually bring the whole edge over, working from one end to the other. This will avoid producing a pucker in the sheet which is hard to remove.

A wired edge is produced by forming the edge of the panel over a length of wire; this not only provides a smooth edge but increases its strength substantially. A line is drawn $2\frac{1}{2}$ times the diameter of the wire in from the edge of the metal. This edge is then bent at right-angles, the wire is inserted and the metal formed round it. Figure 42 gives a step-by-step guide to forming both these edges.

Forming a right-angle bend can be achieved with a pair of folding bars or by clamping the work to the edge of the bench using a strip of wood or angle iron secured by G-clamps. As has already been mentioned, the metal must be malleted over gradually, working backwards and forwards from one end to the other. If the bend is in the middle of a piece of metal and there is sufficient to get hold of, force the metal down with one hand while using the mallet with the other. Obviously a folding machine would make light work of such a

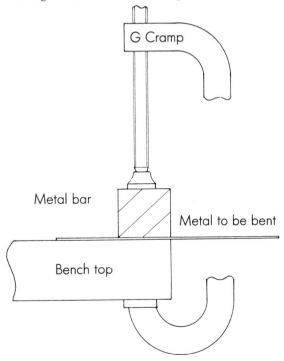

G Cramp

Metal bar

Metal to be bent

Bench top

**Above left** *Bending sheet metal using the bench edge, G-cramps and a bar. (See also diagram on previous page.)*

**Above** *Bending sheet metal using folding bars held in a vice.*

**Left** *A swaging machine.*

**Below left** *A close-up view of the rollers.*

**Below** *A piece of metal in the process of being swaged.*

job, and if you have access to one your work will be that much easier.

Where the edge has to be formed on a curve, it can be tackled in two ways. The first way is to cut the shape out of a piece of wood and clamp the metal to it; this will provide a positive guide. The second way is to use a narrow piece of wood or metal that has a slight curve at the end; this can be moved round the panel while the edge is gradually formed up.

Before we leave the treatment of panel edges, one other forming operation is used where two panels overlap, such as battery box lids or the engine covers on a scooter. To ensure that the two panels are flush with each other, the edge of one panel is swaged down so that the edge of the other panel sits on it. This operation is best done in a swaging machine which will give an accurate swage the length of the panel. A hand tool that does the same job is a pair of joddlers; these have to be moved along the panel edge forming the swage each time the handles are gripped together.

## Shaping sheet metal

When forming curves in a single plane, such as simple legshields, a set of bending rolls is the ideal method. However, a lot can be done using tube of the correct or smaller diameter — the metal can be formed by pressing the sheet over the tube and malleting where necessary. Obviously soft metal such as copper and aluminium can be formed more easily than steel. If you find this process does not work well, most sheet metal firms have bending rolls and if you take your sheet ready cut with the precise instructions as to the dimensions of the curve, it should be a relatively cheap operation. When making replacement panels it is always best to make a paper pattern of the part before you commit yourself to cutting the metal. Offer up the pattern, make sure it is a good fit and that there is an allowance for treating the edge of the metal.

In many instances where a sidecar body frame of wood or metal tube is to be covered, it is possible to clamp the metal sheet, after it has been cut out, directly to the body frame and dress the edges of the metal over the frame. This will work for curves in a single plane and also compound curves, providing the curve is a shallow one over a large area. For this operation you will need a number of G-clamps and pieces of wood packing to prevent the clamps marking the metal. The body panel should be clamped into position, making sure the correct overlap is present all round the frame and that the metal is held in contact with the edge of the frame where it is to be malleted over.

The metal is then malleted over using a rawhide or rubber mallet, remembering to work the metal over gradually along the frame. If you do not have enough G-clamps to hold the metal all along the edge, the part of the metal that has been dressed over can be fixed to the frame before moving the clamps along the frame. The method of fixing will depend on the material of the body frame. Panelling on wooden frames can be held in place with wood screws or pins. If the frame is of metal tube or angle, then 'pop' rivets, self-tapping screws or small nuts and bolts can be used. Avoid using, if possible, steel fixings in an aluminium body — this will prevent any problems in the future with electrolytic corrosion.

### Removing dents

When faced with the problem of removing a dent from part of your motor cycle, the first task is to remove the damaged item, whether it is a mudguard, engine cover or legshield. The one great

*Body panel malleted over the frame and pinned into place.*

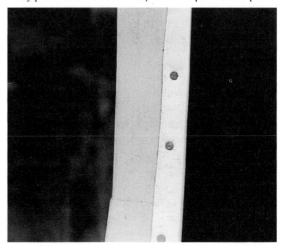

*A Triumph Twin with rear wheel enclosure prone to damage.*

*A 1964 Vespa. Those curved but vunerable engine covers are easily dented in a fall.*

advantage of this is that handling the part and supporting the damaged section while it is being worked on is so much easier.

The next thing you must do is to clean the part thoroughly; if it is a mudguard make sure that there is no grit or rust left behind. Using a hammer on dirty or rusty metal will produce more surface damage and, apart from this, it is much more pleasant to work if there is no rust, dirt or oily grease to handle.

Before starting to use a hammer, assess how the dent was formed. The direction of the dent, whether straight in or at an angle, will tell you where to start the reshaping process. Using a dolly or sand bag, which can be made from a thick plastic bag filled with dry sand and the neck tightly tied, start hammering on the highest part of the dent. Do not use brute force to return the panel to the right shape; the blows from the hammer should be controlled so as not to stretch the metal, which would cause more problems.

Do not expect to be able to return the part back

to a perfect shape with a hammer without a great deal of practise, because you will be disappointed. It is just as important to know when to stop, and finish the job with lead or body filler, as it is to know where to start.

Where the metal has been stretched, usually indicated by a deep dent or crease, do not attempt to hammer out all the damage. Shrinking metal that has been stretched is a very skilled operation and requires the use of heat properly applied. In situations such as this, knock out the dent as much as possible and then use filler. Over-hammering will stretch the metal even more and lead to an ugly bulge on the outside of the part.

Where headlights are concerned, many will have suffered dents and scrapes over the years and be in need of repair. Before attempting a repair the lamp must be removed from the machine and stripped down to the bare shell. If the dents are small it will probably be possible to remove them without annealing the metal. Where the lamp is chrome-plated the annealing process will discolour the chrome, making replating necessary. The dents are carefully knocked out from the inside, using a ball pein planishing hammer, with the lamp shell supported on a polished steel block, or a piece of smooth hard wood.

Where the lamps have painted shells or where they are going to be replated, it is best to anneal the metal first. Obviously painted shells must have all the paint stripped off before this process.

After the dents have been removed, the surface of the metal should be smoothed off with a Water-of-Ayr stone, a very fine abrasive stone sold in sticks and used by hand. Where the metal has been scored, or depressions are left where the metal has been stretched, these can be filled in one of two ways. A shell that is going to be painted can be filled with body filler or, for a better job, with body solder. Both these fillers can be rubbed down to give a perfect finish.

A shell that is going to be replated should have any scores or depressions filled with silver solder and then smoothed off. It is possible to plate over body solder but the heat and the pressure from the polishing mop when the chrome is buffed can cause body solder to move, spoiling the finish.

**Forming compound curves**

Should you want to produce a new lamp shell or some other component that has a compound curve in it using hand tools, you will need a sand bag, a bossing mallet or ball pein hammer, and a planishing hammer for finishing the surface. An alternative to a sand bag is a stout piece of wood with a hollow of the shape required carved into the top.

The first stage is to work out the size of the blank necessary to form the required shape. Figure 43 shows two methods of achieving this. Do not cut the metal too large as this will make the forming difficult, particularly at the edges, where the excess metal will tend to pucker into unwanted folds.

After the blank has been cut to size, file the edges to remove any burrs that may have formed during the cutting out. The next step is to anneal the metal as described in Chapter 3 so that it can be easily shaped. Before the metal can be beaten it must be cleaned of the oxides that have formed on its surface. Aluminium is the easiest to clean; it will

*Fig. 43 Estimating the size of a blank required for a curved shape.*

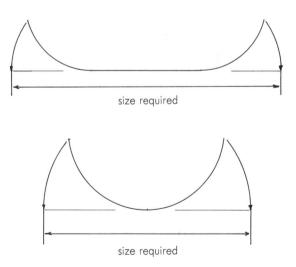

size required

size required

*The metal will stretch as it is shaped to make up the difference in size between the blank and the finished object. A full size or scale drawing will be needed to accurately find the correct measurements.*

only need the blackened soap washed off the surface of the metal.

If you are working in brass, copper or gilding metal, a pickle bath made up from a 10% solution of sulphuric acid should be used. Remember when making up dilute acid solutions to ADD THE ACID TO THE WATER and not the other way round, or there will be a violent reaction and the acid will be thrown out of the container. The solution is best kept in an earthenware or plastic container with a well-fitting lid. For the best results the metal should be dipped when it is warm, but not hot, or it may well make the acid spit and cause injury to you. Brass tongs are the best to use in acid baths as they do not discolour the acid in the same way as steel or copper ones.

Mild steel can also be pickled, but use a separate bath because the acid solution will become discoloured extremely quickly. The other way of cleaning steel is to use emery cloth to remove the oxides. It is important to remove as many of the oxides as possible, otherwise they may be hammered into the surface of the metal, which could affect the later finishing.

After the metal has been dried, a series of lines $\frac{1}{2}$ inch (13 mm) apart should be drawn round the blank, starting from the outside and working towards the middle. These lines are used as a guide for the mallet blows to aid even shaping of the blank.

The blank is held at an angle on the sand bag or block and the blows from the hammer or mallet made a short distance from the edge. The blank is rotated slowly so that the hammer blows are made in the same place on the bag or block. The second course of blows is made just inside the first and the process continues until the required shape is obtained. The work will have to be annealed and cleaned during the shaping as the metal becomes work hardened by the blows of the hammer. The number of times it needs to be annealed will depend on the metal being worked and the depth of the hollowing.

When the shaping operation is complete, the work should be planished to even up the shape and remove any irregularities. It will also harden the metal and produce a more rigid shape. The work

should first be annealed before planishing on a suitably shaped stake (a polished block of steel) with a planishing hammer. It is possible to use an ordinary hammer but the faces of both hammer and stake must be polished, with no flaws in the surface; any flaws will be transferred to the surface of the work, marking it badly.

If you do not have any shaped stakes, a curved piece of work can be planished from the inside on a flat block of polished steel, using the ball pein of a hammer. Planishing is started from the centre of the work with relatively light blows, working in concentric circles towards the outside. The hammer must hit the work where it is supported, otherwise the work will be distorted. As in the first process, the work should be rotated so that the hammer is brought down in the same position on the block each time. The facets formed by the hammer should overlap slightly to make sure that no part of the surface is missed.

When the planishing is finished you will be left with a surface that is evenly covered with facets left by the hammer. The next process depends on the final finish for the work. If it is going to be polished and then plated, all the marks on the surface will have to be removed.

Normally a Water-of-Ayr stone is used to grind away the facets and produce a perfectly smooth surface prior to polishing. Should the surface of the work be fairly rough, fine emery cloth can be used followed by wet-and-dry paper before the final finishing with Water-of-Ayr stone.

If the work is going to be painted, the process need not be so painstaking as the paint will need a slightly roughened surface to act as a key. Any slight irregularities in the surface can also be filled with body filler or leaded if the work is made from steel or copper alloy.

## Working with tube

When making any object out of tube the first decision that has to be made is the cross-sectional shape of the tube to be used. Square or rectangular section tube is far easier to prepare as the ends of the tube can be cut at the required angle and

**Right** *A heat-scorched wooden jig for bending square tube, together with a section of bent tube.*

**Below** *Fig. 44 Bending square tube by cutting.*

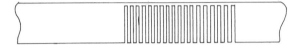

Tube cut through three sides before bending.

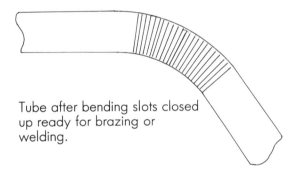

Tube after bending slots closed up ready for brazing or welding.

assembled ready for joining. On the other hand, round or oval tube will have to be shaped at the end to fit round the tube to which it is to be joined.

**Square tube** is more difficult to bend without distorting its shape unless you have access to the specialised equipment that can deal with cross-sections of this type. There are two ways that square tube can be bent. The first involves making up a curved jig to suit the bend you require. If the jig is made of wood it should be covered with sheet metal to protect it from the red hot tube as it is bent round the jig. This operation should be done in a number of stages, so that the tube can be kept in

shape with a hammer should it start to distort. This method is really only suitable for small sizes of tube; larger sections are difficult to handle.

The second method involves making a number of saw cuts through three sides of the tube where the bend is going to be. The number and spacing of the cuts depends on the radius and the length of the bend and is best found by experimenting first with a piece of scrap tube. After cutting, the tube is bent round and the closed saw cuts can be welded or brazed together (see Figure 44).

**Round tube** is easily bent using a tube bender that can be hired from most tool hire shops, but make sure that the formers and guides are correct for the tube you are using. Many firms still supply imperial size tube only, and if you order, for example, 25 mm diameter you will be supplied with 1 inch diameter. Though the difference in size is only about 0.035 inch, a 25 mm former will put an ugly neck in the tube which will spoil an otherwise good piece of work.

Small-diameter cold drawn seamless tubing can be bent without a tube bender if treated carefully. One way is to make a former around which to bend the tube. An alternative is to drill a hole through a piece of strong timber about 100 mm × 50 mm; the hole should be countersunk on both sides. The wood is then held firmly in a vice and the tube placed through the hole and bent over. Quite complex bends can be achieved using

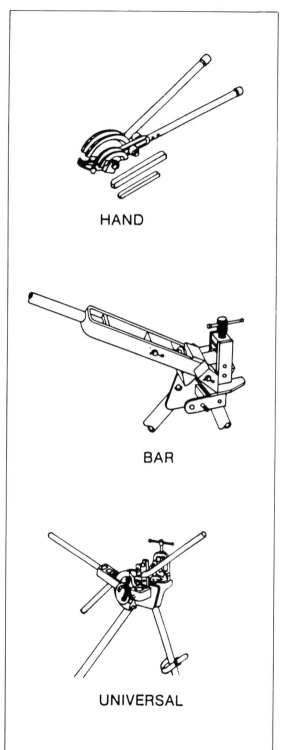

HAND

BAR

UNIVERSAL

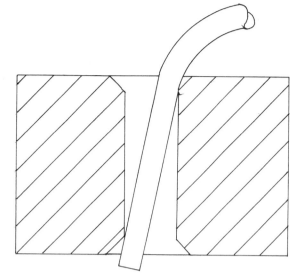

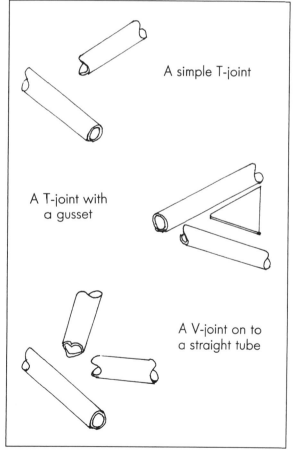

A simple T-joint

A T-joint with
a gusset

A V-joint on to
a straight tube

Far left *Tube, pipe and bar benders. (B.A.H.C.O. Record Tools.)*

Left *Fig. 45 Bending small diameter seamless tube in a wooden block.*

Below left *Fig. 46 Mitring round tube.*

Right *A strengthening gusset on the frame of a 250cc racing Cotton.*

Below right *Uses of tube – an O.E.C. tubular side car frame of 1952 . . .*

Below right *. . . and the famous Swallow Silk sidecar chassis of the early 1950s, a simple but effective design.*

this simple tool, but do not try using seamed tube as the wall of the tube will collapse very easily (see Figure 45).

The third method of bending tube involves filling the tube with sand, rammed hard, to prevent the walls collapsing. The sand must be thoroughly dried before filling the tube to prevent pockets of steam forming when the tube is heated and blowing out the sand and plug in spectacular fashion! One end of the tube is plugged using a tapered piece of wood; when the tube is filled the other end of it is also plugged. It can then be heated and, when red hot, bent to the required shape. The tube and sand take some time to heat thoroughly and care must be taken to ensure that the whole area of the bend is heated, otherwise a smooth bend will be very difficult to achieve.

A pattern should be made from either stiff wire or a wooden template so that progress can be checked. Make certain that you remember whether the template or jig is of the inside of the curve or outside, otherwise the component, while looking the part, will not fit anywhere.

Figure 46 shows some methods of mitring tubes together. It can be seen from this that round tube requires considerably more work than that of square or rectangular section. The strengthening gusset shown in the diagram can also be used on

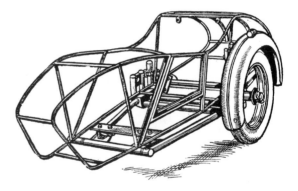

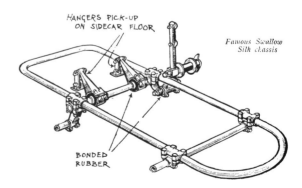

HANGERS PICK-UP
ON SIDECAR FLOOR

*Famous Swallow
Silk chassis*

BONDED
RUBBER

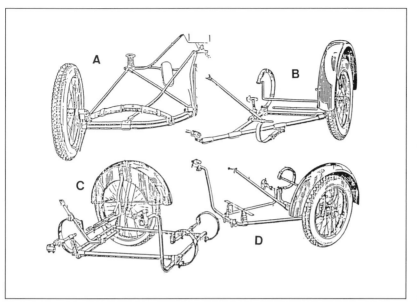

**Left** *Four vintage sidecar chassis frames: A, B.S.A.; B, Ariel; C, A.J.S.; D, Montgomery.*

**Below left** *Awaiting restoration – a Canterbury chassis?*

**Below** *A scooter carrier by Raydot from the early 1960s. Carriers of a similar design are well within the abilities of most amateurs.*

SCOOTER CARRIER

By RAYDYOT

the outside of a joint where tubes of the same dimension are used. For anyone who is at all doubtful of their ability to produce perfect welded joints every time, a simple gusset such as this is easy to weld onto a joint and increases its strength considerably.

Tubing that has been damaged and bent, be it part of the cycle frame or the sidecar chassis, cannot be straightened and should be removed and replaced. Resist the temptation to cut out just the damaged piece and weld a section in. Unless you are an expert welder with first-class equipment, the end result will not be strong enough.

# CHAPTER 11
# Casting and pattern-making

Although casting is usually thought of as a specialised skill beyond the range of the amateur restorer, the production of simple castings is not beyond the abilities of most reasonably competent people. The lack of facilities need not be a handicap; there are many foundries around the country who would possibly be willing to undertake a 'one-off' job at a reasonable price. If you have been able to join a night school class as mentioned in the Introduction, you may find all the facilities you need.

| APPROXIMATE SHRINKAGE OF SOME CASTING ALLOYS | Shrinkage (mm/m) |
| --- | --- |
| Cast Iron | 10 |
| Steel | 20 |
| Brass | 15 |
| Aluminium | 13 |
| Magnesium Base | 13 |

## Sand casting

### Making a pattern

The most expensive part of the operation is the making of the pattern to use in the production of the mould. If it is possible to make this yourself, casting costs will be greatly reduced. It is not possible to use the original part for a pattern because the copy will be smaller, as the molten metal shrinks as it cools. Also, many patterns have to be made in several pieces so that they will lift out without breaking the sand of the mould. The table given here shows the shrinkage rate of various metals, which in the case of steel is quite considerable.

Unless the casting is very simple and dimensional accuracy is not important, a pattern larger than the final object must be made, not only to allow for shrinkage but also to allow for machining where necessary. Pattern-makers allow for this shrinkage by using a contraction rule which is calibrated to produce the correct increase in the length of the pattern. The simplest patterns to make and cast are known as flat-backed patterns; these, as their name implies, have a flat back. This makes them easier to make and cast.

More complex shapes such as circular sections or those having holes through the casting require a split pattern. This may be in two pieces, or in the case of an intricate casting several pieces, which are slotted together to produce the final pattern.

Pattern-makers are amongst the most highly skilled people in the industry as they have to interpret a two-dimensional drawing into a three-dimensional object, making sure that the pattern will lift cleanly from the sand and that the mould is positioned in such a way that the mould cavity will fill correctly and produce a sound casting.

It will probably clarify the process more easily to describe what is involved in producing patterns and the completed moulding box for the two types of casting.

Patterns should be made from a good close-grained wood which can be sanded to a smooth finish. The wood must be painted or varnished, otherwise the damp moulding sand will raise the grain of the wood and it will not lift from the sand

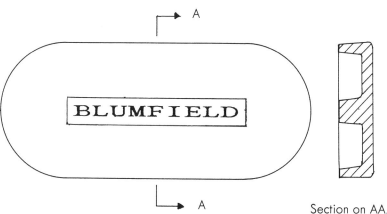

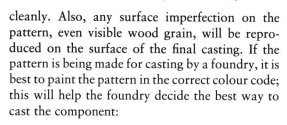

Section on AA.
Note the taper
on the edges.

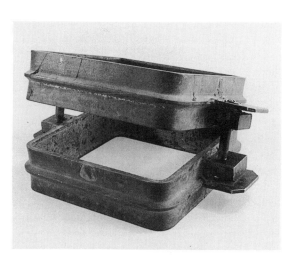

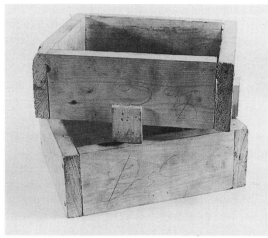

cleanly. Also, any surface imperfection on the pattern, even visible wood grain, will be reproduced on the surface of the final casting. If the pattern is being made for casting by a foundry, it is best to paint the pattern in the correct colour code; this will help the foundry decide the best way to cast the component:

Red — unmachined surfaces
Yellow — machined surfaces
Black — core prints

The pattern must be given a very slight taper of 3° to 5°, called the draw, to enable it to be lifted from the sand cleanly. If you have an original part to work from, study it carefully. It is often possible to see the moulding line where the pattern was split.

Simple patterns can be made from one piece of wood, whereas complex shapes are more easily made by building up the pattern from smaller pieces of wood fixed together. Any internal corners should be radiused using car body filler, or similar. This will produce a stronger casting and reduce the risk of sand breaking from the edge of the mould.

Figure 47 shows a sketch of the pattern needed to produce a timing gear cover for a 1913 Blumfield vee twin engine. Though the pattern is hollowed out it can be treated as a flat-backed pattern for casting. You will notice that both the inner and outer faces are tapered to ensure a clean lift from the moulding sand.

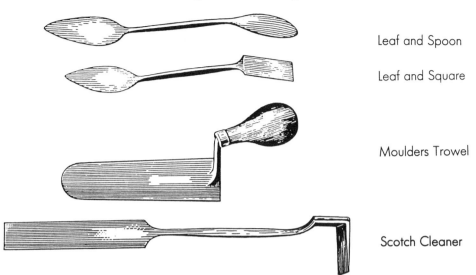

Leaf and Spoon

Leaf and Square

Moulders Trowel

Scotch Cleaner

## Moulding boxes

To produce a mould ready for pouring you will need moulding boxes or flasks, mansfield sand, parting powder, sprue pins and some simple moulding tools.

Moulding boxes, or flasks as they are called in the trade, are normally made from metal when used in industry, but quite adequate ones can be made simply from wood. The important point to remember is that they should be approximately 50 mm wider and longer than the pattern and 50 mm or more deeper than the pattern, otherwise the sand will not have enough strength to stay in the flask when the pattern is removed. The flasks are used in pairs; the top box is known as the cope, the bottom one the drag.

The mansfield sand used in the moulding is sand with a thin layer of clay around each grain. When this is moistened it has the ability to bind together firmly and hold its shape, even when molten metal comes into contact with it. The sand is prepared by first passing it through a sieve to remove and break up any lumps until it is smooth in texture. Water is then added a small amount at a time and mixed with the sand. In industry this is done by special mills, but an equally good result can be achieved by hand. The simplest test for the correct amount of moisture (about 5%) is made by squeezing a handful of sand. The sand should hold together but, when broken in two, the break should be clean not crumbly. Also your hand should not feel wet.

It is important that the moisture content is correct. If it is too dry, the mould will crumble as the pattern is removed or as the metal flows into it. If it is too wet, the molten metal will turn the excess water to steam which will either stay trapped inside the mould and produce a casting similar in appearance to a piece of Gruyère cheese or blow the molten metal back out of the mould with often dire consequences for the person pouring it! Obviously, therefore, proper safety clothing should be worn for this process.

Parting powder is used to prevent the moulding sand from sticking to the pattern, and the sand in the cope and the drag from sticking to each other. Dry sand can be used though it is not so effective. The sprue pins are tapered wooden pegs used to make the holes to allow the molten metal into the mould and the air out. These holes are usually referred to as the runner and the riser.

Moulding tools come in a bewildering array of shapes and sizes, some of which are shown in Figure 48. It is also possible to make usable tools from small spoons or cut pieces of metal.

## Producing a mould for a flat-backed casting

Using the timing case cover described earlier as an

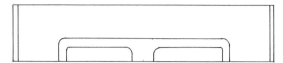

Drag inverted, patterns positioned, dusted with parting powder.

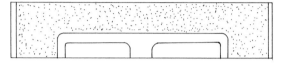

Box rammed with sand strickled flat.

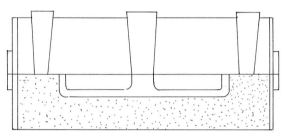

Drag turned over, cope placed on. Sprue pin to form runner inserted. Box dusted with parting powder.

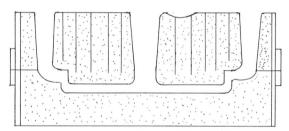

Box rammed with sand, strickled flat. Sprue pin removed, pouring basin cut. Mould vented. Patterns removed. Gates cut. Mould ready to pour.

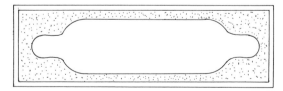

Plan view of the drag, showing gate and vent channels.

*Fig. 49 Making a mould with a flat-backed pattern.*

example, a mould can be prepared in the following manner.

The bottom flask or drag should be placed upside down on the moulding bench and the pattern placed centrally in it. A thin layer of parting sand should then be sprinkled over the pattern and the area of the bench visible inside the drag. Next a layer of moulding sand about 50 mm deep should be sieved into the drag; this should be pressed firmly down with the knuckles of one hand while holding the pattern in place with the other. The sand should then be rammed firmly with the pein or pointed end of the rammer, taking particular care at the edges of the drag.

Another layer of sand should then be sieved in and the process repeated except that the rammer can be used straightaway. Once the pattern is covered there is no need to sieve the sand into the drag, as the purpose of that was to ensure as smooth a finish as possible for the surface of the mould. It is important that too much sand is not put into the flask at any one time as there is the possibility that the bottom layers of sand will not be rammed firmly enough, causing the mould to be weak. Ramming too hard can also cause problems since the gases from the molten metal and the sand will not be able to escape by permeating out through the sand.

When the drag is over-full it should be rammed with the butt or flat end of the rammer to produce a smooth surface. The reason why the butt end of the rammer is not used until the final stages is that it produces a smooth surface which would prevent the next layer of sand sticking to it; the consequence of this is a pile of sand on the bench or more likely in your boots when the flask is picked up and turned over.

The surface of the sand should now be scraped flat with a piece of wood or metal that is long enough to span the flask in one go. Any concave depressions must be filled in and scraped flat otherwise they will cause problems later. The foundryman's term for this 'strickling'.

Next turn the drag over (if your technique is correct all the sand will stay in the box) and place the cope in position. The sprue pins should also now be put in position; it is important that they are placed near the thickest section of the pattern and preferably one on either side of it. They should also be larger in cross-section than the thickest part of the pattern so that their contents can remain molten to provide a reservoir of molten metal as the casting cools and shrinks. If the runner and riser cool before the casting, shrinkage cavities will occur, spoiling the casting.

Parting powder should now be sprinkled inside the cope to prevent the sand from the two flasks sticking together, and the cope should be filled and rammed in the same way as the drag. After strickling the top flat, the mould should be vented with a thin rod to help the gases escape. The rod should not be pushed through the sand to touch the pattern, otherwise the casting could come out looking like a porcupine; $\frac{1}{2}$ inch (12 mm) away is near enough. The easiest way to achieve this is to hold the rod between the finger and thumb the correct distance from its end and push it down until your hand meets the sand. Only a small number of holes is needed; about one every 2 sq inch (50 sq mm) is adequate.

The sprue pins should now be loosened and removed, and a pouring basin should be cut next to the top of the runner; this will prevent the molten metal from passing into the mould too quickly and perhaps causing damage to any frail parts. The top edges of the runner and riser can then be smoothed off.

The cope and the drag should now be parted and the bottom of the runner and riser rounded off. Next the channels from the mould cavity to the runner and the riser should be cut and smoothed off. The pattern can now be removed—a draw spike (or two long wood screws) can be screwed into the pattern and gently tapped to loosen the pattern in the sand, which can then be lifted carefully out. Any damage to the mould can be carefully repaired and all the sharp edges in the

**Above right** *The finished casting of the Blumfield timing case. The letters were formed by using pattern-maker's letters which can be fixed to the pattern.*

**Right** *This cast alloy footboard on a 1924 Beardmore Precision is a simple shape to reproduce.*

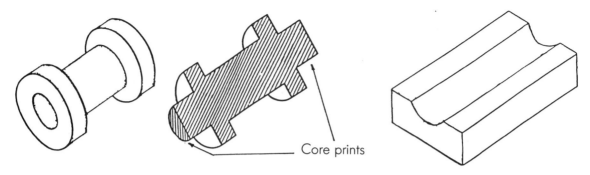

Fig. 50 *Tubular component with half a split pattern.*          Fig. 51 *Half a core box.*

path of the molten metal smoothed off. After gently blowing away any loose grains of sand, the two flasks should be placed together and the cope weighted to prevent it being lifted by the pressure of the molten metal. The mould is now ready for pouring.

### Moulds for tubular castings

Castings that have holes in them require a slightly different technique, in that a solid object the same shape as the holes must be placed into the mould for the molten metal to flow round. This shape, or core to give its correct name, is made from sand mixed with a binding agent which is then cured so that it is strong enough to withstand handling and the pressure from the molten metal when it is in the mould.

The making of the simple tubular shape shown in Figure 50 would be undertaken as follows. First a split pattern is made, the two halves located correctly by two small dowels. Note that the pattern has a circular extension at each end; these are called core prints and they produce the cavity in the mount in which the core will rest. Next a core box should be made (see Figure 51). Again dowels are used to locate the two halves of the core box so that an accurate core can be produced. If the hole through the casting is going to be machined, the core box and core prints should be slightly smaller to allow for the machining. The length of the core box should be slightly less than the pattern and core prints to give the necessary clearance when positioning the core into the mould cavity.

There are two methods of producing cores. The first uses linseed oil as a binder and sharp silica sand. These are mixed in the ratio of 40 parts of sand to 1 part of linseed oil by volume. When the mixture is thoroughly mixed it can be rammed into the core box after the cavity has been dusted with parting powder. Next a thin rod should be pushed through the centre of the core to provide a vent before the two halves of the core box are separated and the core gently removed. The core must be handled with great care as it is very fragile in its green state. It must now be baked at about 200°C until it has the appearance of milk chocolate; do not overheat it as this will destroy the bond and will weaken the core considerably. When the core has cured it can be placed into the mould cavity and the casting poured. Core-making using linseed oil is time consuming, and if domestic oven is used to cure the mixture it is likely, because of the smell, to be very unpopular with the rest of the family.

The second method, the cold process using carbon dioxide gas and sodium silicate as a binder, has two great advantages: the core can be cured in the core box and is therefore hard when handled, and it is very quick, taking only a few seconds to cure.

Carbon dioxide is readily available either in small cylinders or even the small bulbs used for fizzy drink makers. Sodium silicate is available from most chemists, usually under its more common name, Waterglass, used in days past to help preserve new-laid eggs, amongst other things. Silica sand is mixed with about 5% sodium silicate: for small-scale use a tablespoon provides a

*From right to left: the core box, core, split pattern and finished casting for a Singer rear light made by the author.*

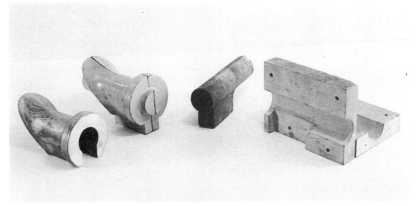

*Assorted casting patterns made by the author.*

**Below** *Fig. 52 Fitting for applying CO₂ to the core sand.*

satisfactory measure, 20 spoonfuls of sand to 1 spoonful of sodium silicate. The mixing should be thorough so that each grain of sand is coated with the sodium silicate. Rubber gloves should be worn as the skin can react to the chemical, and the gloves also enable you to rub the mixture through the fingers to ensure a good mix.

The core box should be dusted with parting powder and the sand carfully rammed into it, making sure that there are no parts of the box left soft. Vent holes should be made right through the core to enable the gas to penetrate the sand. The carbon dioxide is then passed through the sand at a low pressure for a few seconds — the larger the core, the more gas will be needed. The box should be gassed from both ends if possible. This will turn the sodium silicate into silica gel, bonding the grains of sand together. Figures 52 and 53 show two simple fittings that can be used to transfer the gas to the core box.

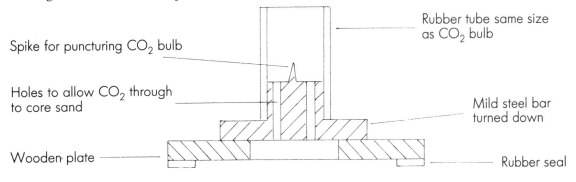

Spike for puncturing CO₂ bulb

Holes to allow CO₂ through to core sand

Wooden plate

Rubber tube same size as CO₂ bulb

Mild steel bar turned down

Rubber seal

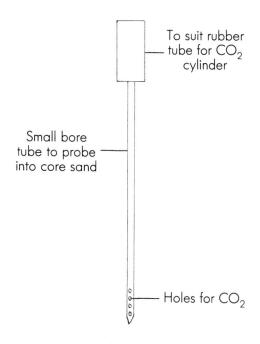

To suit rubber
tube for $CO_2$
cylinder

Small bore
tube to probe
into core sand

Holes for $CO_2$

*Fig. 53 Lance fitting for gassing deep cores.*

# Rubber mould casting with low melting point alloys

While sand casting is ideal for a vast range of work, it is not suitable for castings that require thin sections or fine detail such as mascots, badges and name scripts. Normally items such as these would either be made by the lost wax process or by using pressure die casting with metal moulds. Both these methods are perhaps beyond the scope of the amateur restorer, though a brief description of the lost wax process will be included later. Metal moulds are very expensive to produce and the expense would be difficult to justify for a one-off job.

There is, however, one method of casting that can be accomplished successfully in the kitchen if necessary, and that is with low melting point alloys using silicone rubber for the mould. These alloys have melting points that range from 185°C to 245°C and are capable of being melted in a ladle over a gas stove.

There are two different methods of casting with L.M.P. alloys, either using a small centrifugal casting machine or by hand. Naturally the machine will produce castings that have very thin sections requiring pressure to fill them correctly, and it will also produce several different castings at the same time if necessary. The one drawback is that the best machine costs several hundred pounds. However, it is possible to obtain equally good results by hand casting, providing care is taken in the type of work undertaken and in the production of the moulds.

## Producing the rubber mould

The material used for mould-making is called room temperature vulcanising (R.T.V.) silicone rubber and the two most suitable for hand casting are known as RTV11 and RTV31. Mixed with a catalyst they will produce a cure within 1 to 24 hours, though they should not be used for casting before 72 hours have elapsed to allow the rubber to achieve its full working properties.

The pattern for the casting can be made from almost anything as no heat is involved in the mould-making operation. If you are using an original badge, etc., it must be cleaned up and all the imperfections removed. Any pitting or corrosion must be filled with a suitable material such as car body filler and smoothed down to a perfect finish. The level of finish required can be judged by the fact that the rubber will reproduce even a smudgy finger mark. As with sand casting, time spent getting one pattern right is more effective than time spent having to correct every casting produced.

If the pattern has a flat back such as a badge or name script, a simple mould box ½ inch (13 mm) bigger all round than the pattern can be produced out of wood, cardboard, metal or even Lego bricks pressed firmly together.

The box should be sealed to a smooth base with double-sided sticky tape. If the pattern is a badge or something similar, with legs or lugs on the back for fixing purposes, wood is the best material for the base board, as holes can be drilled in it to locate the legs, allowing the pattern to fit flush with the board. Location key formers are also needed; these provide depressions in the face of the mould, and any domed or conical object can be used if it is large enough to form a suitable depression. A release agent should be brushed onto the inside of the box and on the pattern to ensure ease of removal. If plasticine is used anywhere it must be varnished first and then treated with the release agent, otherwise the rubber will stick to it very easily.

The silicone rubber should be mixed with the correct amount of catalyst, then, when it is ready, it should be poured slowly into a corner of the box and allowed to flow round the pattern and then over it. Allow the rubber to settle for a few minutes and then continue pouring rubber over it until there is at least $\frac{1}{2}$ inch (13 mm) of rubber covering the highest part of the pattern. Leave the rubber to cure, making sure the box is standing level.

When the rubber has cured, lift the mould and the mould box off the base board and invert both onto the board. If the pattern stays on the base board it should be replaced in the mould. A second mould box of the required depth should then be fixed with double-sided tape. The inside of this

box and the surface of the first half of the mould should be given a coating of release agent before the box is filled with catalysed rubber. The rubber will flow into the depression made by the location formers on the first half of the mould. These will ensure that the two halves of the mould will locate together perfectly each time it is assembled.

When the rubber has cured completely, the two halves of the mould can be removed from the mould boxes and the necessary gates and risers cut into the mould with a sprue cutter. For hand-poured castings, the ingate where the molten metal is poured in must not be too small — a reasonable head of metal is required to provide enough pressure to force it into the mould.

When the object to be cast is a more complicated shape, such as a mascot, two different methods of mould-making can be used. In the first method, the pattern is half embedded in modelling wax or plasticine. This should be done carefully so that the surface of the wax follows the centre line of the pattern. Location key formers are placed on the surface of the wax and the procedure is then the same as for the simple mould.

*Fig. 54 The two different methods of producing a mould using RTV rubber. (Alec Tiranti Ltd.)*

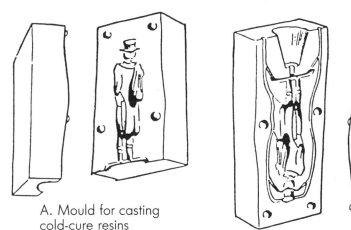

A. Mould for casting cold-cure resins

B. Mould set up for casting hot low-melt metals

The long funnel on top of B allows a good head of pressure to force the metal into the mould; the air goes up the risers and helps the metal to flow freely.

All the sprues and air vents are cut with the sprue cutter after the mould has cured. Do not make them too big to start with; they can always be enlarged later.

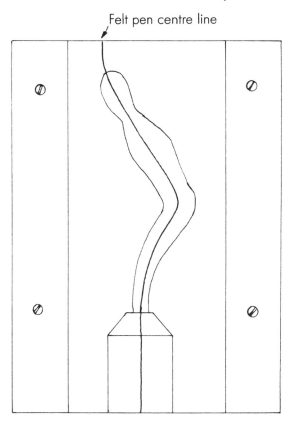

Felt pen centre line

Fig. 55 *A mould box with a perspex front.*

When the rubber has cured, the mould box should be inverted, the modelling wax or plasticine removed and the pattern cleaned up. After the release agent has been applied to the pattern mould and mould box, the second half of the mould can be poured. After the recommended cure time the mould box can be removed, the two halves of the mould parted and the pattern removed. Where required, sprue and vent holes can be cut.

The second method involves making a box with a clear perspex front tapered to the top on all sides. The box should be at least $\frac{1}{2}$ inch (13 mm) taller than the pattern plus an allowance for the ingate. The pattern should be stood inside the box and the parting line of the pattern drawn on the outside of the perspex front with a felt pen. This line should then be redrawn on the inside of the perspex where it will mark the rubber of the mould. After the box

has been reassembled and secured to the base board, the catalysed rubber can be poured slowly and carefully into the corner of the box until it is full. Slow pouring will ensure that no air is trapped in the mould. When the rubber has completely cured, the perspex front of the box can be removed and the mould taken out. A sharp scalpel or craft knife should then be used to cut down the parting line to the pattern. The mould can then be opened and the pattern removed. Before casting, the mould should be replaced in its box to hold the two halves of the mould together accurately (see Figure 55).

### Casting LMP alloys in a rubber mould

The two halves of the mould should be dusted with talc, french chalk or graphite, brushing the powder into all the sections of the mould. The use of graphite helps reduce the risk of porosity in the finished casting. Bang the two halves of the mould together to get rid of any excess powder, then assemble the mould and securely clamp it together ready for casting. The mould should be stood on a metal tray when pouring to contain any spillage that may occur.

Heat sufficient metal in a flat-bottomed ladle on a stove or other suitable heat source. Do not overheat the metal; a good test for temperature is to use a spent matchstick or cocktail stick, which when dipped into the metal should smoke slightly. When the metal is ready it should be poured in one go without a break. Do not flood the metal into the mould as this could cause air to become trapped; a steady pour will give good results.

When the mould is full, it should be carefully tapped to shake down the metal; more should be added if required. If you are undertaking a run of castings using the same mould, allow sufficient time for the casting to cool completely before removing it from the mould. Do not attempt to water-cool the mould; it can be extremely dangerous, and may cause an explosion. Allow the mould time to cool down by itself every few casts, otherwise it may overheat and become damaged.

### Types of low melting point alloys

There are several different low melting point

alloys available, each suitable for different applications. As a general rule, high tin content alloys have better flow and definition, but are more expensive. Generally it will be found that the more delicate castings will require the higher range of temperatures, while bulky castings require lower temperatures; experiment to find the most suitable. The following grades of low melting point alloys are available.

**Lead-free pewter metal alloy** Made to BS 5140(SpecA), pewter is a very high grade alloy, lead-free and tin-rich, suitable for highly detailed castings where good flow properties are required. Castings are reasonably malleable. Pewter is a metal in its own right and, because of the high finish it takes, it does not need plating or painting. Melting point: 245°C. Suggested operating temperature: 280°C–295°C (can go up to 310°C).

**KA low melt metal alloy** A tin-rich alloy, ideal for thin sections and fine delicate castings where good flow properties and detail are required (e.g. filigree). Widely used in the jewellery trade. Castings have a good shiny surface and are malleable. Very prone to porosity if overheated. Particularly suitable for hand gravity casting. Melting point: 185°C. Suggested operating temperature: 240°C–280°C.

**No. 1 Low melt metal alloy** A good all-purpose lead-rich alloy. Suitable for casting larger bulk where detail is more important than flow properties. Useful, like KA, for jewellery manufacturing. Castings are malleable. Melting point: 228°C. Suggested operating temperature: 280°C–300°C.

**No. 2 Low melt metal alloy** A general lead-rich alloy, pouring at higher temperatures than no 1. Suitable for figures, jewellery components and model-making, giving good reproduction of detail and very malleable castings. Melting point: 243°C. Suggested operating temperature: 290°C–310°C.

**No. 3 Low melt metal alloy** An alloy developed especially for flat surfaces, where porosity is giving problems. Good flow properties give a very good reproduction of detail and good surface finish on flat areas. Ideal for making model kits of trams, locos, cars and other vehicles, etc. Low malleability. Melting point: 225°C. Suggested operating temperature: 275°C–295°C.

## Lost wax casting

Although the silicone rubber mould will produce high-quality castings of intricate shapes in low melting point alloy, it is unable to cope with metals having a melting point much above 300°. If castings are required in zinc alloy, aluminium or brass, some other method of producing a mould is needed.

Lost wax casting utilises a pattern made from wax which is placed in an open-ended box, then investment material made from a refactory plaster is poured over the wax pattern. When the plaster has set, the wax pattern is melted out of the plaster, leaving a cavity into which the molten metal is poured.

The wax pattern can be carved from a block of modelling wax, or, if you want to copy an original casting, a silicone rubber mould will have to be produced as already described. The wax should be melted and poured into the mould and left to cool before removal from the mould.

Runners and risers made from wax should be attached to the pattern; this can be done with a small piece of hot metal. The patterns should then be stuck on a metal plate by melting some of the wax; this prevents the pattern moving when the investment material is poured over. A suitable size of metal tube is then placed over the pattern and sealed to the base plate with wax. Next the refactory plaster should be carefully mixed and poured slowly into the tube; do not pour it directly over the pattern as this could damage it. The outside of the tube should be tapped as the plaster is poured to help any trapped air to escape. In industry the mould is placed on a vibratory table while pouring.

Allow the mould to dry for about 4 hours, then remove the base plate and place the mould in an oven set at 100°C–150°C. This melts out the wax, leaving a mould cavity in the investment material.

When the wax has been removed, the mould should be pre-heated before receiving the molten metal. The object of the heating is to remove the last traces of the wax and to ensure that all the remaining moisture is driven out of the investment plaster. A temperature between 200°C and 220°C is needed; higher than this will cause shrinkage or distortion of the mould, whilst a lower temperature will not remove all the moisture, making the pouring of the molten metal very dangerous.

Once the casting has cooled, the investment plaster can be broken away to remove the finished casting.

Small flat-backed castings can also be produced in a two-piece plaster mould by using a wooden pattern, well painted to prevent the moisture from the plaster affecting it, or with an original of the part you wish to reproduce if shrinkage does not matter. A wooden frame should be made, large enough to take the pattern and the runner and riser plus about 1 inch (25 mm) all round. This should be placed on a sheet of glass or metal, after the inside has been greased to act as a release agent. The frame should be sealed to the glass with double-sided tape or plasticine. The pattern should be smeared with thin lubricating oil and placed in the frame; it can be held in place by a nail through a piece of wood which is itself nailed to the top side of the frame.

Mix the plaster carefully according to the instructions and pour it into the box, which should be gently tapped to help any bubbles of air rise to the surface. When the plaster has set it can be carefully pressed out of the frame. Using a penny, cut out four locating dowels by screwing the coin into the plaster. Smear the surface of the plaster with grease and lightly coat the pattern with thin oil.

The wooden frame must also be coated with grease on the inside and then pressed down over

*A Vauxhall Griffon cast by the author using the lost wax process.*

the top of the first plaster cast. The bottom edge should be sealed with plasticine and the second mix of plaster poured into the frame. When this has set, the wooden frame can be removed and the two halves of the plaster mould separated. The runner and riser can be cut into the plaster and the pattern removed. The plaster should then be heated as already described in the lost wax process before clamping the two halves together and pouring in the molten metal.

# CHAPTER 12

# The lathe and lathework

## Buying a lathe

The lathe is a very versatile and useful tool to have in one's workshop, and the amount of time and money that can be saved by being able to repair or make your own spare parts is considerable.

However, not everyone is able to go out and buy a brand new lathe, complete with all the necessary accessories. The vast majority will have to rely on the second-hand market, or use the machines at local night school classes. Buying a second-hand lathe is very much like buying a second-hand bike. There are certain questions and tests you must apply before you make your decisions.

The first concern is the size of lathe that is best suited to both your needs and to the space available to house it. Lathes are sized according to their capacity for machining metal; a 6 inch (150 mm) lathe is capable of turning a piece of metal 12 inches (300 mm) in diameter. In America, and increasingly in Europe, machines are being designated by the largest diameter they can swing,

which avoids confusion. The largest diameter capable of being turned can be increased if the lathe has a 'gap bed'. This is where a short portion of the bed near the headstock can be unbolted and removed, allowing a relatively short, larger-diameter item to be machined, a very useful addition if flywheels or brake drums need attention.

The physical size of the machine must also be taken into consideration. A $4\frac{1}{2}$ inch Boxford lathe is approximately 3 ft 6 inches long and 1 ft 8 inches wide and weighs about 3 cwt. In contrast to this, a $7\frac{1}{2}$ inch Colchester lathe is 7ft 6 inches long and weighs over a ton.

The next question concerns the electric motor — is it to be single or three-phase? Household electricity supply is single phase and considerable expense is required to run a three-phase cable out to the workshop. It would also be expensive to swap the three-phase motor for a new single-phase one, particularly as the output of the motor must be quite high.

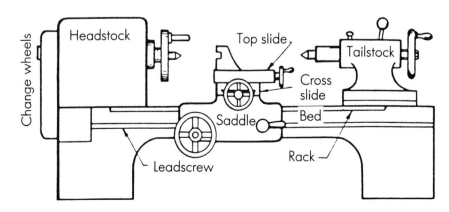

*The centre lathe.*

The physical condition of the lathe should be checked. The bearings in the headstock should have no play in them; check these by attempting to shake the chuck. Some machines use taper roller bearings and these may be adjustable to take up any wear. The saddle, cross slide and top slide must also be checked for play. Try lifting the saddle and pushing and pulling the top and cross slides in their direction of travel — there should be little or no free play. If there is, and there is no method of adjustment, the replacement parts could be costly or, if the machine is old, impossible, without having new parts made. The bedways and other castings should be checked for any damage that could affect the accuracy of the machine.

The accessories that come with the machine should also be checked. The minimum you will require is a three-jaw and four-jaw chuck, a tailstock drill chuck and a tailstock centre. Face plates, etc., are useful but generally are not used as much as a chuck. If either of the chucks is missing, it is as well to remember that a good quality 4 inch (100 mm) diameter three-jaw chuck can cost over £100.

It is important that you see the lathe working so that you can check the accuracy of the machine. A piece of round bar should be held in the chuck and machined along its length. The lathe tool should be moved by operating the carriage rather than the top slide. After the bar has been turned down, its diameter should be checked with a micrometer at both ends of the machined portion. The readings

**Top left** *A lathe bed with the 'gap' piece in place.*

**Centre left** *The same lathe with the 'gap' removed. Note the increased space to swing larger pieces of work.*

**Bottom left** *An Emco Unimat modelmaker's lathe. While these are excellent machines they cannot be expected to produce the same work as a larger lathe. (Elliott Machines Ltd.)*

**Above right** *A $7\frac{1}{2}$ in Colchester lathe.*

**Right** *A $4\frac{1}{2}$ in Boxford lathe. Note its size in comparison to the Colchester behind it.*

should be the same; if they are not then the lathe is producing a taper, so do not buy it unless it is the type of lathe where the headstock is a separate casting to the bed. If it is, then it may be possible to realign the headstock to produce an accurate machine.

Do not worry too much if the piece of test bar you have turned down is not concentric to the original size. After some use a three-jaw chuck is not expected to hold work perfectly true, and an allowance has to be made for this when machining. Obviously if the difference is great, new chuck jaws or a new chuck may be needed. It should be

remembered that any accurate work is usually set up in a four-jaw chuck where the independent adjustment of each jaw can ensure that the work is set up accurately before machining begins.

Try taking a fairly heavy cut on the test bar; this will give you some indication of the state of the motor. There should not be an appreciable change in speed and the lathe should not go slower and slower. If there is a drop in speed and the lathe is belt driven, check that the belt tension is correct and that the belts are in good condition before blaming the motor.

Finally, do not be in a rush to buy the first lathe

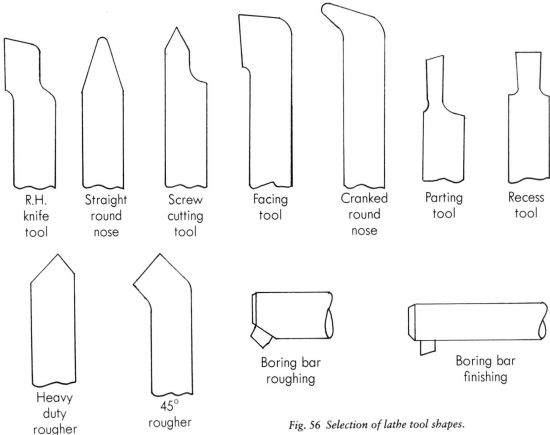

R.H. knife tool

Straight round nose

Screw cutting tool

Facing tool

Cranked round nose

Parting tool

Recess tool

Heavy duty rougher

45° rougher

Boring bar roughing

Boring bar finishing

*Fig. 56 Selection of lathe tool shapes.*

that comes along. With the rapid change in manufacturing industry over the last few years, there are plenty of good second-hand lathes available.

## Lathe tools

The correct type of lathe tool must be used if the lathe is to machine efficiently and accurately. The cutting edge must be correctly ground and set at the correct height.

Lathe tools can be made from either high-carbon steel (H.C.S.), high-speed steel (H.S.S.) or tungsten carbide, the last of which is usually used as a cutting tip brazed onto a steel bar or as an insert that is held in a special holder.

High-carbon steel lathe tools are cheaper than the others, but they are only suitable for softer materials; tackle anything harder than mild steel and the edge will dull very quickly.

High-speed steel tools will cut more effectively than H.C.S. at higher speeds and greater depth of cut, but on hard materials such as alloy steels they need to be sharpened frequently.

Tungsten-carbide-tipped tools will cut all materials more efficiently than H.S.S. and will last longer between sharpening. These tools need a special green grit grinding wheel for sharpening because the ordinary type of wheel will not do the job satisfactorily.

The angles ground on a lathe tool to produce the cutting edge will differ, depending on the hardness of the material being cut, the amount of material to be removed and the quality of the finish required. The harder and tougher the material, the greater the tool angle must be to support the cutting edge of the tool. A large tool angle gives maximum strength to the cutting edge and helps to dissipate the heat produced by the cutting action. It also requires greater power to force the tool through the work. A smaller tool angle gives a better finish to the work with less tearing, but does weaken the cutting edge.

The top or front rake is the angle formed between a horizontal line and the top face of the tool. Tools used for turning some brasses and cast iron need little or no top rake, while those used for aluminium need a large top rake for efficient cutting.

The side rake is the angle ground on the top face of the tool away from the cutting edge. The size of the angle depends on the material being cut; in general, hard metals require a small angle while soft materials have a larger angle. The side rake

will also determine the direction that the swarf will follow off the cutting edge. Because of this, some tools such as parting off tools have no side rake.

The front clearance angle is ground on to prevent the front of the tool rubbing on the work. As with other angles, it is kept to a minimum with hard materials to give extra support to the cutting edge.

The side clearance angle also depends on the material and the rate of feed used. A coarse feed needs more clearance than a fine one.

Figure 56 shows a selection of lathe tool shapes and their applications, and Figure 57 gives a chart showing cutting speeds and tool angles for various materials.

| MATERIAL | CUTTING SPEED | | TOOL ANGLES IN DEGREES | | | |
|---|---|---|---|---|---|---|
| | METRES PER MINUTE | FEET PER MINUTE | FRONT CLEARANCE | SIDE CLEARANCE | BACK OR TOP RAKE | SIDE RAKE |
| ALUMINIUM – SOFT ALLOY | 120–240 | 400–800 | 9 | 9 | 30 | 15 |
| ALUMINIUM – HARD ALLOY | 90–180 | 300–600 | 9 | 9 | 30 | 15 |
| BRASS | 90–180 | 300–600 | 7 | 6 | 0 | 5 |
| BRONZE – FREE CUTTING | 90–180 | 300–600 | 5 | 5 | 0 | 2 |
| BRONZE – TOUGH | 30– 60 | 100–200 | 10 | 12 | 8 | 10 |
| CAST IRON | 20– 30 | 60–100 | 5 | 4 | 10 | 9 |
| COPPER | 20– 45 | 60–150 | 5 | 5 | 20 | 25 |
| DIE-CASTINGS (ZINC) | 60– 90 | 200–300 | 8 | 8 | 8 | 10 |
| MAGNESIUM ALLOY | 180–300 | 600–1,000 | 10 | 10 | 8 | 6 |
| PLASTICS – CAST RESIN | 60–180 | 200–600 | 10 | 12 | 30 | 25 |
| PLASTICS – LAMINATED | 60–180 | 200–600 | 7 | 7 | 25 | 25 |
| STEEL – MILD | 30– 60 | 100–200 | 8 | 6 | 20 | 15 |
| STEEL – HIGH CARBON | 10– 25 | 35–80 | 6 | 5 | 10 | 5 |
| STEEL – STAINLESS | 20– 45 | 60–150 | 8 | 6 | 8 | 5 |
| WOOD | 150–300 | 500–1,000 | 15 | 15 | 25 | 25 |

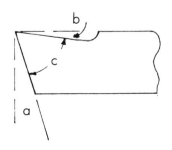

a Front Clearance
b Back Rake
c Tool Angle
d Side Clearance
e Side Rake

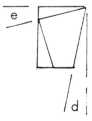

*Fig. 57 Tool angles and cutting speeds.*

**Left** *Facing off.*

**Below left** *Taper turning.*

Having selected the correct tool for the work in hand, it must be set up in the tool post correctly. If the tool is set too high, the front clearance angle will be reduced, perhaps to a point where the tool is rubbing rather than cutting. Setting the tool too low will reduce the top rake angle and will also leave a small portion unmachined in the centre of the work.

# Types of turning

### Facing off
This is the term given to machining the face of the work parallel to the chuck. All work should be faced off before it is drilled or centre drilled or any other machining is undertaken.

### Parallel or plain turning
This is the term used to describe turning at right-angles to the chuck, i.e. parallel to the lathe bed. On a short piece of work the job may be supported by the chuck alone. For longer work the end of the metal is often supported by a centre held in the tailstock of the lathe.

Work can also be held between two centres, one end in the headstock and the other in the tailstock. The work is driven by a dog which is clamped around the metal and a catch or driving plate screwed onto the headstock spindle.

### Taper turning
There are three methods of producing a taper. For short tapers the compound slide should be loosened, set at the correct angle and then re-tightened. The taper can then be cut using the compound slide feedscrew by hand.

Long tapers can be cut by one of two methods. The first involves setting over the tailstock so that it is out of line with the centre line of the lathe. The amount of set-over has to be carefully calculated. One method of calculating it is to take the total length of the work piece and divide it by the length of the taper required, then multiply the answer by one half of the difference in diameters between the start and finish of the taper. This form of cutting tapers can only be used if the work is set up between centres.

The second method uses a taper turning attachment which bolts onto the rear of the lathe saddle and is also clamped to the lathe bed at its other end. The cross slide can then be disengaged from the saddle and clamped to the taper attachment. If the taper attachment is then adjusted to the correct angle, and the saddle moved along the bed, the cross slide will slowly move across the bed of the lathe as it travels along it. The method of attachment and adjustment varies between different makes of lathe, but the basic format remains the same. One of the big advantages of the attachment is that it enables internal tapers to be bored.

## Screwcutting

One of the great advantages of owning or having the use of a lathe is the ability to cut screwthreads of any size or pitch very accurately.

If the lathe has a gearbox, it is only a matter of selecting the appropriate gears to achieve the correct relationship between the speed of the lathe chuck and the lathe leadscrew. If there is no gearbox, the change gear wheels mounted on the back of the headstock will have to be changed to suit the type of screwthread you wish to cut. The correct wheels to use are usually marked on a plate fixed to the headstock. Where there is no indication, you will have to work out the relationship yourself. For this you will need to measure the gears are necessary to cut the correct thread; e.g., if the leadscrew is 8 T.P.I. and you wish to cut a 24 T.P.I. thread, the gearing must be set up so that the chuck revolves three times quicker than the leadscrew.

The thread is produced with a single point lathe tool that has been ground to suit the profile of the thread to be cut. A threading gauge should be used to check the profile of the lathe tool. This gauge has vee slots cut into it, corresponding with the angle of different types of thread, and should be used to set the threading tool square before machining is started.

Once the tool is set up correctly the point can be brought in until it just touches the work. The

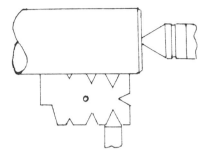

External tool bit set square
using threading gauge

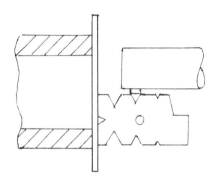

Internal tool bit set square
using threading gauge

*Fig. 58 Threading gauge.*

micrometer collar on the cross slide hand wheel should now be set to zero so that the depth of cut can be measured accurately.

Before the thread is machined it is usual to cut a groove where the thread is going to end. This is to give a small run out area at the end of the thread where the leadscrew of the lathe can be disengaged and the screwing tool wound out away from the work.

The lathe should be set on the slowest speed and a very light cut taken to check that the thread is correct. If it is, the rest of the thread should be cut until it is the correct depth.

The leadscrew must be engaged at the correct place each time and this can be achieved by using the thread dial indicator. The handbook for your lathe will tell you which lines on the indicator to use for different threads. If you have no handbook,

**Left** *A thread dial indicator.*

**Below left** *A hand thread chaser for internal threads.*

**Right** *A knurling tool, showing the two sets of wheels. One gives a straight knurl, the other a diamond knurl.*

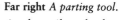

**Far right** *A parting tool.*

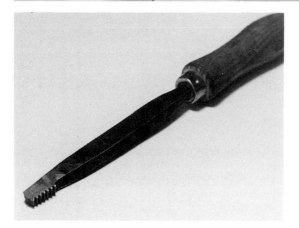

it will be a question of testing on a piece of metal and making a note of the results, or using the same line each time you make a cut.

Once the thread has been cut to the correct depth (see Chapter 7), a thread chaser should be used to round off the crest and root of the thread to produce the correct thread form. The easiest to use is a hand chaser; held in contact with the thread as it revolves, it will remove a very small amount of metal. It is essential to check the thread after each pass of the chaser as it is easy to remove too much metal and produce an undersized thread.

## Drilling and boring

The most common method of drilling in the lathe is for the work to be held in the chuck and the drill to be held stationary in the tailstock chuck. The second method involves mounting the work on the carriage of the lathe and holding the drill in the chuck or the tapered headstock sleeve. This second method is rarely used because in many cases it is easier to use a drilling machine rather than take the time required to mount the work piece accurately in line with the centre line of the lathe.

Before drilling a hole in the end of a round bar, the metal must be faced off. When the work is ready a combination drill should be put in the tailstock chuck and the workpiece drilled with this first. This will locate the twist drill accurately in the centre of the metal and enable it to start cutting correctly; it will not be able to start cutting accurately on its own, and the point will wander and most likely start to drill off-centre. Drill sizes beyond the capacity of the tailstock chuck, usually $\frac{1}{2}$ inch (13 mm), can be held in the morse taper of the tailstock spindle.

A boring tool can be held in the tool post for boring large-diameter or non-standard-sized holes. Before boring a hole in a solid piece of metal, the work will have to be centred, drilled and then drilled to a large enough size to allow the boring tool to enter the work. It is usually quicker to drill the hole as large as possible, leaving only a small amount of metal to be removed by the boring tool.

When a deep through hole has to bored that is beyond the capabilities of a normal boring tool, it is possible to set up a special boring bar held on

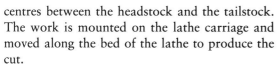

centres between the headstock and the tailstock. The work is mounted on the lathe carriage and moved along the bed of the lathe to produce the cut.

## Knurling

Knurling is a method of raising a surface to provide a grip for holding or turning. Two types of knurling are available — diamond knurling or straight knurling — and they are produced by a knurling tool that has one or two wheels with straight or angled teeth cut into them.

The knurling tool should be mounted in the toolpost with the centre line of the wheels in line with the centre of the work. The lathe should then be set on a low speed and, when it has been started, the knurling wheels will be forced into the work and then moved along, preferably using the automatic feed for uniformity of speed. Plenty of lubricating oil should be used during knurling to help produce good definition. More than one pass may be needed to give a knurl of satisfactory depth.

## Parting off

Parting off is the name given to the process of cutting off a piece of work while it is being held in the lathe. A special narrow lathe tool is required, usually consisting of a blade of H.S.S. clamped into a holder.

The parting tool must be set up correctly; if it is below centre, the workpiece will try to climb over the tool, usually snapping the end of it off.

The lathe should be adjusted to a low speed and the parting tool fed straight in. Coolant should be used on all metals except cast iron, and great care taken not to force the tool into the work.

Should your lathe have play in the cross-slide, it may not be possible to part off work without difficulty. In this case it is much better to saw through the metal and face off the cut surface.

## Mandrel work

When machining the outside of a hollow piece of work, it is often necessary to mount the work on a mandrel. Standard lathe mandrels, hardened and tempered, can be bought in various sizes. The mandrel should be ground to a taper of 1 in 2000 (·0005 inch per inch). The surface of the mandrel should be lubricated and driven into the workpiece and the work set up between centres.

Manufactured mandrels are expensive to buy and it is possible to make a satisfactory mandrel for one-off jobs. A stub mandrel can be made from mild steel, by turning down a larger diameter bar to the size required.

One method of clamping the workpiece to the mandrel is by turning down the end of the mandrel, threading it, and using a nut and washer to clamp the work against the shoulder of the man-

*A stub mandrel.*

drel. The second method involves drilling a hole into the end of the mandrel and threading it with a taper tap only. The end of the mandrel should then be cut down its centre line to beyond the depth of the hole. When a bolt is screwed into the hole it will expand the mandrel, gripping the inside of the work.

It should be understood that only a brief outline of the lathe's uses can be given in this book. Anyone wishing to know more about lathe work will find there are several specialist books dealing with subject including PSL's recently published *Making The Most of Your Lathe*, by Harold and Audrey Mason.

# CHAPTER 13

# Cleaning and protecting metal

Whenever restoration work has to be undertaken there will be the need to clean the various parts before any necessary repair work is started. Having completed the repairs there is then the need to finish the parts in an appropriate way to protect them while in use.

## Cleaning

There are a number of methods of cleaning metal ranging from the simple brush and paraffin bath, for removing loose grease and dirt, to specialised systems for the removal of rust and baked-on carbon. High-pressure water washers, which can remove oil, grease and road dirt quickly and easily, can be hired to clean the outside of the engine and cycle parts before dismantling begins.

Where corrosion, paint or similar hard substances have to be removed from metal, abrasive cleaning equipment must be used. This equipment falls into two catagories: dry blast or wet blast. Dry blast equipment uses air under pressure to shoot an abrasive at the component being cleaned, while wet blast equipment uses air and water under pressure to shoot the abrasive. The abrasives used can be silicon carbide, aluminium oxide, emery, shot, glass beads or any other abrasive material, depending on the material being cleaned and the substance being removed.

There are two main differences between the systems. Wet blasting surrounds the abrasive with a layer of water; this reduces the cutting action, producing a smoother finish but also increasing the time taken to clean the component and adding to the cost. Dry blasting is quicker but much more aggressive, which can cause problems with thin or rust-weakened components. Dry blasting with coarse grit, for example, can cut through thin aluminium or rust-weakened steel, so care must be taken to choose the right system.

Blasting with the water/grit system is ideal for aluminium castings. Apart from the advantage over the dry system of removing less stock from the casting, any grit from the cleaning process is washed away by a clean water/air spray at the end of the process, leaving a bright lustre on the surface.

Apart from cleaning anything from a large frame to a spark plug, components can be strengthened by wet or dry blasting with lead shot or glass beads. These processes are known as shot peening, or vapour bead blasting when using a wet blast system. The process compacts and smooths the surface of the metal, removing scratches and other imperfections that could be the cause of stress failures.

Whatever cleaning process you decide to use, make sure it is suitable for the article involved. Remember that if it is steel that has been cleaned, paint it as soon as possible, because rust will start to form extremely quickly on the surface. If there are no local firms able to offer any of these services it is possible to undertake a number of processes in the ordinary home workshop.

Steel that has carbon or grease baked on to it can be treated with a caustic soda solution. Follow the instructions carefully; the solution will burn unprotected skin, so rubber gloves and tongs to lower the parts to be cleaned into the solution and prevent splashes. DO NOT CLEAN ALUMIN-

**Left** *A Blumfield engine before wet blasting.*

**Above** *The Blumfield engine after blasting and painting the barrels. The process is inexpensive considering the time that is saved.*

IUM in this way, as the caustic will react violently with the aluminium and eat into the surface of the metal.

Aluminium can be cleaned by boiling it in a strong solution of household detergent and allowing it to simmer for an hour or so. Scrub the parts under cold water with a stiff brush and the results can be quite impressive.

Wire brushes fitted into a hand or electric drill will remove baked-on carbon and oil. I would not recommend their use on the outside of an aluminium casting, though, because it is too easy to leave ugly scratch marks which will take a great deal of time and effort to remove.

## Polishing

The practice by manufacturers of polishing engine components has increased over the years as the technology for producing high-quality die-castings has improved. Few manufacturers pre-war were willing to accept the increased cost that time-consuming polishing entailed. Specially prepared show machines were a different matter, but in the main castings were left as they came out of the mould. For this reason I feel it is inappropriate for

engines to be polished beyond their original state, but that is a matter of opinion. However, aluminium does tarnish quickly and, if left for a considerable time, loses any polish it may have had. Whatever metal you are going to polish, be it aluminium, copper, brass, steel, etc., the basic process is the same.

The first thing to do is to clean the metal thoroughly so that you can clearly see the state of the surface. Next any scratches or scores in the surface must be removed using a fine file followed by progressively finer grades of emery cloth. The finest emery should be used with a small amount of oil for the best finish; this will make the subsequent polishing process much easier and cheaper. Awkward corners can be tackled with scrapers, rifler files or emery cloth wrapped around a suitable piece of wood. This dirty, time-consuming process will probably take hours, but the result, a smooth dull surface, will be worth it.

The next stage is to polish the surface to a shine. A proprietary cleaner such as Solvol Autosol can be used to buff up the surface by hand, and though this will take a long time and much effort to produce the required shine, it can be done. A much quicker method is to use a rotating mop attached to an electric polishing machine. A simple machine can easily be made using the electric motor from a washing machine or similar appliance. The motor must be rigidly fixed to a suitable base, which in turn must be fixed firmly to the bench.

Polishing mops come in a range of sizes and types. They are made from circles of cloth stitched to two large leather washers at the centre. The coarseness of the cloth corresponds to different usages — coarse for the initial rough work, fine for the final polish. Coarse mops often have the cloth stitched together away from the centre to make the mop more rigid.

The mop is screwed onto a tapered screw thread on the spindle of the polishing machine. Tapered fittings can also be bought to bolt onto the plain shaft of an electric motor. These fittings, called 'false noses', have either a left-hand or right-hand thread; make sure you buy the correct one.

The polishing compound is supplied in bars and there are different types depending on the type of metal or plastic being polished:

Crocus — general-purpose
Tripoli — finishing non-ferrous metal
Rouge — silver and brass
Greenglo — stainless steel
NCP — plastics

Before using the polishing machine make sure that the mop is firmly in place. The tapered thread on the spindle nose should tighten the mop as the work is held against it.

*Using the polishing machine:*

Once the motor is switched on the polishing compound should be held against the mop. Do not overload the mop otherwise the polishing action will be impaired. Hold the work against the bottom half of the front of the mop (see Figure 59), but do not press too hard or it will slow down the motor and the polishing process. Take care not to round off edges or any lettering, etc. Hollow objects such as headlamp shells or rims should always be polished as shown in Figure 61, otherwise there is the danger that the mop will catch the edge and pull the work from your hands, or at least damage the edge.

The work will get very hot as it is being polished, hot enough to burn your fingers, particularly with a good conductor of heat like copper. DO NOT hold the work with a piece of cloth — this could very easily be caught up by the mop and drag your hands into the wheel, causing a serious injury. Either wear a pair of soft leather industrial gloves, available from most engineers' supply shops, or leave the work to cool at regular intervals. Goggles or safety spectacles should also be worn to prevent pieces of polish or fluff from the mop getting into your eyes.

Thin flat pieces of work should be supported on a suitable piece of wood, held in place by tacks or drawing pins (see Figure 62). The work can be turned to ensure the whole surface is polished.

When the work has been polished, clean it with a proprietary polish such as Brasso or Auto Solvol. This will remove the last traces of polishing compound.

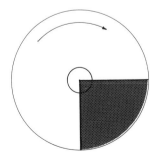

*Fig. 59 Safe working area.*

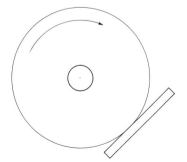

*Fig. 60 External polishing.*

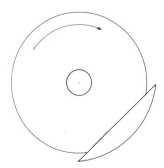

*Fig. 61 Internal polishing.*

POLISH IN THIS DIRECTION

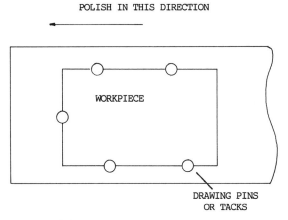

*Fig. 62 Polishing thin sheet using a wooden base board.*

## Protection

Polished metal can be lacquered to protect the surface from tarnishing. There are several brands on the market — before buying one, ensure that it is suitable for the metal *and* the working environment. Some turn brown when they get hot, making them unsuitable for engine components.

There are also other ways of portecting metal from the effects of the atmosphere and of providing a decorative finish. The main examples are described here.

### Electroplating

Electroplating is used to provide a bright decorative finish that will resist tarnishing, or to build up worn components by providing a hard, wear-resistant surface.

Chromium plating is the most widely used form of electroplating for motor cycles, though more manufacturers are using stainless steel in its place. On older bikes, such as those built up to the late 1920s, only nickel was applied as a final finish. Hidden parts of the bike which need protection against corrosion can be zinc or cadmium plated. Of these zinc is the cheaper and its ability to protect steel is the equal of, if not superior to, cadmium.

Other plated finishes that can be used are copper, brass, silver, or even gold, if your taste is that extravagant. Whatever finish you require, the component must first be prepared. Do not expect

to be welcomed with open arms by the plater if you thrust a dirty piece of metal into his hands and ask him to plate it. The component should be clean, and in a rust- and grease-free condition. If the object is made of several parts, it should be dismantled as far as possible. If you are in any doubt, ask the plater for advice.

One of the most difficult metals to replate is die-cast zinc, used for many items such as indicator flasher stalks or rear light holders, etc. The problem arises from the swelling and cracking of the casting as described in Chapter 2. If the corrosion is too bad, do not bother wasting time on it; try to find another in better condition.

While it is possible to electroplate most metals, including aluminium and some plastics, not all plating shops have the equipment to undertake this work. Should you find a good plating firm, treat them well, as by all accounts they seem to be few and far between.

It is not possible to undertake most types of plating in the home workshop because of the dangerous chemicals involved, cyanide being one of them. However, it is possible to nickel plate at

*Nickel plating kits for use in the home workshop.* (Dynic Sales.)

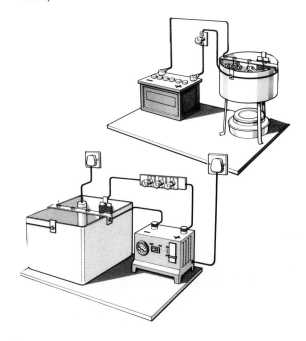

home using a DIY kit such as those supplied by Dynic Sales. Apart from an enamel or plastic container to hold the chemicals, a battery or battery charger to supply the electricity and possibly a fish tank heater to keep the solution warm, everything else comes with the kit. Full instructions are provided and, speaking from experience, if these are followed carefully excellent results are obtained.

## Anodising

Aluminium components can be protected from corrosion by anodising. This produces an oxide of aluminium on the surface of the metal which prevents further corrosion. The anodic layer can be self-coloured or dyed to a number of colours.

Many plating firms will undertake anodising, but one word of warning: make sure that the alloy is of anodising quality, otherwise the component could be ruined. The plater should be able to tell you, but if in doubt do not try it.

## Stove enamel

This is an extremely tough finish that is suitable for wheels, frames and engine parts as it is proof against hot oil. The components are cleaned, painted with enamel and then baked, or stoved, in an oven. Components that have been pitted by rust will need to be filled before the enamel is applied; special heat-resisting filler will be necessary and this will increase the price of the job. Because of the heat involved, any soft soldered items cannot be stoved — these will have to be finished by hand. Most shot blasting firms offer stove enamelling as part of their service.

## Vitreous enamel

Not often seen on motor cycles, this heat-resisting finish can be used on cast iron manifolds, etc. Though the finish is quite tough, it is possible to chip it, particularly on exposed edges.

## Plastic coating

Any metal can be coated with plastic using the hot dip method. The metal is cleaned and heated to a temperature of 190°C–230°C, depending on the type of plastic being used. The metal is then dipped into a tank of plastic powder that is being fluidised by having air blown through it. The plastic powder sticks to the hot metal and melts to a uniform thickness. Once again, the heat involved makes it unsuitable for soft soldered items.

## Powder coating

This is a hard coating of either polyester or epoxy resins. As with stove enamelling and plastic coating, heat is used, again making it unsuitable for soft soldered items. The single coating will allow any flaws to show through, but unlike stove enamelling there are no suitable fillers available.

## Metal spraying

While metal spraying is often used to build up worn components, it can be used as a decorative or protective finish. Most metals can be sprayed on to another metal base; the finish is matt and will require careful polishing.

## Painting

One of the most obvious ways of protecting metal is by painting it. The painting of motor cycles or any other vehicle is a very large subject and it is not possible in a book of this nature to go into it in any great detail. I can only recommend that anyone who requires 'chapter and verse' on the subject should read one of the many books on the market that deal solely with this aspect of restoration.

Before starting the preparation work on a motor cycle, it is necessary to decide whether you are going to brush paint or spray the finish onto the bike. Do not be put off brush painting by the horrific vehicles you may have seen that look like they have been painted by the roadside with a scrubbing brush. They probably have. With a decent brush and the correct method of use, a very good result can be obtained.

The main problem to overcome when using synthetic enamel, irrespective of whether it is applied by spray gun or brush, is the longer drying time before it becomes dust proof; it will take approximately $1\frac{1}{2}$ to 2 hours compared to the very short time for sprayed cellulose.

If you intend using a spray gun, it is possible to hire one from most hire shops to avoid the expense of buying one outright. Where only part of the machine is being repainted, the decision is made

*HobbyAir 70 spray outfit.* (S.I.P. Products.)

for you. You must match the existing finish.

When you are undertaking the total repaint of your machine, it is best to buy the materials you require from a paint specialist. All paint manufacturers supply technical information sheets with their products and these will enable you to ensure that you buy the right primers, undercoats, etc. The information will also include thinning ratios and drying times—everything, in fact, that you need to know to produce a good result.

Problems can arise when only part of the machine needs repainting. All paints fade due to the effects of sunlight and pollutants in the atmosphere, so buying the original colour, either in bulk or in aerosol tins from accessory shops, will not match the faded paint on your machine. This will be more noticeable on machines that have side panels such as the Ariel Arrow and similar models. The best way round the problem is to go to an accident repair shop and ask them to match the colour of the undamaged panels. Specialist sprayers such as these have paint matching cards that have a range of shades from the original paint. The cards can be placed on the panel and the nearest match selected, while on the back of the card will be the ingredients for making up that particular shade of paint.

Whatever method of painting you use, the preparation of the machine is the same. If you are stripping the entire assembly down to bare metal be prepared for a lot of mess. Choose the paint stripper carefully, particularly if fibreglass is involved; some strippers will attack the gel coat. Do give the stripper time to work and wear

protective gloves and clothing.

When all the paint has been removed the parts must be cleaned thoroughly to remove any traces of paint stripper. This is particularly important if there are any areas where stripper could be trapped. If it is not removed it will cause continual trouble with the repainting.

Once the stripper has been removed, inspect all the parts carefully and be prepared to find all manner of things that have been covered over by layers of paint. Do not skimp on the repair work; make sure the parts are as sound as you can make them before you think of applying any paint. Remember that paint will not hide defects, only make them more visible, so ensure that all panels, mudguards, etc., are as smooth as possible, using body filler or body solder to fill any small blemishes. Now you can start applying the paint, following the maker's instructions carefully.

Make sure that the garage, shed, back bedroom or whatever you are going to use has enough space to walk round the parts being painted. Ensure also that there is plenty of ventilation; some modern paints give off toxic fumes and those that do not are unpleasant in a confined space. Remember not to smoke—ash does not improve the finish and most paints are highly inflammable.

If you have nowhere inside to paint, it is advisable to get the work done professionally; painting in the open air will not give good results. You will at least have the satisfaction of knowing that your own preparation work has been done properly and that you have saved a considerable amount of money as a result.

# CHAPTER 14

# Glues

Although I have mentioned glues in several places in this book, a separate section dealing with all the different types would, I feel, be advantageous. The following list, though not exhaustive, gives suitable adhesives for most jobs. When faced with an unusual combination of materials, it may be necessary to experiment with various glues. Perhaps the quickest and surest way is to get in touch with one of the major glue manufacturers, most of whom have an information service to answer such queries.

| | |
|---|---|
| Metal to metal | –epoxy resin |
| Metal to others | –epoxy resin or contact adhesive |
| Wood to wood | –a wide range of wood glues suitable for all purposes |
| Wood to others | –epoxy resin or contact adhesive |
| Leather to leather | –epoxy resin, contact adhesive or P.V.A. |
| Leather to others | –contact adhesives or epoxy resin |
| Textiles to textiles | –natural latex (e.g. Copydex) |
| Textiles to others | –natural latex, P.V.A. or contact adhesive |
| Acrylic to acrylic | –'Tensol' cements |
| Acrylic to others | –acrylic is not usually glued to others. Use screws, etc., or experiment with various types of 'Bostik' |
| Rubber to rubber | –rubber solution, natural latex or contact adhesive |
| Rubber to others | –natural latex or contact adhesive |

| | |
|---|---|
| Glass to glass | - epoxy resin |
| China to China | –epoxy resin |
| Glass or china to others | –contact adhesive or epoxy resin. Glass should not be glued to wood — if the wood warps or shrinks, the glass may crack. |
| P.V.C. to P.V.C. | –P.V.C. cement |
| P.V.C. to others | –P.V.C. cement or contact adhesive |
| Polystyrene to Polystyrene | –polystyrene cement |
| Polystyrene to other | –contact adhesive |

Surfaces that are to be joined must be clean, dry and grease free. Old paint, varnish, glue, etc., must be removed to enable the glue to form a good bond with the material. Plastics should be washed in warm water with a small amount of detergent added to it, then rinsed in clean warm water and left to dry. Smooth surfaces must be roughened slightly to improve the glue bond; this does not apply when joining plastic to plastic because the cements work by dissolving the surface layer.

Always put the work together 'dry' to ensure that the various parts fit together closely before gluing. Use cramps, weights, etc., to hold the parts together until the glue sets; joints that move during the drying process will fail easily. Follow the manufacturer's instructions closely, particularly in respect of mixing and working time available before the glue starts to cure. The setting time is also important. Some glues may appear or feel hard but do not reach their full strength for some

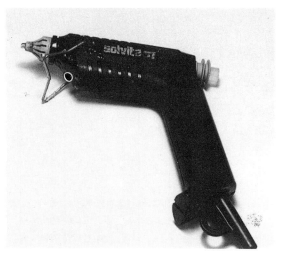

*A hot glue gun, a useful piece of equipment for quick gluing jobs.*

time; to put stress on the joint before a full cure is achieved may well weaken the bond and cause premature failure.

Excess glue should be wiped from the joint before it sets. Most wood glues can be removed with a damp cloth; some other glues have solvents which can be used sparingly to remove the excess. Glues that contain a high proportion of solvent, e.g. contact adhesives and plastic cements, should not be used in a confined space or near a naked flame; the solvents are not only very detrimental to your health but are also highly inflammable.

Recently hot glue guns have become available on the market. These comprise a heating element within a gun-shaped holder, hence the name. Sticks of hot-melt glue are placed in the gun and when melted can be forced from the nozzle of the gun onto the surfaces to be joined. Various types of glue stick are available for different materials and more are being introduced. While these glue guns are excellent for quick small jobs, it is inadvisable to try them on long runs as the glue starts to set before the parts can be assembled.

## Glues for wood

When considering glues for wood in a sidecar

bodyframe, it is essential that only glue that is waterproof be used where there is any possibility of the timber becoming wet or damp.

**Polyvinyl acetate glue (P.V.A.)** is a white liquid usually sold in plastic containers (e.g. Resin W). It is probably one of the most widely used wood glues and is also suitable for some other materials. It has an unlimited shelf life and is reasonably quick setting; approximately 2 hours will give a strong joint. Though the glue is water resistant, it is not waterproof and for this reason I would not recommend its use anywhere on a sidecar where it may come in contact with water.

**Synthetic resin glues** are made from plastic resins and come in two main types. The one-shot type (e.g. 'Cascamite') is in powder form and has to be mixed with water to activate the resin and hardener. The two-shot type (e.g. 'Aerolite 306') consists of a liquid hardener and a resin powder. The resin is mixed with water and spread on one half of the joint and the liquid hardener spread on the other half before the joint is cramped together.

These glues produce a waterproof joint that is stronger than the wood itself and are ideally suited for sidecar work. The one disadvantage they have is that they stain some woods, but this will be of little importance if the wood is not seen in use.

**Resorcinol and phenol glues** are considered the strongest glues for wood and are used especially for laminating work and highly stressed joints. They are completely waterproof but are very expensive and leave dark brown glue lines on the work.

**Impact or contact adhesives** (e.g. 'Bostik', 'Evo-stik', 'Thixafix') are made from synthetic rubbers and solvents, and are best used for gluing dissimilar materials together such as leathercloth to wood. They are ideal for large areas or awkwardly shaped items which are difficult to clamp. The main disadvantage with these adhesives is their relatively low strength, making them unsuitable for joints under stress. They also have a short shelf-life after they have been opened.

# Glues for plastics

Most thermoplastics can be joined by a suitable cement that contains a powerful solvent for the material being joined. There are, however, several thermoplastics that cannot be joined in this way because suitable solvents are not available. Polypropylene, polythene and P.T.F.E. are examples of these.

Though other adhesives are capable of joining plastics to each other and other materials, the joints are usually not as strong as those produced by plastic cements.

**Acrylic** (e.g. 'Perspex', 'Oroglass') can be joined to itself using cement. Some of the most widely used are the 'Tensol' range from I.C.I. 'Tensol No. 12' is a ready-mixed cement which is suitable for most purposes but it does not produce a clear joint. 'Tensol No. 10' is a two-part cement which gives a clear and waterproof joint that is suitable for outdoor use.

**Rigid polystyrene** can be joined with polystyrene cement, readily available in small tubes from any shop that sells polystyrene model kits. It is quick drying and gives a clear joint. Excess glue can be removed with acetone (available in many a home under the guise of nail polish remover). Do not attempt to join expanded polystyrene with this cement as it will dissolve before your eyes as the solvent gets to work.

**Polyvinyl chloride (P.V.C.)** can be joined using 'Tensol 53' cement or a number of other proprietary P.V.C. adhesives. Some of these, such as 'Gloy' P.V.C. repair and 'Vinyl weld' will stick P.V.C. to other materials. Acetone can be used to clean off excess glue.

# Adhesives for metal

For many people the thought of sticking metal to metal has had no place in a properly ordered workshop, but in recent years great strides have been made in adhesive technology. Not many people realise that wing sections of aircraft and rotor blades of helicopters are literally stuck together with adhesive. There are now several adhesives that are very useful to engineers and in many instances, like those already mentioned, they can out-perform more traditional ways of joining metals.

**Epoxy resins** are possibly the best known of the adhesives suitable for joining metals, the most common type being the two-part epoxy which consists of a resin and a hardener; a good example of this is 'Araldite'. These adhesives should be carefully mixed, applied direct to the work surface and allowed to cure. In single-part epoxies, these two components are already mixed and simply require heating to cure. In many applications the new single-part epoxies such as 'Permabond ESP' offer a real challenge to brazing and soldering. They are easier to use, free from lead and flux, and eliminate the need for refinishing.

**Anaerobic adhesives** are often known as sealants or 'locking compounds'. Acrylic based, they normally set in the presence of metal and the absence of air (to be exact atmospheric oxygen). They are used to lock, seal and retain all manner of turned, threaded and fitted parts, and often to seal flanges.

The 'Permabond A' range of adhesives only require the joint to be clean and dry and are applied straight from the container to the workpiece. 'Permabond A136' can be used instead of a thin gasket, saving the time and difficulty of making gaskets.

# Cyanoacrylate adhesives

Cyanoacrylate adhesives are very versatile. With one drop it is possible to bond a wide variety of materials together — plastics, rubber, metals and ceramics. They are solvent free and cure as a result of contact with very small quantities of moisture found on all surfaces exposed to the atmosphere.

As single-part adhesives, cyanoacrylates do not require mixing. They can be applied straight from the bottle or tube to the workpiece and they cure rapidly. One drop will cover up to 1 square inch with a 0·001 inch glueline thickness. The surfaces to be bonded must be free from grease or oil; use alkaline solvents such as acetone or methyl ethyl ketone or, if there is persistant surface contamination, remove it with emery cloth or other abrasive. Apply the adhesive sparingly to one surface (usually one drop is enough) and bring the components together quickly and correctly aligned until curing is achieved, normally in a few seconds. Any surplus adhesive can be removed by the use of acetone or methyl ethyl ketone, observing the usual precautions with these solvents.

Where difficult surfaces are to be bonded, such as acidic, porous or unreactive ones, a surface activator can be used to extend the capabilities of cyanoacrylates. It is usually only necessary to treat one surface, applying adhesive to the other.

Cyanoacrylate adhesive bonds skin and eyelids in seconds, so wear polythene gloves. If contact with the skin does occur, warm soapy water will gradually remove the adhesive. In case of contact with eyes, bathe with copious amounts of water and seek medical advice at once. Keep cyanoacrylate and any other similar adhesives out of the reach of children.

*Fig. 63  Joint design.* (Permabond Ltd.)

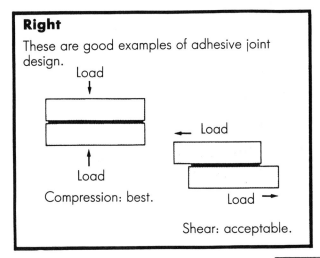

> **Right**
>
> These are good examples of adhesive joint design.
>
> Load
>
> Load
>
> Compression: best.
>
> ← Load
>
> Load →
>
> Shear: acceptable.

## Design to use the benefits of adhesives

There are many ways to reduce or avoid destructive cleavage forces. The 'wrong' examples can be avoided in any of the ways shown, with dramatic improvements in performance.

It is important to remember that adhesives are a separate technology. Joints that are perfectly suited to welding may be unsuitable for adhesives, and vice versa. Here is a brief guide to better joint design.

Is the joint heavily or lightly loaded?

Conventional adhesives may be used wherever loads are light, and components are not expected to suffer heavy impacts. Where there is a risk of impact and/or heavy loading, you should use an appropriate toughened variant.

Wherever possible, adhesives should be loaded in compression and shear, so as to minimise or avoid peel or cleavage forces.

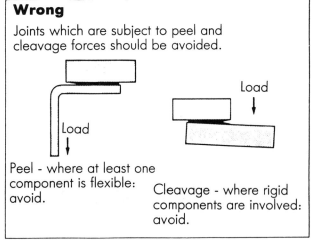

> **Wrong**
>
> Joints which are subject to peel and cleavage forces should be avoided.
>
> Load
>
> Load
>
> Peel - where at least one component is flexible: avoid.
>
> Cleavage - where rigid components are involved: avoid.

## Good practice

1. Do use an adequate overlap, as this gives a stronger joint.

2. Do choose a rigid adherend where loads are carried. Joints formed from thick, rigid sections perform better than thinner ones, as they lower peak stress to the joint.

3. Do avoid butt joints

4. Do talk to the manufacturer. The old maxim 'the thinner the glue line, the better the joint' is not always true. Your supplier will be able to advise you on the optimum amount to use.

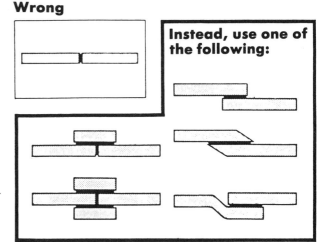

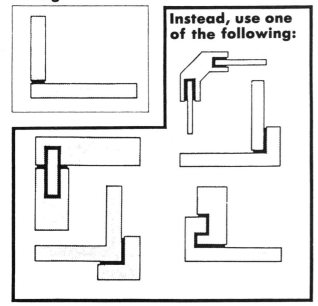

## Toughened adhesives

The latest types of adhesives are known as toughened adhesives, and they combine the best features tures of anaerobics, cyanoacrylates and epoxies with exceptional toughness. They will withstand shock, peel and impact forces that destroy other adhesives. The toughness is obtained by the incorporation of a low modulus rubber phase which prevents cracks from spreading by absorbing their energy before they effectively start. Toughened adhesives can be used to join the majority of materials, such as metals, plastics, wood, glass and ceramics to themselves and each other. They can be obtained in various grades of single-part epoxies and acrylics.

As with any other method of joining materials, the strength of the joint is dependent on good joint design. Figure 63 points the way.

# CHAPTER 15

# Sidecar matters

Having dealt with the metalwork involved in sidecar chassis in Chapter 10, it is now necessary to look in detail at the actual bodyframe of the sidecar.

The vast majority of sidecars have a frame made from wood and require for repair or manufacture a different set of skills and tools compared to the rest of the restoration process.

## Woodworking tools

There is no need to buy a complete set of woodworking tools, but a few basic ones are needed. If you are contemplating undertaking any wood-

work, I would suggest the following as a basic set:

14-inch jack plane
Panel or cross cut saw
Tenon saw
Marking gauge
Marking knife
$\frac{1}{2}$ inch (13 mm) and 1 inch (25 mm) bevelled edge chisels
Try square
4-inch (100 mm) and 6-inch (150 mm) G cramps

I have included illustrations of a number of other tools that could be useful for frame building and other woodworking jobs.

*A small band saw for sawing straight or curves.*

**Above** *A selection of marking out tools. From left to right: square, sliding bevel, marking knife and bevel or mitre square.*

**Above right** *G-cramps.*

**Right** *Spokeshaves – useful for shaping curves both internal and external.*

A power saw is an obvious tool to have if you have a considerable amount of wood to cut. Power saws fall into two groups: circular saws (which can be hand held, table mounted or in the form of a radial arm saw) and band saws. In recent years, several manufacturers have produced small reasonably priced band saws. Of the two, my preference would be for the band saw as it is more versatile, being able to cut curves as well as straight. With suitable blades it will also cut metal and plastic. The main drawback of the small band saw is the difficulty of cutting long lengths of timber accurately unless a fence is used and the saw clamped to a firm surface.

### Tool maintenance

Planes and chisels must be kept sharp if you are going to produce neat, accurate work. Working with hardwoods means that the tool will require sharpening more frequently. A good quality India oilstone will, if used regularly, put a keen edge on the blades. There is no mystery about sharpening blades — they must be held at the correct angle of 30°/35° and moved backwards and forwards along the stone. A few drops of oil on the surface of the stone help the cutting action and keep the fine

particles of metal that have been ground away from clogging the grit of the stone.

Should you have difficulty in obtaining a good flat edge, one of the honing guides that are available from most ironmongers will solve the problem. Once the edge has been sharpened, there will be a fine feather of metal on the underside of the edge. This has to be removed by stropping the blade on the palm of the hand or a leather strop. Alternatively the blade can be placed flat on the stone and the feather ground off gently.

## Choosing the timber

The most widely used wood for sidecar frames is ash. This is a tough, durable timber, cream to pale brown in colour, with good bending qualities and an excellent strength-to-weight ratio; is without doubt the best timber to use for body framing. The main defect to look for in ash is 'black heart'; this occurs in the heartwood of the tree and looks like a black patchy stain. Avoid buying boards that have this appearance.

It is possible to use other hardwoods for the frame; oak, elm or beech are suitable, but use ash for the best results.

Do not use softwoods of the type found in D.I.Y. stores; they are cheaper and easier to work but they are weaker and not so weather resistant.

When buying the timber for the frame, make sure you check the boards carefully; if they are warped or wet, reject them. Wet wood can, if dried very carefully, be used but it will warp if the drying is carried out too quickly. Boards that are split can be used if there is nothing else available, but check that you can cut out the parts you need, and ask for a discount on the price! (It is normal to find splits, or shakes as they are called, in the end inch or two of a well-seasoned board.) While on the subject of cutting boards, remember to allow in your calculations for the width of the saw cut and for planing up afterwards. Most hardwoods in timber yards are sold roughsawn, so if your timber needs to be 1 inch (25 mm) finished size, you will need to buy a board thicker than that.

Reject boards that have a bleached appearance, which oftens means that they have been left out in the weather unprotected. This usually causes a multitude of fine shakes along the length of the board.

Any sheet material for floorboards, etc., should be plywood. This is made by gluing thin layers of timber, called veneers, together, with their grain directions at 90° to each other. Because of this cross-bonding, shrinkage and warping are minimal. Plywood is made up from an odd number of veneers to give even stresses in the sheets. Plywood with five or more layers is called multi-ply.

Some manufacturers panelled the sidecar frame with thin plywood on the outside. This increased the strength of the frame considerably and also enabled them to stick very thin gauge aluminium or steel sheet to the plywood to provide the outer panel.

It is possible to make the sidecar out of plywood, cutting out the body sides from a large

sheet, and number of successful homemade sidecars have been produced by this method. The biggest drawback is the increased weight that this method entails.

For use in sidecars or as footboards on vintage machines, it is essential that only exterior-grade or marine ply is used, because moisture will attack the adhesive of the plywood and soften it, causing the sheet to de-laminate and fall apart. Exterior-grade plywoods are marked as follows according to the type of adhesive used in their manufacture:

M.R.   Moisture resistant and to some extent weather resistant. Will stand exposure to water for a short period, but boiling water will cause the adhesive to fail.

B.R.   Boil resistant. These plywoods will accept exposure to weather conditions.

W.B.P.   Weather and boil proof. The adhesive used in these plywoods will resist all weather conditions. They are the best to use for such items as floorboards and footboards.

Plywoods are manufactured in a range of thicknesses from 4 to 25 mm and in sheets normally 8 ft × 4 ft (2,440 mm × 1,220 mm) or 6ft × 3 ft (1,830 mm × 915 mm). Some plywoods are also available with a hardwood veneer on one side for more decorative work.

Resist the temptation to use other manufactured boards; the majority of them are not waterproof and will start to disintegrate in a short space of time.

## Woodworking techniques

When faced with the task of repairing a wooden body frame or even making a completely new one, do not allow despair to engulf you. The basic skills are quite straightforward; you do not have to be a master craftsman or craftswoman to cut fancy joints such as dovetails because they do not appear in body frames. If you can use a plane, a chisel and a saw, you have all the skills that are needed. However, for those who need a reminder of one or two of the basic points, the following will prove useful.

*From left to right: try, jack and smoothing planes.*

## Planes

Wood should always be planed with the grain to produce the smoothest possible surface. It will soon become apparent if you are planing the wrong way — the wood will tear and leave a rough surface. To achieve a good finish on wood that has awkward grain, the plane must have a sharp blade set very fine.

Stand in a position where you can plane without leaning over the bench, with your left foot parallel to the wood being planed (right foot if you are left-handed). Your bodyweight should move on this foot as you push the plane forward. Make sure that you feel balanced throughout the length of cut; any tendency for your body to wobble will make planing an accurate surface difficult.

The plane should be gripped with the thumb and first finger of the right hand guiding it, the other three fingers gripping the handle. The other hand grips the knob at the front of the plane. If you are left-handed, the grip will be reversed.

When you are planing narrow edges, do not grip the knob at the front of the plane as this could cause the plane to wobble. Grip the toe of the plane and use your fingers as a fence. Frequently check the side of the timber you have chosen to plane first with a straight edge until it is flat. Next look at the two edges and decide which will need the least planed off to produce a good edge. When you have decided which edge you will plane first, the side you have just finished planing should be marked

with a face side mark P with the tail pointing towards the edge to be planed next.

This edge should now be planed and should be checked frequently with a straight edge for flatness and with a try square from the face side for squareness. When the edge has been planed smooth, flat and square you can put on the face edge mark ∧, with the point of the inverted vee touching the tail of the face side mark. The face side and face edge should be used for all subsequent marking out of the timber and this will ensure that the finished piece will be as accurate as possible.

When planing across the grain at the end of a piece of wood, do not plane right the way across otherwise the grain will split at the edge as the plane passes over it. To prevent this happening, a scrap piece of wood can either be cramped to the edge of the board with a sash cramp or, if the wood is narrow enough to fit sideways in the vice, placed in the vice with the wood to be planed. This scrap wood will support the grain at the edge of the board, preventing it from splitting away. If the wood is wide, it is possible to plane from the sides towards the middle, so preventing the splitting.

## Chisels

Before using a chisel make sure that it is sharp; this will make working much easier and more accurate. My old woodwork teacher was fond of saying: 'Sharp chisels cut wood, blunt chisels cut

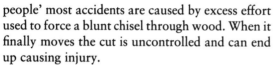

*Firmer and bevel-edged chisels.*

*Mortise chisels.*

people' most accidents are caused by excess effort used to force a blunt chisel through wood. When it finally moves the cut is uncontrolled and can end up causing injury.

Use the right chisel for the job in hand. Using the wrong chisel means that not only will the work be less well finished, but the chisel will also feel wrong. For example, a mortise chisel is no good for removing the waste from a halving joint; the blade is too thick and too narrow, causing the wood to split rather than be cut. Take great care if you use a mallet on a chisel with a fine blade, which, being made from hardened steel, can break if too much force is used.

A good chisel is not that expensive and if treated well will last a lifetime. There are two types which will be useful for body frames: firmer chisels and mortise chisels.

**Firmer chisels** are for general-purpose work and are available from $\frac{1}{8}$ inch (3 mm) to 2 inch (50 mm) widths. They are used for cutting with hand pressure, called paring, or with light blows from a mallet.

Bevel-edged firmer chisels are available in the same sizes as the normal firmer chisel, the only difference being that the sides of the blade are bevelled for cutting into acute angles such as the corners of dovetails. Because of its bevelled edge, the blade is not as strong as the firmer chisel and must be treated with care.

**Mortise chisels** are used for heavy-duty work such as the cutting of mortise joints. They are specially designed to withstand heavy blows from a mallet, and the thick blade prevents twisting in the mortise and enables the waste to be levered out without straining the blade. A leather washer is fitted between the handle and the blade to act as a shock absorber. The width of the blade varies from $\frac{1}{4}$ inch (6 mm) to $\frac{1}{2}$ inch (13 mm).

Plastic end caps are available to fit over the end of the blade to protect the cutting edge from damage while it is being stored in a tool box or rack — one is shown in the illustration.

### Saws

Good-quality hand saws are needed if you are going to cut a large amount of timber and you do not have access to power machinery.

For cutting down the grain of timber, a rip saw will cut most efficiently. A panel or cross cut saw will cope with cutting across the grain and a tenon saw will be needed for joint work. For cutting curves, a bow saw will be necessary, the smaller coping saws being too small for all but the lightest work.

Making friends with the local timber merchant can pay great dividends. If you know what basic sizes of wood you want, he will usually put it through his saw at a reasonable cost and this could save you hours of hard work with a hand saw.

**Right** *Rip and cross cut saws.*

**Below** *Tenon and dovetail saws.*

**Below right** *Coping saws for cutting small curves.*

**Bottom** *A bow saw for cutting larger curves.*

**Bottom right** *Marking and mortise gauges.*

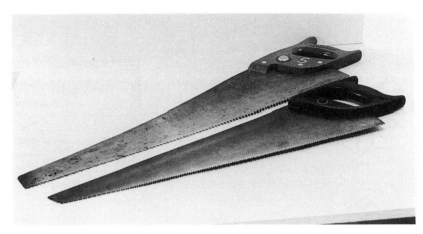

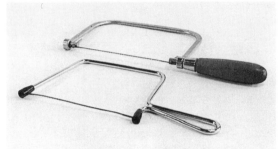

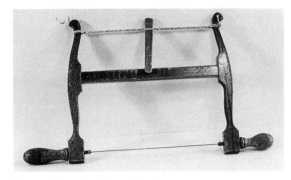

# Repairs to body frames

### Halving joints

The most commonly used joint is the halving joint (see Figure 64) where, as its name suggests, half the thickness of each of the two pieces of timber is cut away so that when the joint is put together the pieces of wood are flush with one another. There are two types of halving joint: one where the ends of two pieces of timber are joined; the other where the end of one piece of timber meets another piece somewhere along its length.

Halving joints are marked out using a marking gauge set to half the thickness of the timber. The length of the joint should be marked out with a square and then the centre line is marked with the gauge. It is a good idea to mark with a pencil the part of the joint to be cut out, to eliminate the frustrating discovery that you have removed the wrong piece of wood! A tenon saw can then be used to cut across the timber, first down to the line and secondly down the length of the timber to remove the waste. Remember to keep to the waste side of the line otherwise your completed joint will

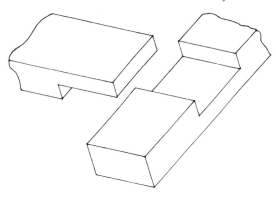

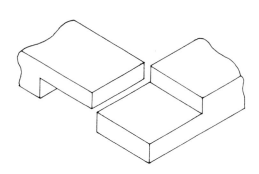

Fig. 64 *Halving joints.*

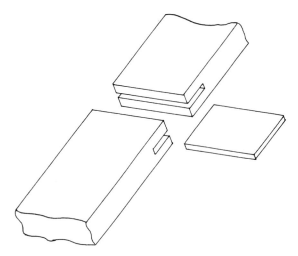

Fig. 65 *Spliced joint.*

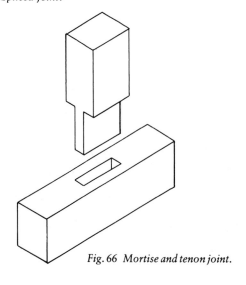

Fig. 66 *Mortise and tenon joint.*

be thinner than necessary and the two faces of the frame members will not be flush with one another. Once the bulk of the waste has been removed with the saw, the joint should be pared down to the line, if necessary, with a sharp wide-bladed chisel.

When removing wood from the middle of a piece of timber, saw down to the centre line at each end of the joint. Depending on the width of the waste wood to be removed, it may be possible to use the saw at an angle to saw some of the waste out of the joint. After this, use a chisel with a wide blade to cut out the remaining waste. The joint should be pared out at an angle, working from the sides of the timber towards the middle. Do not chisel straight across the timber as this could cause the grain of the wood to split on the far side of the joint. Ensure that the faces of the joint are true, otherwise the timbers will be angled in relation to each other.

There are times when a joint has to be cut to achieve an angle between the timbers. Doors, for instance, are built with a certain amount of twist so that they do not rattle when shut. This twist is referred to as 'wind' or 'slam' and is carefully arranged so that the door makes contact with the dovetail rubber just a few millimetres in advance of the lock meeting the striker plate.

If you are rebuilding a door, take careful note of the joints in any remaining pieces of timber and reproduce them as accurately as possible. It is not necessary to cut each item to the finished size; indeed, it is an advantage to leave them oversize to allow for adjustments to be made without spoiling the finished piece. The final shape of the door can be achieved by planing off the excess wood. Always cramp the door together dry and offer it up to the frame. If the 'slam' of the door is incorrect, small wedges of timber can be placed in the appropriate joints until the door is correct. This will then show which joints need adjusting and the amount of wood to be removed.

Halving joints should be screwed together as well as glued, to ensure that they withstand any stress that is put on them. I would advise the use of stainless steel screws in any body frame; they are more expensive than other types of woodscrew, but once in place you can forget about them with peace of mind. Normal mild steel screws will rust very quickly, especially in an acidic timber like oak. Even plated screws will rust in the end and brass screws, while non-rusting, are not really strong enough for the job.

Do not drive a screw directly into the timbers. Not only will it be very difficult to drive in, but the joint will not be pulled together properly. The outer half of the joint should be drilled to provide a clearance hole for the screw to pass through. This hole should then be countersunk, deep enough for the head of the screw to be below the level of the surrounding timber. The second half of

the joint should be drilled to suit the core diameter of the screw and its depth, exclusive of the tapered point of the screw. The accompanying table shows the sizes for clearance and core diameter drills. The timber can then be glued and screwed together. Make sure that you use the correctly sized screwdriver on the screw otherwise the slot will become damaged and you will have difficulty driving the screw fully home.

### Spliced joints

It is not every time that a whole frame member has to be renewed because of rot. You may find that only a portion of the timber is affected and that a replacement section can be fitted in.

The first thing to do is to assess the extent of the damage or rot. Be generous in your calculations — 'if in doubt, cut it out' must guide what you do. Having decided what needs to be replaced, take all the necessary measurements to enable you to reproduce the part. Do not cut out the old timber from the frame until the new part has been made and compared to the original.

There are two joints you can use to join the new wood to the old: a halving joint, which has already been described, and a spliced joint. The latter is basically a butt joint that has a rebate in the face of each piece of timber. A tongue, usually of plywood, is tapped into the rebates to provide the strength of the glued joint (see Figure 65). You may

| GAUGE NO. | 2 | 4 | 6 | 8 | 10 | 12 | 14 |
|---|---|---|---|---|---|---|---|
| CLEARANCE | 2.2 | .8 | 3.6 | 4.4 | 5.0 | 5.8 | 6.4 |
| CORE | | 1.2 | 1.4 | 1.8 | 2.2 | 2.6 | 3.0 | 3.2 |

*Wood screw sizes.*

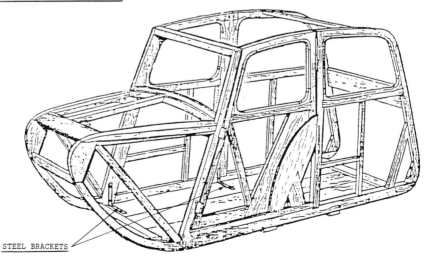

*Sketch of the body frame for a 1952 Canterbury sidecar. Note the steel brackets where the body sides meet the floor.* STEEL BRACKETS

find this joint more awkward to cut than a halving joint if the rebate that has to be cut in situ is in a difficult position.

Whichever joint you decide to use, do not glue the joint before you have had a 'dry run' at assembly. The most usual problem is the tongue in the spliced joint. This should be a push fit when dry; do not force it into the joint as you are liable to split the timber of the frame. Check also that no parts of the frame near the new section are under undue strain caused perhaps by badly fitted joints or the new section being forced into place. When you are satisfied that all is well, the joints can be assembled with glue and firmly screwed together.

One point to remember when using screws is to put the screws into the wood at a slight angle. Not only does this improve the strength of the joint by increasing the leverage required to pull the screws out of the wood, but also if they are angled towards the shoulders of the joint, they will pull the shoulders together as they are tightened.

### Mortise and tenon joints

Another type of joint found on some body frames is the mortise and tenon joint (see Figure 66), usually used to join centre rails to outside rails. To enable you to mark out the joint accurately you will need a mortise gauge; it is possible to manage without one but accuracy is likely to be lost.

First decide on the thickness of the tenon; one-third of the thickness of the wood is considered correct. This then has to be matched to the nearest mortise chisel size, usually $\frac{1}{4}$ inch (8 mm), $\frac{3}{8}$ inch (10 mm), or $\frac{1}{2}$ inch (12 mm).

The length of the tenon, which is equal to the width of the wood containing the mortise, is marked around the end of the piece of wood. The mortise gauge points should now be set to the chisel that is going to be used to cut the mortise, then the stock of the mortise gauge set so that the pins are equidistant from either edge of the wood. Place the stock of the gauge against the far side of the timber and scribe the lines right round the end of the timber.

The position of the mortise should then be marked out on the other piece of timber. First mark the length of the mortise and then the width, using the mortise gauge from the face side of the timber.

### Timber protection

Once the frame is finished or repaired, it is important to consider how to protect the timber from the effects of the weather. In my opinion there is only one effective method of protection and that is a complete and thorough application of exterior grade paint.

As with all types of finish, careful preparation is the key to success. It is best that all the metalwork (hinges, brackets, etc.) on the body frame should be removed and the timber rubbed down with fine glass paper to provide a key for the primer. Two coats of aluminium wood primer should be

*1934 Swallow single seat sidecar.*

*1934 Watsonian Airflow saloon.*

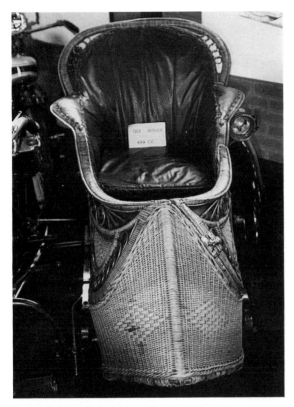

**Above** *1913 Rover wicker sidecar. An occupational thera-pist's delight!*

**Above right** *Freddie Dixon with his famous 'Banking' sidecar.*

**Right** *Freddie Dixon at Brooklands. The obvious qualities for the passenger are strong neck muscles and no imagination!*

applied and left for two or three days to thoroughly harden. Next apply at least two coats of undercoat to make sure that every section of the frame is adequately covered; this should also be left for two or three days to harden off properly.

When you are sure it is hard, it can be rubbed down with fine carbide paper. Do not use any water with the paper; undercoat is not waterproof, and if water soaks into it, this will prevent the top coat from adhering to it. After rubbing down, use a tacky cloth to remove any dust particles. Tacky cloths are available from good accessory shops or paint factors. The top coat can be applied by brush and if done carefully you can obtain a good finish,

although to achieve the best result the top coat should be sprayed on.

It is not advisable to use cellulose paints for the timber of the frame. Cellulose is very brittle and is more likely to crack as the frame flexes when the bike is driven or when the timber moves, as all timber does, in reaction to the weather.

## Making curved timber components

### Laminating

On many original body frames, curved pieces of timber were cut from wide boards. Not only was this wasteful and expensive but the short grain on parts of the curve meant weak areas in the timber. A much more satisfactory method of producing curved pieces of timber is to laminate them up from thin strips of wood glued and clamped to a suitable former. This produces an extremely strong and stable body component, much stronger than the original piece.

Ash, elm and beech are all suitable timbers for laminating and will bend around a surprisingly tight radius, depending on the thickness of the laminates. For curves whose radius is less than 12 inches (300 mm) the laminates should be $\frac{1}{8}$ inch (3 mm) in thickness. For a curve whose radius is greater than this, $\frac{1}{4}$ inch (6 mm) laminates will be satisfactory. The laminates should be wider than the finished size required to allow for planing up afterwards. Extra length is also needed to allow for final cutting, and also saves the needless problems of trying to get the ends of the laminates neatly together and also of remembering that the laminates on the outside of the curve are longer than those on the inside of the curve.

A circular saw or large band saw will be needed to cut the laminates out of the board, for there is no point in attempting such an exercise by hand. Once the laminates have been cut, some people advocate that they should be planed to produce as smooth a finish as possible to obtain a stronger join line. In my experience if the saw has a tungsten-tipped blade, the finish will be very

nearly as good as that of a plane, and will produce a perfectly good lamination. Should your ability to produce a perfectly flat surface with a plane over a long piece of timber be in doubt, leave the wood as it came from the saw.

If the saw has left a rough surface, the laminates will have to be planed. Perhaps the easiest way of holding thin pieces of timber for planing is to pin them to the bench top and punch the heads of the pins well below the surface. When that face has been planed, the laminate can be carefully levered up from the bench, turned over and the process repeated.

The jig around which the laminates are formed must be an accurate copy of the inside shape of the final component. For one-off or short runs of laminations, the jig can easily be made from fairly heavy sections of scrap wood. The thickness of the timber for the jig should be the same as the width of the laminates; this makes it easier to check that the laminates are lying flat together. If you are producing a long lamination, you may find it easier to bolt the jig to a large board. This makes clamping the laminates easier as they can rest on the board instead of flapping about in mid-air.

*Fig. 67 Laminating wooden frame parts. The jig is screwed to the baseboard while the outer formers are clamped to the laminates by G-cramps. In practice more G-cramps would be required than the number shown here.*

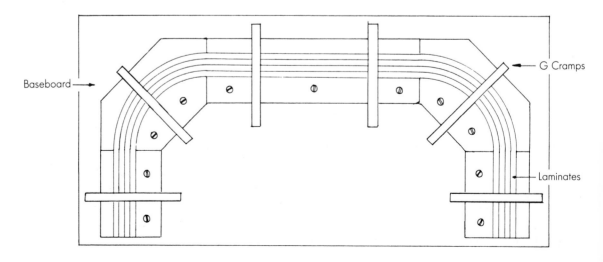

The formers and the board should be protected from the cramps by either a steel strip or a wooden former that corresponds to the outer shape of the component. Naturally the surfaces of the formers must be smooth, without any bumps or hollows, as these will cause uneven pressure under the cramps, weakening the glue line. Notches should also be cut, where necessary, to allow the cramps to grip without sliding.

The formers and the boards, if they are fitted to one, must be protected from the glue used on the laminates. It would be extremely frustrating to find your perfectly laminated component stuck fast to the former. A couple of coats of varnish will prevent the glue sticking; as an extra precaution a layer of polythene or aluminium cooking foil can be placed between the former and the laminates.

Before gluing the laminates together, cramp them up dry on to the former. I have found it easier to mark each laminate halfway along with a pencil and then start at the middle of the former and work towards the ends. This method also needs less physical space in the workshop. Cramping them together dry will also show up any problems you may have with the jig and also how many G-cramps you will need to pull the laminates together evenly. When the laminates are all cramped in place, check the join line between each piece; it should be tight together around the whole of the former. When you are satisfied that everything is right, the laminates can be glued and cramped back onto the former. Use either 'Cascamite' or one of the 'Aerolite' glues for laminating; the glue must be strong and waterproof. On long laminations use a paint brush to apply the glue and make sure you cover all the mating surfaces. When the laminations have been cramped onto the former, remove as much of the surplus glue as possible. A damp cloth will remove it easily and make cleaning up much easier. Glue, especially 'Cascamite', is extremely hard to remove when it has fully cured.

### Steam bending

Should you want to bend timber above $\frac{1}{2}$ inch (7 mm) in thickness, you will have to use steam to make the wood pliable enough to bend around the former. Ash, beech and elm are all suitable for steam bending.

To make a steam chest you will need a vessel of some kind in which to boil the water. This can range from an electric kettle to a special steaming pan which has a conical lid with a funnel for the steam to escape. I have seen an old tea urn pressed into service, and an excellent job it did too! You will also need a length of pipe slightly longer than the longest piece of timber you wish to steam. P.V.C. pipe is ideal, but any waterproof pipe will do. The lid of your steamer must have a hole cut in it so that the pipe can be fitted there. The piece of timber should then be suspended from the top of the pipe and the outlet sealed with polythene. The steam chest can then be filled with water and heated, so that the steam will rise up the pipe and saturate the timber. Check the water level regularly to prevent the chest boiling dry; much of the steam will condense on the polythene and return to the bottom.

The length of time the timber will need to be left in the steam chest will depend on the thickness of the component and the efficiency of the chest. Several hours may be needed but an occasional test will help you to discover how long is necessary. The timber should bend easily, without strain, around the former; if it does not, steam it for a further period and try again.

Once the timber is ready, cramp it to the jig as quickly as possible. Naturally you do not use glue yet if you are building up a component from steamed laminates. The timber will take a couple of days to dry out and you must resist the temptation to remove it too soon. If you are using laminates, they should be marked with a pencil to show their relationship to each other and the jig before being removed. This will prevent the individual laminates becoming a sticky puzzle if you forget which went where after they have been coated with glue. They should then be cramped back onto the former and left while the glue cures.

One word of warning—use only the best quality timber for laminating and steam bending. Reject anything that has any defects such as knots, shakes or uneven grain; these will almost certainly break when they are bent.

## Fabric tops

If your sidecar has a fabric roof needing replacement, the best material to use is double duck. This consists of a fabric-rubber-fabric sandwich and it is still available from most restoration specialists. Some manufacturers did use man-made materials such as 'Rexine' or its replacement, P.V.C.

Whichever you decide on as a replacement, use the original as a pattern. The stitching will require a heavy duty or industrial sewing machine, unless you do it by hand; a domestic sewing machine will not be robust enough to sew through the material. Since most tops are of a simple shape and very visible, it may be best, if you have doubts about your ability to sew this material, to farm out this piece of work to a specialist.

## Upholstery

The material used for upholstery will fall into two main types: leather or P.V.C. Both will respond to cleaning, with possibly some extra treatment to bring out their best qualities.

The decision whether to renovate or replace is one that only you can make, but there are one or two points to consider. If only part of the interior is replaced it can make everything else look worse than it did before. However, total replacement in leather can be very expensive and may not justify its cost when compared to the value of the sidecar, but that is something you must decide. I feel that a slightly careworn interior is more in keeping with the age of the outfit, but that is a matter of opinion.

Many sidecars were fitted with leather upholstery, and though this is a very hard-wearing material it does need periodic attention to keep it in the best condition possible. Connolly Brothers Ltd, who have suplied the majority of manufacturers in this country with upholstery hide, recommend that their leather be cleaned with a damp cloth dipped in a solution of mild soap and water or with 'Connolly Leather Cleaner'. After cleaning, a light application of their 'CeeBee Hide Food'

**Below left** *A nicely upholstered seat from an early Forecar – a straightforward piece of work not beyond the careful amateur.*

**Right** *A leather-fronted toolbox from a TT Panther, a fairly simple piece of leatherwork.*

should be given to help maintain the supple feel of the leather.

If the leather has faded or there is minor damage to the surface, Connollys will supply their 'Connollising Kit' to rectify the trouble. They will need a small piece of unfaded hide, cut from somewhere where it will not show, to use as a colour match for the range of dyes.

After the leather has been cleaned, the dye should be sponged onto the leather using long, even strokes, and left to dry. Once the dye has dried thoroughly, hide food can be rubbed into the surface and buffed with a soft cloth.

P.V.C. or its forerunner, 'Rexine', are both man-made materials. P.V.C. can be cleaned and if necessary recoloured with a variety of products manufactured for the purpose, but be cautious about using these on Rexine since some of them may soften the surface of the material and leave a sticky mess. Try out the preparation on a piece of upholstery that does not show. One method of determining whether the upholstery is Rexine or P.V.C. is to cut off a small piece where it will not show (e.g. underneath the seat) and put a lighted match to it. If it is Rexine or some other nitro-

cellulose cloth it will burn quickly and smell of burning castor oil. If it burns very slowly or not at all it will be P.V.C.

Nitro-cellulose material can be painted with 'leatherpaint', which is usually sold in craft and D.I.Y. shops. Follow the instructions carefully and it will do a good job on the upholstery.

## Carpets

Carpets should be removed and given a good shake or beating before using a vacuum cleaner to remove the fine dust. Grit is the major cause of carpet wear, because the sharp edges of the grit cut into the fibres and weaken them. Once all the loose dirt has been removed, the carpet can be cleaned with a proprietary carpet shampoo and left to dry.

If the carpet is sound but faded in parts it can be dyed to a uniform colour using a suitable dye. Carpets with frayed edges will be improved greatly in appearance if the edging or binding is renewed. Should the carpets be beyond redemption or missing altogether it is possible to buy suitable carpet from the roll at many car restoration specialists.

Where you have the remnants of carpets from which to take measurements it is best to lay them out on a large flat area. Make sure that the pile of the carpet runs the same way if there is more than one piece of carpet. Take your measurements, making allowance for cutting and seaming. If any of the carpets are made up of more than one piece, check carefully how the pieces are joined together before taking them apart to use as patterns.

If the carpets are missing altogether, patterns made from thick paper will have to be produced.

Make sure that the patterns are big enough; skimping on the material will leave unsightly gaps around the edges of the carpet.

Ensure that you buy carpet that does not fray as soon as it is cut, and bind the edges unless they are fitted underneath sill plates or similar fittings. Where carpets are going to be fitted to existing fixing studs on the floor, chalk the top of the stud and then press the carpet down onto it. This will show clearly where to put the other half of the fastening in the new carpet.

# CHAPTER 16

# Fibreglass and other plastics

In recent years fibreglass, or glass reinforced plastic (GRP) as it has become known, has come into widespread use by manufacturers and specialist producers for such items as fairings, top boxes, panniers, etc.

The glass in GRP is strands of silicon which are bonded together or reinforced by the plastic, which is a resin. When the resin is mixed with a hardener or catalyst, the resin will cure and set solid. Fibreglass is sold either as mat, woven roving, tissue or tape. Resin is sold as general lay up or gel coat resin which has an additive included to make it thixotropic or non-drip. The hardener is usually supplied in the correct quantities when you purchase the resin.

When working with fibreglass there are some important points to remember for health and safety. Many people find that working with fibreglass mat will produce a localised rash on their hands and arms. If you are affected, wear gloves or use a barrier cream. Some people are very allergic to the glass fibres and suffer such painful rashes and swellings that they would be well advised to ask someone else to do the job for them.

Always work in a well-ventilated area because the resin gives off styrene vapour which is highly inflammable and can cause drowsiness. Acetone used for cleaning purposes is also inflammable, so the rule must be no smoking or naked lights when working or while the fibreglass is curing.

## Repairing fibreglass

Apart from the obvious crash damage, the most common cause of deterioration in fibreglass is stress cracks in the laminate which can be caused by a variety of things. But whatever the cause, the remedy is the same. The paint layers must be ground away, then the gel coat of resin and into the top layer of the laminate. The ground out area should extend 1–2 inches (25–50 mm) beyond the crack and the edges of the area should be angled rather than vertical. Always remember to wear a face mask when grinding fibreglass or body filler.

Once the grinding is finished, the edge of the area should be feathered with abrasive paper, used dry. This will remove the grinding marks which would otherwise show after painting.

Next cut a piece of tissue large enough to cover the area of the cracks and, after applying a thin layer of mixed resin, place the tissue over the cracks. This should now be brushed gently with resin until it is thoroughly soaked, then left to cure.

Depending on the depth of the ground-out area, it may be possible to apply more than one layer of tissue giving more strength to the repair. However, it is important to ensure that the level of the tissue does not end up above the level of the panel, since it is not possible to grind down the repair without ruining the surface finish.

The final stage necessitates completing the repair with filler paste, then smoothing it down to achieve the correct contour of the panel.

Should the panel be cracked all the way through it will have to be repaired from both sides. If the inside of the panel is visible it should be repaired in the same way as the outside. If it is hidden from view, two or three layers of mat should be laminated onto the back of the panel, after it has been lightly ground to form a key for the laminates.

A. R. RACE

A. R. ROAD SPORTS

AVON HANDLEBAR FAIRING

BMW EARLS FORK AVONAIRE

A. S. / CLUBMAN

AVONAIRE ELITE

**Left** *Classic-style fairings are available for many bikes.* (Sprint Manufacturing.)

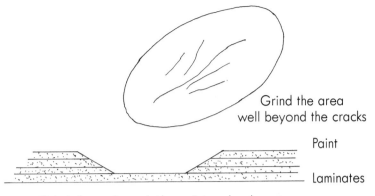

Grind the area well beyond the cracks

Paint

GEL COAT

Laminates

**Right** *Fig. 68 Repairing cracks in GRP.*

Grind down through the paint and gel coat and into the laminates before building up with tissue

Again, make sure the repair is taken well beyond the split, to spread the load. When the repair has thoroughly cured, the outside of the panel can be treated in the same way as a stress crack.

## Making fibreglass components

If you want to make a new moulding or some other article from scratch you will first have to make a mould. Moulds may be either male or female (a male mould is laid up on its outside surface, a female on its inside surface) and can be made from any rigid material. Porous materials such as wood or plaster must be sealed with varnish before use.

As with any other type of mould, you must ensure that there are no re-entrant angles or curves on the mould which would prevent the finished moulding from being lifted off. If you do require such a shape, the mould must be designed so that it can be dismantled with the moulding in place, to allow it to be removed.

Male moulds are easier to make than female ones and for this reason it is often best to make a male mould first. When the mould is complete, it should be coated with release agent, following the instructions on the tin carefully. A female mould can then be formed over the male one, using fibreglass. It may be necessary to incorporate strengthening ribs into the mould to prevent it flexing too much. These ribs can be made of any material such as wood strips or metal tube, providing they are clean. Wood bonds very well to

fibreglass because its porous nature provides an excellent key for the resin. Best results are obtained if it is wiped over with acetone before laminating into the mould. When the laminate has cured, it can be removed and the inside face cleaned up. It is now ready to be used as a mould.

Existing mouldings can be used as a male mould from which to take a female mould. The surface must be free of any defects and supported if necessary. Any defects must be rectified before use otherwise they will be reproduced in any subsequent mouldings.

The polyester resins used in GRP are known as thermosetting plastics. These cannot be re-shaped by the application of heat after they have been formed and the only way to shape them is with normal cutting tools. Thermoplastics on the other hand can be shaped by being heated to the correct temperature and formed by different methods.

## Working with 'Perspex' and other acrylics

Polymethyl methacrylate (acrylic) is perhaps best known under its I.C.I. trade name 'Perspex'. It has exceptional durability for outdoor use and in its clear form has excellent transparency. It has been used for many years as a substitute for glass in the windows of sidecars and for streamlined headlamp covers and windshields.

Perspex is available in sheets of varying thickness as well as rods or tube. The sheets are covered

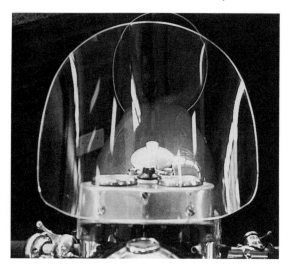

*An aero screen on a 250cc Royal Enfield. Screens like this can be produced quite simply.*

with protective paper and this should be kept in place for as long as possible during working; not only does it protect the surface of the sheet from being marked, but it also makes marking out much easier.

Like other thermoplastics, acrylic can be cut and drilled with normal metal or woodworking tools. When sawing acrylic sheet, it is important that the saw is fed slowly and steadily into the sheet to prevent a build-up of heat which will soften the plastic. The sheet must be well supported to avoid snapping and care is necessary to avoid splintering by over-vigorous sawing. The rough edge left by the saw can be smoothed with a file or, if it is a straight edge, a smoothing or block plane can be used. The blade of the plane must be sharp and set fine.

Normal drills are suitable for acrylic providing that they are not run too fast and so generate excessive heat; water or soluble oil can be used as a coolant. Make sure that the acrylic is clamped down onto a piece of wood, to prevent the sheet from riding up the drill as the hole is completed, and the bottom of the hole from splintering.

It is possible to cut screwthreads into acrylic using standard taps and dies. A coarse thread form will be the strongest and soluble oil or water should be used as a lubricant. However, screw-

threads in acrylic will not last long if used frequently; in a situation needing regular dismantling, a metal insert should be used.

Acrylic rod can be turned on a lathe using H.S.S. tools. The tools should have zero top rake, 15°–20° degrees front clearance and be kept sharp at all times. Coolant must always be used and the work must be held firmly and positioned correctly to prevent chatter. Rigid plastics can usually be machined using the same techniques as those used for light alloys.

Acrylic sheet can be bent easily if heated to 160°–170°C. For work at home the best heat source is the domestic oven. A polished sheet of metal should be used to support the plastic while it is being heated. Otherwise it will sag between the bars of the oven shelf when it becomes soft. An approximate estimate of the time required to heat the sheet can be found with the following formula: time in minutes = 10 + (3 × sheet thickness in mm).

If only a simple bend is required in the sheet, a former made of wood or metal can be used around which to bend it. The surface of the former must be clean and smooth otherwise the soft surface of the plastic will be damaged. Soft leather or cotton gloves should be worn when handling the heated plastic to prevent burns to the hands.

If a compound curve is required, a male and female mould can be made from wood or other rigid material, but the surfaces of the mould must be perfectly smooth before use. The softened sheet of plastic, which has already been cut to shape, should be laid over the female mould and then pressed down into it with the male mould. Only hand pressure is required, but the pressure must not be released until the plastic has cooled sufficiently to become rigid.

**Above right** *Though Halfords are still prominent in the accessory business they no longer market Celastoid as they did in the late 1950s. However, similar materials are available from restoration specialists and plastics retailers.*

**Right** *'Perspex' is still the most famous trade name for acrylic sheet. Bending a piece of sheet this size does pose some problems for the home restorer; a bath full of very hot water might do the trick.*

**Left** *The Honda CD175 with self-coloured plastic mudguards, headlamp shell and battery box.*

**Below left** *Fig. 69 A simple method of forming a concave shape in thermoplastic.*

Hand pressure

Top former

Plastic

Bottom former

Remember to allow for the thickness of the plastic when making the formers.

Any surface scratches can be removed using perspex polish or metal polish, though deeper scratches are best removed by using progressively finer grades of wet and dry paper before using the polish. It is possible to polish plastics on a polishing machine, but if you do so there are one or two points to remember. First, use a clean polishing mop and keep it for use on plastics only. Second, do not use too much pressure between the mop and

the plastic; the heat generated will soften the plastic, often forcing particles of polish into its surface which will spoil it and give you a great deal of extra work.

Nylon is another plastic that is being used more and more in the motor cycle industry. It is a tough, creep-resistant plastic that has excellent resistance to oils, fuels and solvents. It is used for light engineering components such as gears, bushes and bearings where its major asset of not requiring lubrication can be utilised to the full. There are a number of different types of nylon available but they can all be easily machined if the basic guidelines already mentioned for machining plastics are followed. In the late 1960s several motor cycle manufacturers began using other plastics for cycle parts; Honda amongst others used plastic for mudguards, battery boxes and legshields.

While plastics enable manufacturers to produce quite complex shapes easily by moulding they can be a cause of concern to restorers trying to deal with cracks or pieces that have broken off. Not all parts are still available and this leaves the problem of repair unless non-original steel or aluminium parts are used.

Most thermoplastics can be joined together either by adhesives (see Chapter 14) or by hot gas

**Right** *The Honda C90. A large self-coloured plastic moulding forms the legshield and engine cover; the mudguards and battery box are also plastic.*

**Below right** *Fig. 70 Welding plastic with a hot air torch.*

welding. This uses a hot air or nitrogen torch to soften the plastic; when the material is soft a filler rod of the same material is fed into the joint and the plastic fuses together. The torch is moved slowly over the joint until the weld is completed. When it has cooled the excess plastic can be filed off and the surface polished as described earlier.

The joint should be prepared by careful cleaning and by cutting a bevel on both sides to accommodate the filler rod. For anyone contemplating trying this process at home, it may be possible to convert a hot air paint stripper into a suitable torch by making a fine nozzle for the hot airstream.

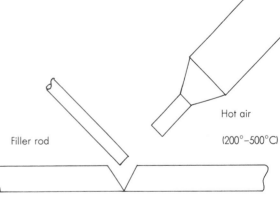

Filler rod

Hot air

(200°–500°C)

Crack or join veed, 65°–70°

# CHAPTER 17
# Chains and belts

No book on motor cycles would be complete without a chapter on chains and belts, the two items that have propelled enthusiasts along the roads for nearly a century. Very few bikes have been produced that do not have one or the other in their construction, either in the engine or transmission.

## Chains

Avoid buying cheap chains—as with so much else, you get what you pay for. A good quality Renold chain will last, if cared for, for a long time and give excellent service.

The accompanying diagrams from the Renold catalogue show the method of shortening or lengthening a chain. Avoid having more spring-links than necessary in the chain; they are the weakest link and should be replaced once a year for peace of mind.

Chains should be checked frequently for wear. The easiest way of doing this is to lay the chain out on the bench, fix one end and then see how much movement is produced by pushing the links back and forth. The recommended movement is 2%, that is a maximum of $\frac{1}{4}$ inch per foot, or 6 mm per 300 mm. If your chain is near this limit, change it.

It is essential that the sprockets are in line so that the chain runs true, otherwise the increased loading on the side of the chain will cause undue wear on both chain and sprocket.

Sprockets should also be checked before using a new chain. If the teeth are worn in any way the sprocket must be replaced or it will soon ruin the new chain. Those with more modern bikes may be able to buy a replacement over the counter, but if you are in the position of needing a new sprocket but there are no replacements you have two courses open to you. One is to have a new sprocket made by an engineering firm, if your budget can stand it. Second, it is possible to restore the sprocket by turning off the worn teeth and welding on a new ring which can have teeth cut on it. Or, if you can obtain a new sprocket of the right size and number of teeth, the centre of this can be machined out to fit your own centre. The join should be at least $\frac{1}{4}$ inch (6 mm) away from the tooth bottom. A full weld all round the sprocket is not needed from the strength point of view; several stitch welds approximately $\frac{1}{2}$ inch (13 mm) long will be adequate, unless you intend to grind down the weld to prevent it being seen. In this case a bevel must be machined on the two parts to allow the weld to penetrate. Great care must be taken when welding the parts together to avoid distortion. The easiest way is to put two small stitch welds opposite each other on one side first. Then turn the sprocket over and put two more at 90° to those on the other side. Repeat the process until the weld is finished; though this is time-consuming it is preferable to spoiling the work by distortion. Depending on the steel used for the sprocket it may be necessary to soften the metal first or use carbide-tipped lathe tools.

If you have no welding facilities, the two parts can be riveted together. In this instance a rebate will have to be turned on each piece so that they fit together as in Figure 71. Use at least six snap head rivets, $\frac{3}{16}$ inch (5 mm) or $\frac{1}{4}$ inch (6 mm); on larger sprockets use more rivets to withstand the power.

## CHAIN LENGTH ALTERATIONS

All drives should be designed wherever possible with sufficient overall adjustment to ensure the use of an even number of pitches throughout the useful life of the chain. Cranked links should never be used on impulsive, highly loaded or high speed chain drives.

In less arduous conditions where there is no other solution and the use of a cranked link unavoidable the diagrams show how length alterations can be accomplished.

A chain having an even number of links requires the incorporation of a cranked link to effect an alteration of one pitch.

A chain having an odd number of links incorporates a cranked link which must be removed to effect an alteration of one pitch.

By removing the parts shown in dark blue and substituting those in light blue a chain can be shortened or lengthened by one pitch.

No joint which relies on a press fit for assembly should be re-used after removal, a new joint should always be employed.

**Using Cranked Link Double No. 30 (or No. 12 where 30's are not available).**

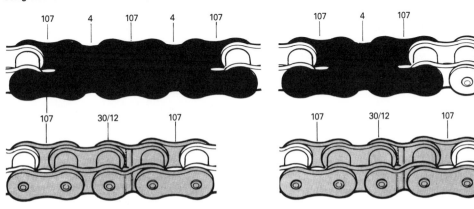

To shorten an even link chain by one pitch

To lengthen an even link chain by one pitch

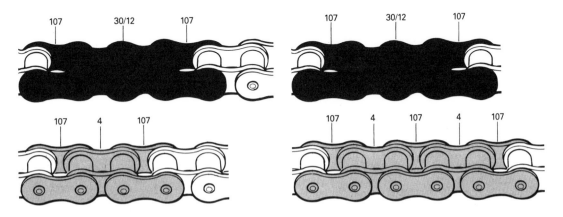

To shorten an odd link chain by one pitch

To lengthen an odd link chain by one pitch

**This page and overleaf** *Chain length alteration.* (Renold Ltd.)

## CHAIN PARTS AND CONNECTING LINKS

The chain parts and connecting links illustrated are only indicative of types available. Please refer to the appropriate chain pages for parts relevant to individual chains.

**No. 4**
**Inner Link (BS/DIN)**
**Roller Link (ANSI)**

Complete assemblies for use with all sizes and types of chain. The unit consists of two inner plates pressed on to the bushes which carry the rollers. (Inner links for use with bush chains have no rollers).

**No. 107**
**Outer Link – Press Fit (BS/DIN)**
**Riveting Pin Link – Press Fit (ANSI)**

For use with all sizes and types of chain where optimum security is desired. The link is supplied with the two bearing pins riveted into one outer plate. The other outer plate is an interference fit on the bearing pins, the ends of which should be riveted over after the plate is fitted.
Press fit connecting links can only be used once; new links must be used to replace dismantled links.
(See separate paragraph overleaf for full riveting instructions).

**No. 11**
**Connecting Link – Slip Fit**
**(BS/DIN/ANSI)**

A connecting link supplied with two connecting pins riveted into one outer plate. The other outer plate is a clearance fit on the connecting pins and secured in position by either a split pin or a spring pin through the projecting end of each connecting pin.

**No. 26**
**Connecting Link – Slip Fit (BS/DIN)**
**Double Cotter – Slip Fit (ANSI)**

Used on short pitch chains only. Supplied with two connecting pins riveted into one outer plate, the clearance fit connecting plate being secured by means of a spring clip, No. 27, which snaps into grooves in the pins.

**No. 11 or No. 26 joints should not be used where high speed or arduous conditions are encountered. In these, or equivalent circumstances, where safety is essential a riveting link No. 107 must be used.**

**No. 58**
**Connecting Link – Press Fit**
**(BS/DIN/ANSI)**

The standard connecting link for all ANSI series detachable chains, also used on riveted chains where high speeds or arduous conditions are encountered. Supplied with two connecting pins riveted into one outer plate, the other outer plate being a press fit on the pins and secured by split pins or spring pins after assembly. Press fit connecting links can only be used once; new links must be used to replace dismantled links.

### Cranked Links

Apart from the specialised series chains, where the cranked link is an essential design feature, cranked links are used only where the chain length must be an odd number of pitches. This practice is not recommended; all drives should, wherever possible, be designed with sufficient overall adjustment to ensure the use of an even number of pitches throughout the useful life of the chain. **Do not use cranked links on impulsive, highly loaded or high speed drives.**

**No. 12**
**Cranked Link – Slip Fit (BS/DIN)**
**Offset Link – Slip Fit (ANSI)**

A single link with cranked plates pressed on to a bush and roller assembly at the narrow end. A clearance fit connecting pin (No. 128) is fitted at the wide end, and is secured by either a split pin or spring pin, according to the pitch and type of chain.

### Loose Fastener

**No. 128**
**Cranked Link Pin – Slip Fit (BS/DIN)**
**Offset Link Pin – Slip Fit (ANSI)**

Used with a single cranked offset link (No. 12 joint). The pin is a clearance fit in the connecting link and is retained by a split pin.

**No. 30**
**Cranked Link Double (BS/DIN)**
**Two Pitch Offset Link (ANSI)**

Double cranked links are available for most sizes and types of chain. The unit consists of an inner link (No. 4), with cranked links retained permanently in position by a riveted bearing pin.

### Tools

Screw operated extractors are available for removing the plate from the outer link of riveted chain by forcing out the bearing pins after first grinding away the rivet swell.

---

The holes must be a good fit for the rivets to prevent any movement; ream the holes if necessary and make sure that the tail of the rivet is firmly clenched.

Chain wheels can also be repaired in this way, either by welding or riveting. It is possible to use bolts instead of rivets if there is enough room for clearance between the frame or wheel. In this case ream out the bolt holes carefully and use nyloc or other self-locking nuts.

For bikes that are in use regularly the teeth on the sprocket should be heat treated to withstand wear, though if your bike is going to be used infrequently then mild steel will suffice.

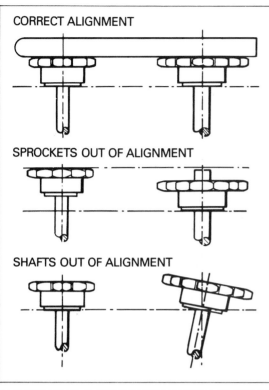

CORRECT ALIGNMENT

SPROCKETS OUT OF ALIGNMENT

SHAFTS OUT OF ALIGNMENT

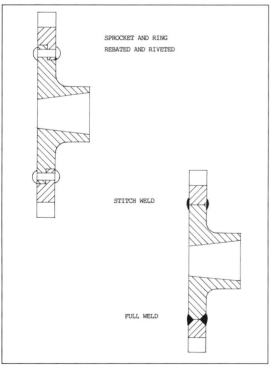

SPROCKET AND RING
REBATED AND RIVETED

STITCH WELD

FULL WELD

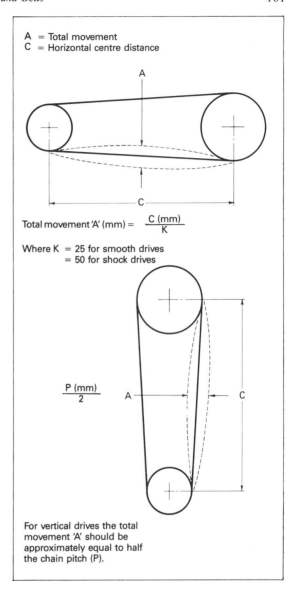

A = Total movement
C = Horizontal centre distance

Total movement 'A' (mm) = $\dfrac{C\ (mm)}{K}$

Where K = 25 for smooth drives
= 50 for shock drives

$\dfrac{P\ (mm)}{2}$

For vertical drives the total movement 'A' should be approximately equal to half the chain pitch (P).

**Above left** *Correct alignment of sprockets is essential for long chain life and preventing power loss.* (Renold Ltd.)

**Above** *How to correctly calculate chain adjustment.* (Renold Ltd.)

**Left** *Fig. 71 Two methods of fitting a new tooth ring to a sprocket.*

# Motorcycle chain maintenance - 1

## CLEAN AND LUBRICATE CHAIN REGULARLY

Exposed chains without oil feed should be cleaned every 1,000 miles. Soak in paraffin and scrub with brush until perfectly clean. Immerse in melted chain lubricant for ten minutes. Allow lubricant to cool, remove chain from bath and wipe off surplus.

CHECK OIL FEED — With drip feed or breather lubrication the feed should be arranged so that oil drips on to the inner edges of the links on both sides of the chain.

# RENOLD MARK 10 MOTORCYCLE CHAIN

# Motorcycle chain maintenance—2

## CHECK CHAIN ADJUSTMENT

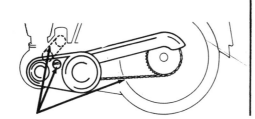

Adjustment must be correct. Test periodically for up and down movement. Make several tests at different positions of rotation and do not over-tighten. Correct amount of chain movement—rear $\frac{3}{4}$ in., primary $\frac{3}{8}$ in., magneto $\frac{1}{4}$ in. If yours is a spring frame machine, check rear chain at a position of the suspension in which the chain will be tightest. In this position the chain should be just free.

# Motorcycle chain maintenance—3

## CHECK WHEEL ALIGNMENT

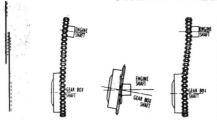

Chain wheels should be accurately aligned. Mal-alignment will result in unnecessary wear of chain and wheel teeth. Both shafts and wheels should be absolutely true. Replace excessively worn and "hooked" chain wheels—they wear out chains.

CHECK CHAINS FOR WEAR—A simple test for chain wear is to remove chain from machine, clean thoroughly, lay on a flat surface and stretch to its fullest extent. Measure 24 pitches between bearing pin centres—if chain shows more than $\frac{1}{4}$ in. elongation it should be replaced.

*Three information advertisements from Reynolds in the late 1950s. (Renolds Ltd.)*

**Above** *A vee belt on a 1914 4½ hp Sun.*

**Above right** *A 'Brammer' link belt on an early Norton.*

**Below** *A link belt on a 1907 Peugeot.*

Lubrication is important — chains that are left to work in layers of grit and road salt will not last. The most thorough method is to remove the chain regularly and give it a good wash in paraffin, making sure that it is dried thoroughly afterwards. Then soak the chain in a bath of molten graphite grease. Take care when taking the chain out of the grease, making sure that the tin is stable on the heat source. Hot grease burns as well as making an awful mess — this is not a job to be tackled in the kitchen.

# Belts

The most suitable belting available for vintage motor cycles is probably the link belt, made with the correct 28° angle for vintage pulleys. Bought by the foot it is easy to fasten together and obtain the correct length for your machine. Modern pulleys use a 40° angle, so any modern endless belts are not suitable for vintage machines even if you could persuade them into place.

Pulleys should be checked for wear or damage. Try the belt into the groove — it should not reach the bottom. If it does the wedging action will be lost and the belt prone to slip. If this is the case, the pulley will need to be re-machined. Where there is not sufficient metal left for re-machining, the pulley will have to be built up by metal spraying and machined back to the correct size.

Belt tension is also important — too slack and it will slip easily causing excess wear; too tight and the bearings will be put under unnecessary strain. As with chain sprockets, the pulleys should be in line and the pulley on the rear wheel as concentric to the hub as possible. A small error is permissable but too much will cause the brake to grab on the rim.

Belt dressing compounds are not recommended for the materials used in modern belt manufacture.

# Conclusion

I hope that having read this book you will have been given the confidence to try processes that you might have avoided before, or sent out to the professionals. No matter what level of skill you feel you have or hope to achieve, I have always found this quote from one of the greatest engineers of this century helpful: 'Whatever is rightly done, however humble, is noble.' Sir Henry Royce

# List of suppliers

**Adhesives**

Perma Bond Ltd,
Woodside Rd,
Eastleigh,
Hants, SO5 4EX.

**Brakes/Clutches**

Harglo Ltd,
462 Station Rd,
Dorridge,
Solihull.

Supreme Motor Cycles,
1 High St
Earl Shilton,
Leicestershire.

Classic Brake Services,
P.O. Box 5,
Whaley Bridge,
Stockport, SK12 7LL.

**Carburettors**

Alan Lines,
70 Blakemore Drive,
Sutton Coldfield,
B75 7RW.

Precision Engineering Services,
Cromwell Rd,
Saffron Walden,
Essex, CB11 4AX.

**Casting supplies**

F. L. Hunt,
Salford,
Manchester.

Alec Tiranti Ltd,
70 High St,
Theale,
Berks, RG7 5AR

**Engine balancing & crack testing**

Basset Down Ltd,
Basset Down,
Swindon,
Wilts, SN4 9QR.

**Engine rebuilding & components**

Final Cut Engineering,
Aultone Way,
Carshalton,
Surrey, SM5 2LH.

Serco,
2 Bracken Rd,
Brighouse,
West Yorks, HD6 2HW.

WDB Engineering Services,
75 High St,
Winslow,
Bucks, MK18 3DG.

**Instrument repairs**

A. E. Pople,
10 Grenville Gardens,
Frimley Green,
Surrey, GU16 6NH.

Vintage Restorations,
The Old Bakery,
Tunbridge Wells,
Kent, TN2 4UU.

**Metal cleaning, stoving, powder coating & plating**

Rugeley Motorcycles,
38 Coronation Rd,
Stafford.

Derby Plating Services,
148 Abbey St,
Derby DE3 3SS.

Vehicle & General Polishers & Platers
Unit 8,
Fairfield Industrial Estate,
Arlesey,
Beds.

Dynic Sales,
Bell View Cottage,
Ladbroke,
Leamington Spa,
CV33 0DA.

Long Eaton Enamellers,
Acton Ave,
Long Eaton,
Nottingham.

Larog Finishers,
328 St. James Rd,
Southwark,
London, SE15 5JX.

Spraymaster,
Unit 16 Thorne Way,
Woolsbridge Industrial Park,
Three Legged Cross,
Dorset.

**Nuts, bolts & other fixings**

Harmsworth Townley Ltd,
Riveting Systems,
Harehill,
Todmorden,
Lancs, OL14 5JY.

C&I Threading,
P.O. Box YR8,
Leeds, LS9 9HX.

Custom Fasteners,
Unit 64,
Mochdre Industrial Estate,
Newtown,
Powys, SY16 4LE.

K. Whiston,
New Mills,
Stockport.

**Thread inserts**

Hurley Engine Services,
Unit 7,
The Maltings Industrial Estate,
Brassmill Lane,
Bath, BA1 3JL.

**Plastics & fibreglass**

Classic Plastic,
MSO Ashwellthorpe Industrial Estate,
Ashwellthorpe,
Norfolk, NR16 1ER.

Sprint Manufacturing,
30a Upton Lovell,
Nr. Warminster,
Wilts, BA12 0JW.

## Petrol tank makers/repairers

Terry Hall,
59 The Hill,
Quarry Hill,
Shropshire, SY4 3BU.

The Tank Shop,
Glenview Glenmidge,
Auldgirth,
Dumfries, DG2 0SW.

## Transfers

V.M.C.C. Transfer Service,
Arosfa,
Cwmpennar,
Mountain Ash,
Mid Glamorgan, CF45 4DL.

Phillips Transfers Ltd,
15 Stock Rd,
Billericay,
Essex.

## Sidecars

Charnwood Classic Restorations,
107 Central Rd,
Hugglescote,
Coalville,
Leics., LE6 2FL.

## Seat & seat recovering

DLC Products,
366 Woodside Rd,
Wyke,
Bradford, BD12 8HT.

R. K. Leighton,
Unit 5, Gunsmith House,
50-54 Price St,
Birmingham, B4 6JZ.

## Electrical services

Motorcycle Electrical Services,
Unit 10,
Ladbrook Park Industrial Estate,
Millers Rd,
Warwick, CV34 5AE.

E. Jenkins,
90 Elliman Ave,
Slough,
Berks, SL2 5BE

D. Lindsley,
196 Pilsworth Rd,
Haywood,
Lancs, OL10 3DY.

## Frames

Barber Engineering,
Attleborough,
Norfolk, NR17 4NZ.

John Hall,
102–108 Devonshire Rd,
Blackpool,
Lancs.

## Forks

R. Daniels,
Unit 3,
Stechford Trading Estate,
Stechford,
Birmingham, B33 8BU.

## Exhausts

Newton & Sulley,
68 Leen Valley House,
Cinderhill Rd,
Bullwell,
Notts.

Armours,
784 Wimbourne Rd,
Bournemouth,
Dorset.

## Wheels

Rossendale Wheels,
Grange Works,
Rawtenstall,
Lancs, BB4 8HY.

Richards Bros,
56 Clive Rd,
Canton,
Cardiff.

Central Wheel Components,
Lichfield Rd,
Water Orton,
Birmingham, B46 1NU.

Devon Rim Company,
20 South St,
South Molton,
Devon, EX36 4AG.

## Workshop equipment

R&R (UK) Ltd,
14 Tower Square,
St. Peter's Industrial Park,
Huntingdon,
Cambs, PE18 7DT.

## Interior trim & accessories

Paul Beck,
Vintage Supplies,
Folgate Rd,
North Walsingham,
Norfolk, NR28 0JA.

Woolies,
Off Blenheim Way,
Northfields Industrial Estate,
Market Deeping,
Nr. Peterborough, PE6 8LD.

Edgware Motor Accessories,
94 High St,
Edgware,
Middx.

Alan Abrahams,
38 Charles Drive,
Cuxton,
Kent, ME2 1DR.

# Index

Page numbers in brackets refer to illustrations or diagrams.